Routledge Revivals

Cosmic Theology

First published in 1964, *Cosmic Theology* introduces a work, little known to English readers, which has influenced theological and mystical writing for at least fourteen hundred years. It is, in effect, a synthesis of Christian teaching, particularly on the nature of the Church, in which science and religion, the other world and the values of the present world may be seen in their source and original harmony. Written before the division between Greek and Latin Churches, and later between Catholic and Protestant, it affords a convenient point from which to view later speculation and controversy in its true perspectives. Apart from helping those interested in the ecumenical movement and in the liturgical revival, this work will serve as a bridge to the understanding of Eastern, and particularly Hindu, religion.

Cosmic Theology
The Ecclesiastical Hierarchy of Pseudo-Denys: An Introduction

Dom Denys Rutledge

First published in 1964
By Routledge & Kegan Paul

This edition first published in 2024 by Routledge
4 Park Square, Milton Park, Abingdon, Oxon, OX14 4RN
and by Routledge
605 Third Avenue, New York, NY 10017

Routledge is an imprint of the Taylor & Francis Group, an informa business

© Denys Rutledge 1964

All rights reserved. No part of this book may be reprinted or reproduced or utilised in any form or by any electronic, mechanical, or other means, now known or hereafter invented, including photocopying and recording, or in any information storage or retrieval system, without permission in writing from the publishers.

Publisher's Note
The publisher has gone to great lengths to ensure the quality of this reprint but points out that some imperfections in the original copies may be apparent.

Disclaimer
The publisher has made every effort to trace copyright holders and welcomes correspondence from those they have been unable to contact.

A Library of Congress record exists under LCCN: 64007036

ISBN: 978-1-032-66800-0 (hbk)
ISBN: 978-1-032-67008-9 (ebk)
ISBN: 978-1-032-67007-2 (pbk)

Book DOI 10.4324/9781032670089

COSMIC THEOLOGY

The Ecclesiastical Hierarchy
of Pseudo-Denys: An Introduction

by

DOM DENYS RUTLEDGE

Routledge and Kegan Paul

LONDON

*First published 1964
by Routledge & Kegan Paul Limited
Broadway House, 68–74 Carter Lane
London, E.C.4*

*Printed in Great Britain
by Richard Clay & Company Ltd
Bungay, Suffolk*

© *Denys Rutledge 1964*

*No part of this book may be reproduced
in any form without permission from
the publisher, except for the quotation
of brief passages in criticism*

Nihil obstat A. M. Young, O.S.B., *Censor*
Cong. Angliae, O.S.B.

Imprimatur B. C. Butler, O.S.B., *Abbas*
Praes. Cong. Ang.
May 3rd 1963.

Nihil obstat Joannes M. T. Butler, S.T.D.,
L.S.S., *Censor deputatus.*

Imprimatur Georgius L. Craven. Epūs Sebastopolis
Vic. Cap.
Westmonasterii, die 27a Maii 1963.

The *Nihil obstat* and *Imprimatur* are a declaration that a book or pamphlet is considered to be free from doctrinal or moral error. It is not implied that those who have granted the *Nihil obstat* and *Imprimatur* agree with the contents, opinions or statements expressed.

Contents

Preface   *page* ix

I. Introduction

COSMIC THEOLOGY   3
THE ECCLESIASTICAL HIERARCHY   26
THE TWO HIERARCHIES   30
PSEUDO-DENYS AND PLATO   37

II. Text

1. The Ecclesiastical Hierarchy   47
2. Mystery of Illumination   60
3. Mystery of the Synaxis or Communion   85
4. Mystery of the Sacrament of Unction   119
5. Mystery of the Priestly Consecration   141
6. Mystery of the Monastic Consecration   166
7. Mystery over Those Who Have Fallen Asleep in Holiness   186

Index   205

Preface

THE following pages attempt to introduce a treatise written not later than the beginning of the sixth century and to suggest its relevance for the contemporary world. The *Ecclesiastical Hierarchy* is one of four small works believed until modern times to have been written by a contemporary and convert of St. Paul. Although perhaps the least known of the four—certainly to the English-speaking world—it seems to form the best approach to the author's thought. I would suggest that, incidental to its primary purpose, it forms also for western man, particularly for the western Christian, a unique guide to the understanding of the eastern mind and of the mode of thought, common to East and West, in which the Christian tradition received its material expression.

Until we have a critical edition of the original Greek text it is impossible to produce a wholly satisfactory translation; an introduction seems the best beginning. The text in Migne's *Patrologia Graeca* has been the only one accessible to the present writer, and that, owing to the conditions in which the work has been done, only with difficulty. It seems, nevertheless, reasonably certain that a modern critical edition would not do more than establish matters of detail without affecting materially the main structure of the author's scheme; it is this with which the present work is principally concerned. Although the book does not, therefore, offer a formal, critical translation, it does in fact include a translation of practically the whole of the treatise in a running commentary: nothing of moment is omitted. My own translation has been compared with modern German and French works, principally those of Stiglmayr and de Gandillac, and in places modified in consequence. In passages where a matter essential to the author's teaching turns upon the exact translation of a word or phrase I have added the Greek in a footnote.

I have tried to make the translation as literal as is consistent with the interpretation of the author's thought, expressed, as this is, in a style and vocabulary that have been described as 'fantastic' and 'uncouth'. I have, however, deliberately omitted or modified a number of stock epithets where I am satisfied that these are merely conventional, not only not adding anything to the meaning but rather serving as a kind of verbal smoke-screen obscuring the thought one is trying to elucidate. This has the effect of lowering the temperature of the text several degrees; but perhaps this may have the result of making its impact on the English reader more comparable to that of the original on those to whom it was first dedicated.

To illustrate my point: I have normally been content to translate θεαρχία (*thearchia*) as 'Divinity' or 'Deity'. It is formed of two words meaning God, and origin, source, beginning. As used by this author it seems commonly to mean God who is the origin, source and beginning of all things; but it is also used with a distinction, for instance to denote God abstracting from the distinction of persons, or as the origin of the processions within the Godhead (Stiglmayr: *Urgottheit*; de Gandillac (evading the issue): *Théarchie*; Rolt (*The Divine Names*, S.P.C.K. 1951): 'Originating Godhead', 'Super-Essential Godhead'). In this, as in similar cases, there is a reason for the choice of such a word; but its discussion belongs rather to the treatise on *The Divine Names*. As normally used in the present treatise its meaning is sufficiently conveyed by 'Deity' or 'Divinity'. That might appear fairly satisfactory, until one finds that Jesus is described in one passage by the superlative adjective formed from this word. Once one has said God and Deity, and even gone a little further to say 'Super-Essential Godhead', it would seem that little more remains to be said. What, then, of the superlative, as an epithet applied to one who, in order of origin, is the second person of the Trinity, and as incarnate is 'less than the Father' ('The Father is greater than I': John xiv, 28)? It is clear from the context that the author is concerned simply to emphasise the divinity of Jesus, to make the point that he is in all things equal to the 'Super-Essential Godhead', but it would be helpful if he could just say so in plain Greek. It illustrates the difficulty of translating his work. In this instance I translate 'truly God', which seems to me to give a clearer and more accurate meaning than, for instance, de Gandillac's *très théarchique* (much as I admire his scholarship).

It has, however, been suggested—I think by no less than Thomas Aquinas—that the author is deliberately obscure, that he wishes to veil his teaching from all but the few who are capable of rising to it. This is for him no mere academic exercise, or light reading for the dilettante; it is the way of life, the way of all life, and the way of the whole of life. I do not believe the obscurity is deliberate; but there can be no doubt that this is the kind of writer one has to live with in order to understand: and even at the end one can never be quite sure that one has understood. He is not given to the concise lapidary phrase. His own St. Paul's 'All things are yours, and you are Christ's, and Christ is God's' (I Cor. iii, 22–23) might have stood very well at the head of his work; but it is not his style. In fact, as one reads on and ponders, and ponders again, the conviction grows that the attitude of the writer to his reader is simply this: If you will take the trouble that I have, undergo the toil and discipline, with the purgation involved, then you will come to see what I see: there is no other way. It is not an unreasonable attitude; it may in fact be the fruit of high wisdom.

The present writer can only hope that his own efforts to elucidate this work, and so make it available to a wider public, have not been unwisdom and served rather to add to its obscurity. Any obscurity that is found will have been unintentional.

I
Introduction

COSMIC THEOLOGY

IF the title of this book, *Cosmic Theology*, should appear to my readers too sensational, I can only say that it seems to me a better description of the work I am introducing than the subtitle, *The Ecclesiastical Hierarchy*. To the author of this treatise 'hierarchy' means no less than the divine economy by which the visible world emerges from the invisible, elaborates its purpose and achieves its final destiny. The subject is, moreover, treated in such a manner, the author's mind ranging in one comprehensive sweep from the depths of the Godhead to the least of created things, that to one coming to his works for the first time they commonly open up what seems to be almost literally a new dimension. Such seems to have been the experience of, for instance, Archibishop Ullathorne, 'the last of the vicars apostolic'. Having come upon them when a young monk at Downside, he describes them as 'theology in its purest form, divested of controversy and written as if by a spirit with a pen of light.' He considered that their study had 'formed a real epoch in the history of his mind'.[1]

In the particular treatise we are considering here the author is more directly concerned with the sacramental system of the Church, but he sees this as the indispensable link between the invisible and eternal and the visible and transient. It offers man an entry to the invisible world, yet in such a way that, far from leaving behind the visible world, he in fact carries it with him to partake of the eternity of the invisible. But to make this distinction between the invisible and visible planes is misleading to begin with. In the author's view they interpenetrate and are inextricably united—to the extent at least that the things on the visible plane *are* at all, to the limit of what is good and desirable in them, of their positive being; the evil and undesirable element is in this scheme a lack of being.

[1] *Life and Times of Bishop Ullathorne*, Butler, Vol. 1, p. 23.

INTRODUCTION

The general reader may wish to know a little more of this wider significance of the author's teaching, in order to assess its practical value for himself, before considering the details of the treatise we are about to introduce. I shall therefore proceed to be still more sensational by attempting to present an outline of the whole system in the context of contemporary thought. I shall stress especially the place of this present visible world in the scheme of things and its connection with the invisible. This, I think, is what the average man wants to know; not unreasonably. We shall find no trace in this author of any stifling of human feelings and desires, of 'apathy' in the sense in which the Greek word is commonly translated. It is nevertheless no armchair religion that is offered to us here; the Christian is invited to a progressive withdrawal from things of the visible world culminating only in the complete withdrawal of death. There is no compromise; 'Every one of you that doth not renounce all that he possesseth cannot be my disciple' is accepted in its most literal sense. Yet the aim is to make man not less but more human; to apply his human feelings and desires to their true end, to lead him from the external manifestation of things, which serves only to tantalise without satisfying his desires, to the reality behind them. In this, too, he is representative of the patristic, the truly Christian, tradition. It seems also possible that the coming age will be marked by a higher, more truly human, Christian humanism; one might perhaps say a truly Christian humanism for the first time. If this should be so, then this little body of works could be of inestimable value, for it presents what is in effect a complete synthesis of cosmology, anthropology and theology, in which the things of this world are seen in their proper proportion, and true significance.

This may perhaps have also the incidental effect of contributing to a more balanced judgement of the author and his writings. Since, in England especially, his very brief *Mystical Theology* is best known, most commonly indirectly through the late medieval *Cloud of Unknowing*, while the present treatise is comparatively unknown, an exaggerated concept has been formed of the writer's 'otherworldliness', omitting to notice that the Christian is invited to walk away from things only in order to find them. The result has been to remove the lower rungs of the ladder of the hierarchy (the subject of this treatise), reducing it almost to a variety of Indian rope trick, with no visible means of support and stretching up into the unknown.

Immediately after the end of the last world war the headquarters of a British army corps, then settling into the task of becoming the military government of one of the German districts, received a dramatic message from an underground resistance organisation: unless the allied forces left Germany by a given date an atomic explosion would be effected with a chain reaction that would destroy the whole earth. The threat was not taken very seriously, and for obvious reasons it was not made public, but as the 'last day' approached one noticed that those who knew of the threat tended to glance more often than usual at the calendar. Since those days we have become more accustomed to the possibility of the imminent destruction of all life on earth, and possibly even of the very earth itself. Christians had indeed from the beginning been taught to look forward to such a universal conflagration, at first thought of as immediately imminent, then, until lately, taking its place in the background of the consciousness, to be revived on the occasion of funerals and at the close of the liturgical year—*dies irae, dies illa, solvet saeclum in favilla*.[1]

It has indeed been suggested that we may be already in the midst of this final dissolution, that the apparently 'expanding universe' implies that we are at the centre of a cosmic explosion, sometimes called, irreverently, the 'big bang' theory,[2] and our long, painful years are but the split second in which occurs the disintegration of all things. Whether, on this hypothesis, the *dies irae* is to be considered as being always with us, though only just realised, and this is indeed 'the last hour', enclosing the whole of our earthly time, we are not told. There is, in any case, a more subtle approach, calculated to arouse alarm and despondency not only in those who have not the hope of an

---

[1] 'That day, that day of wrath, shall dissolve the world in ashes': beginning of the sequence of Mass for the Dead.

[2] It has also been suggested that this phenomenon is best explained on the hypothesis of a 'continuous creation', apparently meaning creation in the literal sense (*ex nihilo sui et subjecti*). Cf. *The Nature of the Universe*, Fred Hoyle (Harper, 1950), p. 111 (of the American edition). For a further discussion of this question see p. 164.

INTRODUCTION

'eternal dwelling',[1] but perhaps also in those of the Faith who may wonder wistfully what resemblance, if any, the 'new earth' that is promised may bear to the one they have known.

The physical scientists are in fact not only threatening the existence of our world; there is a sense in which they may be said to have taken it from us already, to have dissolved it into 'air, thin air'. Our seemingly solid earth, they tell us, is mostly sheer nothingness, emptiness with, revolving in it as a couple of specks of dust might revolve in the vast caverns of one of our larger London railway stations, a few centres of energy, themselves so insubstantial and elusive that they can be neither seen, felt nor heard; their existence is divined, and their probable effects are forecast, only by a process of mathematical calculation. From this is drawn the conclusion that the apparent extension of things, their solidity, colour, sound and taste, is in fact caused by our senses, is 'our way of observing non-material things',[2] and that the senses themselves are but the expression of an invisible force or energy. By some this theory is taken to imply a denial of the validity of sense knowledge. Popular reaction to all this, on the part of the minority who think seriously about such things, is a certain unease and insecurity, a feeling that the reality of the material world is somehow being undermined, that the very foundations of our lives are rocking, and that not only are things not what they seem but that we ourselves are being faded out along the lines of the Cheshire cat. The subject is ventilated periodically in letters to the press, in books, articles, and radio and T.V. discussions; and, very oddly, it is generally assumed that the Church is somehow 'against it'. This line of thought is in fact commonly taken as the latest attack of science on religion, as though it threatened in some way the basic principles of religion, presumably because it appears to contradict the Aristotelian philosophy at present current in our theology schools. Yet it does not deny the reality of objects external to the self, nor need it be taken to imply this; our scientists have not claimed that their atom bombs do not exist. Some of them claim to examine more closely (though per-

[1] From the Preface of Mass for the Dead: 'when the house in which we dwell on this earth is dissolved we acquire an eternal dwelling in heaven', echoing St. Paul, II Cor. v, 1.
[2] So Sir James Jeans.

haps still not closely enough) the meaning of the term 'matter',[1] yet the material world is not less real because we may have to revise our views of its ultimate constitution.

Perhaps the most disturbing factor for the majority of people, were they to analyse their feelings, is the discovery that this apparently solid earth is in fact the least solid and stable of all things, at the very fringe of reality beyond which there is nothing, a manifestation of a higher, invisible reality. But this, after all, is only what all religions have always told us, and if atomic science has awakened us with something of a shock to the full realisation of the truth of this, then surely it has rendered an immense service to religion. In fact, it has done more; it refers us back, as we shall see, to our own earlier and more deeply spiritual Christian tradition.

There is no doubt that such a realisation does come frequently as a shock. It is sometimes said of exceptional people—it was said of Newman—that the unseen world was more real to them than the seen, implying that this was an oddity or abnormality. It is, of course, the abnormal, 'fallen' condition of the ordinary man that makes it appear so. Shakespeare considered the question in *The Tempest*, written in his maturity, and seems to express his conclusion towards the end in the lines beginning: 'These our actors . . . were all spirits.' Prospero has at his command spiritual forces that can produce at will a world of appearances such as ours; when he has finished with them they melt and vanish. They still exist; it is only their temporary, sensible, material appearance, the less real that seems to us the greater reality, that has disappeared, and can, presumably, be made to reappear at will.[2]

The current tendencies, therefore, of physical science, in so far as these are regarded as conveying a threat of extinction, or a disintegration of our world already accomplished, seem to carry also their own solvent or antidote, suggesting that it is nothing but the most superficial aspect of reality that is destructible. It raises the question: Would it be any great loss—or,

[1] Cf., e.g., *The Philosophy of Physical Science*, Sir Arthur Eddington (Cambridge, 1949), and 'the knowledge (that) abolishes all dualism of consciousness and matter' (p. 150).

[2] Cf. the commentary of Alfred Noyes (an exceptional combination of poet and scientist) on these lines, in *The Unknown God*, Chapter XV.

INTRODUCTION

more simply, would it be any loss at all—if a colossal atomic explosion did destroy the earth together with everything on it? This suggests a further question: whether in fact the world can be destroyed, in the sense that we can ever lose it or get away from it.

Theologians commonly assure us that there will always be a *place* where human bodies can live, where in fact at least two human bodies[1] are already living, and that it is infinitely better than the one we know here. Yet many are still left a little worried. Will it bear any resemblance to this world? Is there any connection? Shall we have to lose for ever all we have known and loved here, or is there any form in which we may possess it for ever? May we have all this and heaven besides? Can our world be destroyed, or may we, perhaps, to take an illustration from the world of the cinema, regard apparent destruction as simply a momentary interruption, like a single blank in the series of pictures on a reel of film, showing no apparent discontinuity when projected? Or—many must have watched a town or village being subjected to an intensive bombardment, disappearing in a cloud of dust, smoke and flame, only to reappear when the bombardment has ceased, apparently—from a distance—unchanged. Something like this is suggested by the latest theories of the physical scientists, as also by the earlier, commonly accepted Christian view.

It seems in fact that these very physical scientists who are suspected of having robbed us of our world as we thought we knew it have, in reality, given it to us in a more portable form. There is a sense in which we may be said to carry our world everywhere with us, the world depending on us and at our disposal and not we on the world; our own personal world, with all our own special points of contact, in much the same way—to use a crude image—in which one might carry in one's pocket in microfilm a complete pictorial record of one's life: *This is Your Life (and Your World)*.

In the world in which the Church was founded the Greek

---

[1] Many of the Fathers, e.g. Epiphanius, Ambrose, Jerome, Cyril of Alexandria, also modern Catholic and Protestant theologians, hold that the 'many bodies of the saints that had slept [and] coming out of the tombs after his resurrection came into the holy city, and appeared to many' (Matt. xxvii, 52 f.) did not die again but entered heaven with Christ.

word for this was *microcosm*, meaning, when applied to man, that man *was* the world in miniature, that all that is unfolded and extended into this world of space and time is contained in man in, so to speak, its concentrated essence. Looking into oneself one could, therefore, see the world; go deep enough and one could control it to the extent of being no longer subject to its laws; observe the embryonic development of man and one might deduce therefrom the development of the cosmos or, by comparison of the two, found a school of medicine; abstracted from the world one might survey all time and being; insert a tentative hand at the source and one might influence the flow of history and the destiny of others—and so on in varying degrees ranging from rational science to black magic. The word itself sometimes, and always the view of life contained in it, became the common heritage of both East and West; but it had already long been, and still remains in one form or another, the basis of eastern religious thought.[1]

The mode of thought that gave rise to this conception of the microcosm is most readily accessible to western readers through these works of the probably fifth-century writer now known as the pseudo-Denys.[2] His writings form an early comprehensive *summa* of Christian revelation in which this idea is central. They are not easy reading; the style is diffuse and repetitive. St. Thomas found many obscure passages, and the full meaning of a vital phrase often has to be gathered from *obiter dicta* scattered throughout the works. His main thesis is, however, clear enough, and he has exercised a unique influence on the course of Christian theology down to the present day. This writer claims

[1] Cf., e.g., the fifteenth-century Indian Kabir. Traditional Tibetan Medicine is based on it. Cf. *Tibetische Medizinphilosophie*, Cyril von K. Krasinski (Zurich, 1953).

[2] He claims to be the Aeropagite mentioned in Acts xvii, 22 ff., who became a disciple of St. Paul after listening to his discourse on the Unknown God. He wrote in Greek, was probably a Syrian, and his works were certainly known by the early sixth century. Scholars are generally agreed that, on internal evidence, these works could not be of the first century. In antiquity he was identified with both the first Bishop of Athens and with the Denys, Bishop of Paris, who suffered martyrdom in the third century. There can be no doubt that the belief that he was indeed the disciple of St. Paul added greatly to his prestige in the past; in the Middle Ages his authority surpassed that of any other Father of the Church, and he is one of the authors most frequently quoted by St. Thomas. His true identity is still unknown.

INTRODUCTION

—and there is no reason to doubt his claim—that he is transmitting simply what he has received from sacred scripture, in which he includes, as he tells us, oral tradition.[1] His cast of thought is illustrated at the beginning of this present treatise by the fact that he considers oral tradition to be a higher mode of transmission than the written word as being 'less material', a mode 'more like that of the angels', direct 'from mind to mind, corporeal since they speak, but immaterial in so far as they do not write'.[2] In common with the Greek and Latin Fathers of the Church he uses the philosophical terms and concepts of Plato to express his teaching. In fact, this teaching is set in a scheme so closely resembling in its main lines what one might call Plato's primary intuition, as distinct from his efforts to explain this intuition and present it in a rational scheme, that one can be illustrated by the other. It has even been maintained that his system is the fulfilment of what Plato sought but never quite found.[3]

For this author, then, all created things are manifestations, revelations of God in decreasing degrees of perfection, the visible creation with man at its head being the lowest in the scale. God himself is utterly transcendent, beyond all that we can affirm or deny of him. He is unknowable, yet he is known in all things; he is nothing that is, yet at the same time he is the cause of everything and is thus the object of our reason, touch, sensation, imagination.[4] The vehemence—for that is the word— with which the transcendence of God is asserted is nicely balanced by the continual repetition of the statement that it is God who is the being of all things. Following St. John and an immemorial tradition, our author finds it most convenient, in describing the work of creation and conservation, to speak of God in terms of light, of light manifesting itself in varying degrees of concentration and brilliance.[5] M. Gilson describes this very neatly in saying that 'the Divine Light and the being

---

[1] *Eccl. Hier.* 376B. References throughout are to Migne's edition in the *Patrologia Graeca*.   [2] *Eccl. Hier.* 376C.

[3] The resemblance is especially evident in Plato's allegory of the Cave, *Republic*, Bk. vii, 514 ff. Cf. below, p. 40.   [4] *Div. Names*, 872A.

[5] To appreciate the peculiar aptness of this metaphor, one should recall that for the author and his contemporaries (as later for, e.g., St. Thomas) light is immaterial, diffusing itself and transmitting light to others without any loss or change in itself. Perhaps it may be useful to add that creation is stated explicitly to be a free act. Cf. *Div. Names*, 825A.

which it confers are the illuminative cascade whose steps are described by the treatises on *The Celestial Hierarchy* and *The Ecclesiastical Hierarchy*. This "illumination" must not be conceived as a simple gift of light to already existing things but as a gift of a light which is their very being'.[1] Moreover, the higher orders contain all that is in those beneath them and the lower orders are, for their part, but a less intense form of all that is in those above them, 'imitating' them (a favourite phrase) in every way. All are, so to speak, in the same 'shape' or pattern, increasingly imperfect images or manifestations of the Light that is God.[2] It is not a question, that is, of having parts of a whole, of some having something that others have not; each has the whole—adapted to his capacity, remembering that the capacity also is received. In this sense is to be understood the statements quoted above that God is transcendent, unknowable and incomprehensible, yet known and grasped in all things. All that we know is knowledge of God, all that we have and are is the being of God; yet God remains infinitely beyond the creature.

Stated in this way, the author's teaching is deceptively simple; it contains in germ all that can be said of created being in its relation to its creator, but as capable of indefinite development: and the writer's own development was to be followed by a series of commentaries and developments not always strictly orthodox. It will be necessary to examine the writer's own thesis a little more closely in order to see how he would have disposed of the atom bomb.

In *The Celestial Hierarchy* the angels are arranged in their correct sequence and their nature explained in accordance with the indications given in sacred scripture.[3] *The Ecclesiastical*

---

[1] *History of Christian Philosophy in the Middle Ages* (New York), 1954, p. 83.

[2] Cf. Plato's ascent from the Cave to the upper world, p. 41 below.

[3] Fr. Stiglmayr (in his translation of the *Celestial Hierarchy*, Bibliothek der Kirchenväter (Munich, 1911), p. 34, n.) notes that no writer before the pseudo-Denys places the nine choirs of angels in this precise order, and that Augustine, for example, confesses that he does not know the distinction between the thrones, dominations, principalities and powers. It is, of course, possible that our author is transmitting an 'oral tradition', but I fear that he may be arranging the *details* of this hierarchy to suit his convenience. However, it is clear that the angels are a hierarchy, he claims to reach this order through an interpretation of their names, and his system does not stand or fall by the precise details of the ordering of the hierarchy.

INTRODUCTION

Hierarchy (of sacraments, clergy and laity) reflects the hierarchy of the angels both as a whole and in the details of its organisation; it is a faithful reflection of this on its lower plane. There are, it is obvious, innumerable degrees within each of these orders of heavenly spirits and men—it is probably true to say that there are as many degrees as persons—and only the main stages are indicated by our author; but they all follow the same pattern, unfolded in greater detail and consequently in a lower concentration. Accordingly, a study of the working of the hierarchy of the angels helps us to understand our own in its ideal form.[1] What must be realised as essential to this scheme, as a principle valid throughout the hierarchies, is the doctrine that the light passes through the higher degrees in order to reach the lower, that it is transmitted from one to the other with the necessary modification and diffusion.[2] No creature has anything that it has not received through this line of communication, and this includes, startling as it may seem, its whole being in all its aspects,[3] its actions, its whole history, its life with all its details.

[1] This is also the significance of the long tract of St. Thomas, in the *Summa Th.*, *De Angelis*: knowledge of them helps us to understand the spiritual nature of fallen man and the qualities and powers he is regaining through the Redemption.

[2] In the *Celestial Hierarchy* (301B), but speaking of a general principle operative throughout the hierarchies, our author suggests that their members become increasingly more 'opaque' (παχυτέραις, a word that is also used to mean 'thick-headed') as one descends the hierarchy, so transmitting less and less light to those below. He nowhere explains exactly how this works, but there is a vague suggestion (cf. *Div. Names*, 697C–700A) that when one is more 'opaque' than his position warrants—more opaque than he will be (in the case of men) when he has removed all that obscures his due degree of illumination, whether here or in purgatory—that then the Light, the Light at this precise degree of intensity, passes on to the next without any diminution from the accidental, temporary opacity of this member of the hierarchy. This could be of importance for the principle, not discussed by this author (but see p. 177 below), that the efficacy of the sacraments does not depend upon the sanctity of the minister. In a more general way we may see it operative in the case of an ill-advised, or even deliberately unjust action of a superior working for the good of the subject—'all things work together unto good . . .' (Rom. viii, 28).

[3] Cf. *Div. Names*, 693B, 821B. No attempt is made by the author to reconcile this with the free-will of the individual, but he has no doubt of the existence of free-will. Similarly, position in the hierarchy is apportioned, in a phrase used repeatedly, 'according to the merit of each'. There is no trace of

COSMIC THEOLOGY

At the lower end of the scale, then, is man, in the ecclesiastical hierarchy; below him is the rest of his world of animals, birds, fish, reptiles, plants, vegetables, etc. Logically, therefore, in accordance with the strict uniformity of the hierarchies, we must understand man as possessing in all its aspects all that is below him in the scale.[1] The divine light that is the being even of these lowest things, that enjoy the 'least vestige'[2] of being, is

---

[1] Our author does not state this explicitly, since it does not come within his argument, but it is implied in all he does say, is in the tradition he represents, (cf. p. 17 n. 1) and seems to have been so understood by his first commentators. Among the latter are particularly noteworthy Maximus Confessor and Scotus Erigena, with their startling conception of a kind of final 'folding-up' or 'telescoping' of created being, sensible into spiritual, body into soul, etc., a flowing back of the stream to its source until at last only God remains, 'all in all'. On the other hand, he has no doubt of the objective, external reality of the sensible world, nor is there any trace of Plato's attitude to the body as the 'prison' of the soul; for him the body, having shared the labours of the soul, will enjoy hereafter its immortality (see below p. 187). Rather similarly for Gregory of Nyssa, considered by some to have been one of the principal sources of the pseudo-Denys; all reality is essentially spiritual, the material, sensible character of this world has no existence apart from man, yet though it will be finally resumed into the spirit, in the sense that it will be 'spiritualised', it will still remain. But for Erigena, too, there is no annihilation, no confusion or blending of individual beings and substances; rather is it in this way that the human body and other material things receive their full reality. Cf. Gilson, *op cit.* p. 126.

[2] Cf. *Div. Names*, 856B. 'vestige': lit. 'feeblest echo' ($\dot{α}\pi\dot{η}χημα$). Cf. also *Div. Names*, 696C, where there is a fuller list of 'birds, animals, reptiles, fish, amphibians, plants, things without life'. It is not wise to read a whole theory into a single word unless there are other clear indications that the writer saw a special significance in it; still the peculiar aptness of this word is worth

---

quietism or determinism. Maximus Confessor thinks the degrees were apportioned in foreknowledge of the position each would reach by the exercise of his free-will. This is a way of describing it from a viewpoint in this world, but these writings suggest that the author is rather viewing all this as one single act of God: the decision and activity of the individual—Belloc's 'word which each of us has passed before he was born in Paradise'—and the corresponding place in the hierarchy, before the stream of illumination began to run its course; what we see here is simply the working out of this in space and time. Cf. the comments of M. de Gandillac on this question (*Œuvres Complètes* (Paris: Aubier, 1943), p. 41 f.). Abbot Wiesinger has an interesting comment on this general question of 'illumination' of the mind and will (*Okkulte Phänomene*, (Graz: Verlag Styria, 1952), pp. 67, 135 ff.; there is a translation by Burnes and Oates, not at the moment accessible to the writer).

INTRODUCTION

present first in man and passes through him. It is not that he is just the model or blue-print on which they are fashioned; they are first present in him in their more perfect, and what one might call their more 'concentrated', form, just as all that is in man is present first in the angels. Expressed in the later scholastic terminology, not only their formal and exemplary causes but also their efficient cause passes through man.[1] Being made a little lower than the angels, his world is so much less perfect and compact than theirs, further extended into what, for want of a better term, we must still call matter, the proper concern of the senses. In terms of our original metaphor we might perhaps visualise such things as the living, multi-coloured rainbow spray cast off by the 'illuminative cascade' as it reaches in man the end of its course. To take an anology from the sphere of knowledge, while remembering that each of these degrees *is* both knowledge and being,[2] one might recall the way in which a

---

[1] This includes also the material cause. The fact that matter is received by way of the hierarchy from the Good is used by the author as an argument that it cannot be evil (*Div. Names*, 729).

Some commentators, and notably M. René Roques (*Sources Chrétiennes*, No. 58 (Paris. Éd. du Cerf, 1955), find it necessary to say that the orders of the hierarchies do not *create* those subordinate to them. This is true, but it is not the whole truth, and to leave it like that would, it seems to me, be a serious misrepresentation of the author's mind. In his scheme the individual member becomes so closely identified with the One, the Light, that he forms with it one principle of operation. If the whole being and activity of each member is received it seems to matter little whether we say he or God creates the one immediately below. The immanence and transcendence of God, the unity of the creature with his creator and the distinction of his identity, must be stated with *exactly* the same emphasis. It does not help to emphasise the one just a trifle more than the other, but rather adds to the difficulty, veiling the fact that we have come here to the plane of the indefinable. It is St. Paul's 'I, yet not I.' If we say that God creates each member of the hierarchy immediately, then, if we are to preserve this author's scheme, we must add immediately that each member *is* God, at *exactly* this level of manifestation or creation. Cf. in connection with this p. 10, n. 5 and p. 12, n. 2, p. 38, below and p. 126, n. 2.

[2] I.e., 'A gift of a light that is their very being' (cf. M. Gilson, p. 11 above). Modern theological manuals tend to speak of the glory of the soul in

---

noting. Besides its original meaning of 'echo', it is used of a re-echoed or reiterated utterance or statement passed on from one to another. Thus, it recalls neatly the primary 'utterance', the Word, and the transmission of man's world down the hierarchy.

teacher will break down a proposition for a child, dividing up and illustrating by concrete examples what he himself sees as a whole in one single glance.[1] Something analogous occurs in the descending degrees of the hierarchies of angels and men; less is 'seen' in one glance, less 'done' in a single action; they live less intensely, 'get less out of life' as the Light that is their life becomes more widely diffused and less intense. In our case, when the Light that is our being finally arrives at the world of men, it is of our nature that we should have always this 'concrete example' of the external world throughout our whole activity, the activity of the soul finding its reflection in the act of the body, and our mental processes and communication with others expressed in terms of the sensible world.[2]

A goat before a 'flower in the crannied wall' sees only something to eat; for man it is an experience of God, in which he

[1] One might compare the manner in which the Church, in the same tradition and teacher *par excellence*, presents the *opus redemptionis* to us as one whole in the Mass, at the same time spreading it out for our contemplation over the day, the week and the liturgical year, so resolving its light as by a prism.

[2] Cf. the teaching of St. Thomas on the knowledge of man before the Fall (especially S. Th. I, 94, 1, c. and *De. Verit.* 18, 1 ad 12). This seems to be the reason for his intensive study of the angels.

---

heaven as 'redounding' or 'overflowing' into the body, somehow managing to convey the impression that the body may be a slight embarrassment. For this author and his tradition it is less the glory than the body itself which flows from the soul. If St. John is able to speak of heaven simply in terms of the intellect: '*This* is eternal life, that they may *know* thee . . .' (xvii, 3), or the Angelic Doctor to adopt Aristotle's description of the soul as *quodammodo omnia* (in a way all things), it is because they are both in a tradition in which the sharp distinction of modern times, amounting to almost an opposition between matter and spirit, knowledge and being, is less a distinction than a matter of degree; the higher degree contains the lower, knowledge of it is possession of its being, all knowledge being the knowledge of God, which is a participation in his being. (Cf. St. Augustine: *Nihil sunt angeli nisi videndo te* (Migne. Patr. Lat. 36, 331).) But this does include the lower manifestations of the hierarchy, so that our Lord is able to describe the same thing in the most carnal terms of eating and drinking: 'I dispose to you, as my father has disposed to me, a kingdom, that you may eat and drink at my table in my kingdom' (Luke xxii, 29). Cf. the belief common in the East that to know the true name of a person is to acquire a certain power over and possession of him, and (*Nouv. Rev. Théol.*, December 1958, p. 1034) the 'effective' power of the utterance of 'prophetic' words in the Old Testament.

INTRODUCTION

'sees' and 'touches' God.[1] It is already within him in its higher form as one aspect of a life and activity that is a reflection of the life and activity of God himself. God, in the contemplation of himself, produces also outside himself created being reflecting his perfections. Man, in that participation in the contemplation of God which corresponds to his place in the hierarchies, participates in God's production of that last degree of being which is the sensible world; a transient transformation into terms of the spatial and temporal of a continuous contemplation of God which is the proper life of the soul. Man *is*[2] all these things, but only gradually and by long and careful discipline does he, in his fallen state, come to see 'everything in everything else' and all things as expressions of a single unity which is God. At this stage (though it is not in fact assumed that men do in this life reach it in its perfection) man passes freely between the two, combining the unceasing, motionless contemplation of the highest of the celestial hierarchy with activity about the minor details of the sensible world.[3] A realisation of this present world as somehow included in the world of the soul and reflecting it, with a sense of the unity of all things and the ability to 'see the world in a grain of sand', seems to have been an experience common to the mystics and to all thoughtful men in a greater or less degree; a comprehensive glance such as that with which a returning tripper in a space ship might view the details of his 'fretful

[1] *Div. Names*, 872A. Cf. the argument of St. Augustine (*De Civ. Dei*, xxii, 29) that after the general resurrection men may see God with their bodily eyes. In this tradition bodily sight is but the lowest, the most superficial, 'material' aspect of a single activity in which all sight and knowledge, and indeed the very being of man and his world, is 'sight' and 'knowledge' of God.

[2] The phrase of St. Thomas quoted above, that the human soul is *quodammodo* all things implies, of course, that the mode of being things have in the soul of man is superior, not inferior, to that which they enjoy in their material manifestation; otherwise the angels, who do not possess the things of this world in their material form, would be to that extent inferior to men.

[3] Cf. (1) the unceasing contemplation of the seraphim, p. 132 below; (2) the bishop proceeding to the exercise of his office, yet never leaving the contemplation of 'spiritual realities', so 'imitating' (in the later hymn) *Verbum supernum prodiens, nec Patris linquens dexteram*; (3) Plato's prisoner from the Cave (p. 42 below) gradually accustomed to pass without difficulty between the darkness of the cave and the light of the upper world and, having contemplated all things in their source, to return and order human affairs on the pattern of what he has seen.

midge' of a world opening out beneath him. Perhaps such a vision was that recorded by Gregory of St. Benedict, seeing 'the whole world gathered as it were under one beam of the sun', or Julian of Norwich's 'sight', in her more homely simile of a hazel-nut, of 'all that is made'.

In such a scheme, therefore, it seems that there would be no loss, could be no loss, if the world of the present moment were suddenly wiped out. Man himself possesses the world in its 'microcosmic' form; its essence is an aspect of his own being and, some would say, his consideration of what he has *is* its projection in material form. It is, in any case, an inevitable consequence of man's nature, of his place in the hierarchy of being, that the material world should continue to be projected through him as a picture is projected through a film by the light shining through it; that we carry our world always with us, our own world with its own special characteristics, the slant given it by our own personality, and that there will follow us our own world of earth, sky and sea, of birds and animals, plants and flowers, that this final, perfect subjection of the material to the spiritual will, in fact, be the 'new heaven and new earth' we look for. But our author is well aware that man is not of himself capable of this, though he will experience a vague, possibly only half-conscious desire for it, with a feeling after it. Man as we first meet him in this world is cut off from the source of his being in the hierarchies. He regains it only in consequence of the Incarnation and Ascension of Christ, through his reception of the Body of Christ.

It has been suggested that there is logically no place for the Incarnation in our author's scheme, but there is no indication that the author himself saw any difficulty in this, and St. Thomas accepts the scheme without demur. Unfortunately for us, since he sees no problem, he sees no need for explaining how exactly the Incarnation does fit into his scheme, and we have to deduce this from what he has said. The fact seems to be that the *nauta mundus naufragus*[1] has been carried to destruction through coming adrift from its moorings, severing its connection with the hierarchy, the source of all its being. Man, by cutting

[1] A striking phrase from a Passion-tide breviary hymn: Christ is represented as coming to the assistance of a 'seafaring (lit. *sailor*) world that has suffered shipwreck'.

INTRODUCTION

himself off from God, has carried his world with him to destruction.[1] The incarnation of the Word has bridged the gap, enclosing man and his world in himself and uniting them once more to the Father.[2] Our author's exposition assumes the fact of

[1] I think our author's explanation would be essentially that given me by a Hindu monk to the question: Did he believe that after what we call death the body and a material world would still remain, and for ever? His reply (in essence that of Samkaracharya, and in effect neatly evading my question) was that 'when the consciousness is turned towards God, there is nothing but God; when it is turned away, then there is the material world'. (Cf. *In Search of a Yogi* (Routledge and Kegan Paul, 1962), pp. 216 f.) This seems, with a difference, to be the teaching of some of the Greek Fathers, notably of Gregory of Nyssa and Evagrius, probably following Origen, that the 'materiality' of this present world (of which that evil which is essentially a tendency towards non-entity, non-being, is an inevitable aspect), is caused by the turning of man from God, that it is the very separation of things from God that gives them this material aspect. The body and this 'material' world are not, however, to disappear with the redemption (cf. also Scotus Erigena, p. 13, n. 1), but are to return to their true, original 'spiritual' state; this, in their teaching, will be the 'new heaven and new earth'. The system of the hierarchy seems to imply this in a slightly different way, that man, the being of man, is rather a simultaneous turning to God and to the world, a reception of being from God which he transmits further to the world below him. So long as he remains in contact with the hierarchy, and so turned towards the source of the Light, the world below him is drawn back through him to its source at the exact moment when, of itself, it is plunging into that non-entity of which evil and sin are aspects. For an interesting discussion of *The Earthly Paradise* in such a context cf. *Downside Review*, Summer, 1954, Dom Mark Pontifex.

[2] In order to avoid giving at this point a false emphasis to the author's thought, it should perhaps be added that he sees the Incarnation not so much as an improvisation to meet a situation that had got a little out of hand (the impression sometimes given by modern text-books), or to satisfy a legal claim of justice (though he does not deny this), but rather as a stanching of the *lacrimae rerum* at their source, the Redemption as already achieved at the source of the Light before sin appeared in 'history'. History is here the working out in space and time of both sin and the Redemption. The same situation, that is, is seen from a different viewpoint, less in its temporal and spatial extension than in its source in eternity, where God 'chose us in him [Christ] before the foundation of the world' (Eph. i, 4). Cf. *Div. Names*, 869A, '[God] knowing and creating angels before there were angels'; and 820A, 'all things pre-exist in him'. (There is, of course, no question here of Plato's doctrine of the pre-existence of souls. There, is, however, a certain parallel between the latter's doctrine of 'remembrance' or 'recognition' and the teaching of St. Thomas (implicit in these present works) of knowledge by infused species, possessed by the angels by nature,

the Incarnation, and man, at the point at which we meet him, is only at the stage of 'becoming', of being inserted into his place in the hierarchy; his whole life in this world is conceived as a progress to true being through reception of the Light in increasing fulness by way of the hierarchy.[1] In himself he is simply non-being; cut off from the source of being, he could have no existence of any kind, and the stages of his birth and growth are the degrees of his incorporation into Christ through the hierarchy.[2] The Word is the uncreated source and pattern of all created being throughout the hierarchies, including the world of men; all were in him before they were given existence outside him and continue to have their being in him as the spring of their life and being.[3] The normal distribution of light

[1] This idea is basic to the author's thought. All that is in this world is an extension into time of a reality that in its essence is One. The way back is the reverse of the process, from extension and division to unity.

[2] It may be asked how a creature cut off from the hierarchy could have any being at all. The answer cannot be sought in any actual distinction between a natural and supernatural order, of which our author knows nothing. (Modern theologians, in their desire to stress the gratuitousness and nobility of grace, sometimes give the impression that there do actually exist two separate, independent orders, of nature and grace, so that one can have one's choice between them, or perhaps alternately one or the other.) This author knows only the existing order, of man fallen and restored. In the order actually existing he sees the Light (for man his complete being) as offered to all, at every moment and in every circumstance, and in the least of things of the material world, 'never ceasing to offer itself to the eyes of the soul', a light which is still present when they close their eyes and follows them when they turn away (*Ecc. Hier.* 400A). Logically it seems that we must interpret the 'natural' world in such a scheme, and our own 'natural' being, as simply the first glimpses of a Light (and a Being) which, if accepted, will increase in volume until it has finally established man in his due place in the hierarchy (through a process, as we shall see, of purification, illumination and union). It follows that rational thought and scientific knowledge would be but the first stage of a regular, harmonious ascent to God. For a fuller discussion see p. 68 below.

[3] Cf. p. 18, n. 2. The author's explanation is equivalent to the scholastic expression of things pre-existing in the 'mind' of God, but in his anxiety to

by man by grace before the Fall and, with the Redemption, gradually restored. In this teaching knowledge through the senses, from material things, adds nothing to the knowledge already possessed in the source, so to speak, of these things; is a 'recognition' of what is already known by infused species.)

INTRODUCTION

down the hierarchy having ceased, man and the world beneath him had become something almost more negative than non-being, a positive lack of being, an unquenchable thirst for being it could never attain to, a living death, perhaps the nearest our minds can approach to a concept of hell. The Word, by his incarnation, has, if the phrase may be used without irreverence, by-passed the celestial hierarchy, becoming not just an abstraction, humanity, but all men in all their manifold external manifestations.[1] By his ascension he has taken back into the hierarchy man and his world in indestructible form, *aeternitatis aditu devicta morte reserato*.[2] He has bridged the gap between the hierarchies and this world, re-established the lines of communication. His birth on the lowest plane of being, where it verges on non-entity, is thus virtually a new creation, in which he has become all things, taking up all men and things into himself, drawing them up from their plunge into nothingness, recapitulating them in himself and presenting them back to the Father. God is, then, once again all in all, the Holy Trinity once again reflected faithfully in all creatures, and we see again a dynamic pulse of being from God and back to him; God present in the hierarchy as a whole and in each part of it, wholly transcendent while wholly present in each of his creatures.[3]

In such a scheme of things, then, our life and world, with all its details, its history and its continuation after death of the

---

[1] Cf. *Div. Names*, 897A–B: 'Theologians speak of the Deity under the name of Redemption because he does not allow beings that exist to fall through into non-being (διαπέσειν πρὸς τὸ μὴ εἶναι)'. Cf. also S. Th. III, Q. 8, 3, and 4 ad 1; *De Malo*, Q. 4. 1.

[2] From the Collect of Easter Day: 'overcoming death and reopening the way to eternity'.

[3] A consoling thought that seems to follow logically from such a scheme is that one's own small efforts, even if they produce no apparent fruit in the present, yet are one with the activity of the Logos and have served to inspire all the great men of the past, and will just as surely be active in those who shape the destiny of the future. What is to come in the immediate future we cannot know, but the great 'folding-up' of Scotus Erigena, the 'heavens folded up as a book [a scroll]' of Is. xxxiv, 4 and Apoc. vi, 14, has already been accomplished in Christ.

---

preserve the unity of God he would probably object that this phrase suggests that God 'has a mind' to do something and then does it, whereas he, in the author's phrase, 'knows and produces all things in one single act'.

individual, is seen as contained in the Word incarnate, extended into us individually in the sense that Christ is wholly present as the particular limited being of each. So, in the 'new creation' which the present generation is in process of becoming, sensible phenomena are seen as projections of the Word incarnate, an extension of the Incarnation, and we ourselves, wrapped and enfolded in him, 'living, moving and being' in him, 'seeing' and 'feeling' it all through his creative eyes.[1] Modern physical science, as we saw, suggests that our world seems to be in some way the production of our senses; not that, with some modern idealists, they necessarily deny its objective reality as something external to themselves, or declare that their atom bombs are merely an illusion, but as assigning its ultimate origin to a cause beyond the senses and operating through them. The school of thought we are considering would apparently take us back one step farther to find the source in Christ; and in him all has been taken up from time into eternity.

That before the Incarnation men already existed to be taken up into Christ, and that we who live after it have already before baptism an existence of a kind, a 'becoming' rather than a fully achieved existence, a 'groaning within ourselves', presents no difficulty to our author from his viewpoint of eternity. In this view the Word with his humanity, embodying the whole human race and its world, already existed in the source of the hierarchies before these began their flow through space and time. The purpose of the treatise we are about to study is to demonstrate that all that was, that is, in Christ flows still into this world down through the stages of the ecclesiastical

[1] For Plato (*Timaeus*, 37 c6–d7) time and the world of change is 'a moving likeness of eternity'. For our author it is more precisely through the Incarnation (*Div. Names*, 592A) that 'the Eternal assumes an extension in time and is born in our nature'. The same seems to be implied in St. Thomas's teaching on the mode of operation of the sacraments, as the continuous presentation under specially designated material forms of the whole activity of Christ. All the actions of his humanity, from his going out from his Father to his return, the 'mysteries' of the life of Christ, are the real, the physical efficient causes, of grace, of the Light that is the life and being of God in us, each mystery conveying its appropriate grace; and they flow first into the spiritual aspect of man and through that into the material. Cf. S. Th. III, Q. 48 ff., Q. 8, 2, and W. Barden, O.P., *What Happens at the Mass* (Clon. and Reynolds), pp. 71 ff.

INTRODUCTION

hierarchy, made really present in the Holy Eucharist with its clothing of ritual, words and actions; and flowing into each soul at need through the sacraments, flowing even into those outside the visible communion of the Church and, according as they 'open their eyes to the light', slowly but inexorably leading them from the adumbrations of their present faith to the source of the Light itself.[1]

It seems, therefore, a logical conclusion from such a cosmic view that all that is good, in the philosophical sense of all that is positive reality, in our lives, only its undesirable elements shed, has passed over in Christ back to its source, and that with our death, *transitus*, or passover in Christ we shall, as the material reflection of a direct contemplation of God imitating that of the seraphim in its intense, motionless activity, enjoy as our human nature demands, unfolding unceasingly before our astonished gaze, vista after vista of what we see and possess there; perfect possession of our world, able to switch to any aspect or part of it at will into past, present or illimitable future. In the meantime our life is a becoming, a passage to that permanent state. *How this happens, imperfectly here, and perfectly after death, the mechanics of it, though a matter pre-eminently worthy of study, matters comparatively little.*[2] Whether we care to por-

---

[1] The Light was offered (and is offered) to all nations, not only to the Jews, but whereas the Jews accepted it, the others (considered generally, as nations or people as a whole) refused, and turned 'to the worship of false gods' (or, according to another MS.: 'to that which does not exist'). Cf. *Cel. Hier.* 260C ff. and *Ecc. Hier.* 397D–400A. More particularly, the Old Testament saints in the 'Hierarchy of the Law' are seen as carrying men on, as it were, into the ecclesiastical hierarchy of the New Testament, the fulfilment of that (cf. St. Paul's 'pedagogue' and Christ's: 'I came not to destroy, but to fulfil'), inserting them in it to be carried up by that back to union with God. Cf. p. 142 below. Newman was in the same tradition when he said (*Parochial and Plain Sermons* (Longman), Vol. VII, pp. 85–6) that 'God contemplates from everlasting the one entire work—introducing them once and for all, though they are but gradually unfolded to our limited faculties and in this transient scene—[even at the time of the calling of Abraham] both the course of the Jewish dispensation and the coming of Christ were (so to say) realised'. (Cf. an article in *Pax*, Spring, 1955, on 'Newman and Contemporary Theology'.)

[2] It will help to keep a sense of proportion in this matter if we reflect that, even if there were no resurrection of the body and no 'new earth' adapted to it, if we became literally a lower species of angel, we should be more fully 'human', so to speak, than we are now. In this author's scheme all that is in

tray our world to ourselves as an electrical phenomenon; as a kind of super-television projected by our eyes and other senses; as water, fire, number; as composed of countless 'tiny billiard balls', or simply as a superior quality of green cheese, it remains what it is; its effect on us and our action on it are the same and, in the mind of the author, if that has been correctly interpreted, it shares the indestructibility of man himself. Man is a microcosm; each man is all that is, within his own personal manner and limitations, to the extent of his capacity a manifestation of God himself.

Our physical scientists seem, therefore, to be ranged with us on the side of the angelic hierarchy and, as I hope to show, of the ecclesiastical hierarchy. They are in an immemorial tradition. Newman, on the occasion of the gift of a 'fiddle', wondered 'if music may be thought'.[1] Alfred Noyes, echoing, whether consciously or not, St. Augustine and the tradition exemplified by the pseudo-Denys, thinks of it as memory,[2] as God's

[1] He had feared that the violin might be a temptation to waste time, but found instead that it enabled him to get through more work than usual, since 'thought seemed to flow from the music'.

[2] For Augustine 'memory' is the first of the trinity of powers in the human soul, by which man passes from time to eternity, from transient, partial phenomena to their undivided, eternal source in God. In the context of this work it would, I think, be the point at which the being of man issues from the flow of the Light, what, I assume, the mystics are trying to describe by such phrases as 'summit', 'apex', 'spark' of the soul. This concept of 'memory' is important for an appreciation—I prefer to call it this rather than 'understanding'—of the Mystery of the Synaxis (Holy Eucharist) (cf. p. 113 below) and for this author's doctrine of 'contemplation' (cf. p. 67 below). I think our author would see the 'memory', 'commemoration', that is the Mass as the archetype and source of all memory, of all the partial, divided fragments of memory that we call by that name, yet which achieve full reality only from union with this. As a current example of the rediscovery of this principle cf. J. Dupont, O.S.B. (*Nouv. Rev. Th.*, December 1958, p. 1035), who quotes with approval Leenhardt on the significance for the Jewish mind of

man is present in the angels in a higher way; one might say, using an inappropriate quantitative term, in a higher 'concentration'—anyway, really present. It is not possible for us to visualise or describe it adequately, because it is on this higher plane, but it is probable that most men have glimpses of it, through, rather than in, such moments of complete harmony and happiness as they may enjoy in this world. It will be understood that in all this I am trying only to interpret the author's mind and teaching; my own mind is still in process of formation, of becoming.

INTRODUCTION

'memory' present in us as the source of our being, the point at which our life begins:

> Music that is God's memory never forgets you. . . .
> All, all that we ever loved, though it sleep in the silence,
> At a touch of the Master shall wake and be music again.[1]

I have tried to demonstrate for the general reader the practical value of this line of thought and the advantages to be gained from a link with the ecclesiastical hierarchy, by relating it to modern theories of physical science. In the more restricted field of that liturgical renewal which is being so stoutly resisted by so many of my brother clergy, its value for a full appreciation of the nature of the Church's liturgical worship will be obvious. The general spirit of the scheme we have considered, especially in this matter of the relation of the visible world to the invisible, was the spiritual climate in which was born and developed the *lex orandi* of the Church, her liturgical worship; and the shape and vocabulary of the liturgy carry the associations and presuppositions of this school of thought. Further, it was this liturgical worship that formed the mind of the West down to the dawn of modern times; until the Counter-Reformation intelligent participation (though, one must admit, progressively less intelligent participation) in the Church's liturgical worship formed the basis of the religious education of the faithful. A simple and striking example quoted by Mgr. Knox some years ago[2] illustrates well the mentality formed by such an education. He refers to our Lord's description of himself as the *real*, the *true*, bread (John vi, 56). It is not the bread of this world that is the standard loaf by which to measure and judge all others. The

---

[1] Alfred Noyes, *The Unknown God* (Sheed and Ward, 1941), p. 79.
[2] In an American edition of sermons not at the moment accessible to the present writer.

---

the word 'commemoration' (*anamnesis*, I Cor. xi, 24) when applied to the Mass: 'Se souvenir, c'est rendre présent et actuel.—Le passé et le présent se confondent. Une ré-actuation du passé devient possible.' I think, however, that our present author sees the 're-presentation' of the Mass not so much as a 're-actualisation', or a juggling with time, as a 'revealing' and 'putting in touch with' something that is always present. We shall find this concept recurring continually, e.g. p. 165, n. 1, p. 18, n. 2, p. 163, n. 1, p. 109, n. 8, p. 197, n. 4.

COSMIC THEOLOGY

Real Bread, the source and support of all our being, is in the other world, and what we have here is only an inferior imitation.

There is a further important implication. Some understanding of this mode of thought is necessary for a full understanding of the Church's liturgical worship; it is also essential for an understanding of the East, to which this climate of thought has always been native.[1] This becomes of more immediately practical importance if we consider that Russia, linked in our minds with the more sinister aspects of atomic science, is of the East rather than of the West. Now Plato stood, geographically and spiritually, at the meeting-point of East and West. There was a constant interchange of ideas so that it is not possible for us to know for certain what was Plato's own contribution to philosophical thought. It is, however, certain that what we have called his primary intuition, which became the basis for this first theological *summa*, was commonly accepted by the Fathers, and is implicit in the Church's liturgy, was common currency in the East; it formed, and still forms, the basis of eastern theological speculation. With the coming of Christianity, with its great central fact of the Incarnation, as the fulfilment and crown of this common philosophical heritage, there were the makings of a religion and culture uniting the two, common in essentials, infinitely diverse in accidental local expression. This unity was never achieved, for reasons that cannot be discussed here, and the meeting-point became a parting of the ways. These led in one direction to a hesychastic content to live in the world within oneself, letting the world of phenomena go by, and, in the other direction, to a frantic pursuit in ever-increasing tempo of a world one could never quite catch up with. The whole, balanced view of life is that now in process of being formed anew by renewed intelligent participation in the liturgical worship of the ecclesiastical hierarchy.

Today the two, East and West, are meeting again, but, generally speaking, at only the most superficial level. The need for mutual understanding is great; it may be necessary for the survival of the world of phenomena, it is certainly essential for the business of living together in a contracting world. Is it too

[1] Cf. *In Search of a Yogi* (Routledge and Kegan Paul, 1962), p. 31 and *passim*.

INTRODUCTION

fanciful to see that liturgical renewal that is still feeling its way to a more complete appreciation of the true nature and spirit of the Church's life—indeed of all life—as designed by divine providence to be the bond of reunion between East and West?

I would be unwilling that anything said in these pages should appear to support the suggestion sometimes heard that 'Thomism' is outmoded in so far as contact with the East and the requirements of 'adaptation' are concerned. The contrary is probably nearer the truth, that such a synthesis is particularly valuable when the meeting of East and West is proceeding so rapidly. I would, however, like to register a protest against styling St. Thomas Aristotelian without any qualification. What he attempted was a harmony or synthesis of Plato and Aristotle, and it appears there is more in him of Plato than of Aristotle. However that may be, might one, with all due deference, suggest that a little more attention might profitably be given to that component of the Thomistic synthesis that is being considered here (to this particular mode of thought rather than necessarily to this particular author)? It is not easy to piece together the teaching of St. Thomas on a particular point, and from the neat little highly polished bricks provided by the Angelic Doctor in such embarrassing abundance men have raised edifices of strikingly different shape. Even with an electronic brain and twelve million cards (the latest 'aid') it is likely that the student in our theological schools will still need the digests and text-books at present compiled for his assistance. It is these that commonly relegate this whole great sphere of thought to a short section on asceticism or mysticism.

THE ECCLESIASTICAL HIERARCHY

The ecclesiastical hierarchy forms in our author's scheme the vital link between the visible and invisible worlds, between the transient world of becoming and that of true, permanent being. Since his aim is the limited one of explaining the nature and economy of this hierarchy, he does not, except by implication and casual references, go beyond it. He does, however, refer repeatedly to the celestial hierarchy on which this is modelled, an 'imitation' or reflection of it. The 'mysteries', or sacraments, form the direct link with the invisible world. They are, in fact,

THE ECCLESIASTICAL HIERARCHY

more than a mere link; they actually bring the invisible world into the world of space and time. Their external 'shape' or pattern is, on this lower plane, the 'shape' or pattern of the invisible spiritual reality above them which they contain; to one looking down the scale, into the world below them, they are, as it were, the summing up, the recapitulation in the literal sense, of the whole of this material world. The 'mystical', symbolic, language of the external form of these mysteries—the whole rite, that is, of words, things and actions—unlike ordinary, 'philosophical', language, 'requires an initiation';[1] its meaning can be understood only by those who, through this initiation, are able to penetrate through the external form to the 'contemplation of and participation in' (a regularly recurring phrase) the spiritual realities. This is the reason why the profane are excluded from the mysteries: the external form could convey no meaning to them; divorced from the upper end of the scale it could, in many cases, appear sheer nonsense and have the effect of repelling them from religion. The contemplation of these outward forms—and at this period attendance at the Holy Eucharist, for instance, was assumed to include, almost as an integral part, the reception of Holy Communion by all—was simply the lower end, so to speak, of a range of sight, of contemplation, that led up into the unseen: the one was contained in the other, an aspect of it, the two interpenetrated.[2]

Beginning, then, with the sacraments our author sees the ecclesiastical hierarchy flowing from the invisible world in a series of steps, stages or waterfalls of the 'illuminative cascade'. He envisages the flow as descending in three main steps or degrees: (1) the 'mysteries' or sacraments; (2) those who administer, transmit the sacraments, the clergy or 'initiators'; (3) the laity, the people, those who receive the sacraments, the 'initiate'. Each of these three degrees has three divisions, so that we have a ninefold hierarchy 'imitating' the nine choirs of angels. Even within the individual members of each of these subdivisions, it is possible to make a threefold distinction; each proceeds to its fulfilment by a threefold movement of purgation, illumination and union. That, at least, is from our way of viewing it; fundamentally, it is a simple reception of Light, a movement from non-being to being. It is an acceptance of Light

[1] Letter ix, 1105D.   [2] Cf. p. 16, n. 1.

INTRODUCTION

which is at the same time the effect of the possession of a degree of Light; purgation is the effect of illumination, as well as the preparation for it, and illumination is already a union with the Light. Each moment reproduces in its degree the whole, as each member of each subdivision reproduces the whole subdivision in its own degree, and the subdivision is a reflection of the whole and ultimately of the whole hierarchy. So, too, the union of one member is the beginning of the moment of purgation in the next member above in the ascending order.[1] This principle is seen as so fundamental to both hierarchies that even the angels, we shall learn, have something corresponding to what in men is purgation.[2]

The three sacraments forming the first, or highest, degree of the ecclesiastical hierarchy are for our author Baptism, Unction[3] and Holy Eucharist. Not that he does not recognise any others,[4] but these are for him the three essential for the initiation or introduction of man into the stream of Light. Others are limited to special needs and classes of men already initiated. So Holy Order, 'consecration to the priesthood', is seen as establishing the vital link between the sacraments and those with the office of transmitting the Light to others, the clergy; and this means primarily the bishop, through whom it flows by way of his subordinate clergy to the people.

Only three orders of clergy are mentioned in this second degree, corresponding to the three divisions of the first degree, bishop, priest and deacon. This is, of course, correct for the period at which the treatise pretends to have been written; by the early sixth century, the most likely date of composition, there were minor ministers.

The people, the laity, are divided into: (1) those not admitted to the sacraments, composed of catechumens preparing for baptism and public penitents and lapsed of varying degrees not easily distinguished in the author's account; (2) the initiate, the 'holy people' or 'contemplatives'; (3) the highest degree, the monastic order.

Instead of treating of these in their logical order of descent, so

---

[1] Cf. p. 141 below.   [2] Cf. p. 184 below.
[3] I use this word in preference to 'anointing' because it may mean both the act of anointing and oil used. It is used in these works to include all the rites of anointing with holy oil.   [4] Cf. p. 119 below.

to speak, out of the invisible world, from the sacraments, through the bishop and down to the lowest degree of the laity, the author adopts a method psychologically more attractive. After a short introductory chapter on the principle of hierarchy he introduces one seeking enlightenment, 'illumination' or baptism. This provides an opportunity of introducing all his characters already in the first scene. The congregation of the faithful is summoned. We see the three orders of the clergy co-operating in the rite of baptism; confirmation is administered[1] immediately after baptism, and the neophyte is admitted to communion in the Holy Eucharist. This forms a natural transition to a chapter on the *Mystery of the Synaxis* (Holy Eucharist), followed by one on the *Sacrament of Unction* (Anointing). This last deals in fact rather with the blessing of the holy oil for use in the sacrament of confirmation and, in the author's own phrase, 'in almost all the rites of the hierarchy'.[2] Here, then, we have his trinity of sacraments. The next chapter treats of ordination to the priesthood and is followed by one on the degrees of the laity. This latter deals, however, almost exclusively with the *Consecration of a Monk*, which is shown as modelled on the rite of ordination to the priesthood: it reflects this on its lower level.

Although the author's style and diction have been described, with some justification, as 'fantastic' and 'uncouth', it will be seen that he displays considerable skill and artistry in thus linking up the three principal divisions of his hierarchy. Holy order is seen as primarily establishing a link between the sacraments, and the clergy, the 'initiators', channelling the flow into them in such a way that it can be transmitted to others. So we shall find, in the episcopal consecration, that there is placed on the head of the bishop (as it still is) the book of sacred scriptures, revealing 'all his [God's] words and all his acts, in a word all that the Deity in his goodness has wished to transmit to the human hierarchy of what has been said and done by God',[3] with the implied suggestion that all this is being literally infused into him for transmission further. Similarly, the monastic consecration forms a bridge between the second and third principal divisions, between the clergy and the laity. The monk, as monk (he may also, of course, be a priest as well), is still of the laity, yet he has

---
[1] I think it is confirmation that is intended here, but the question is disputed. Cf. p. 66 below.   [2] P. 122 below.   [3] P. 157 below.

INTRODUCTION

something in common with the clergy too, and his 'consecration' is similar in form to that of their ordination, and even gives him a degree of life, a communion in the mysteries, 'in a manner different from that of the holy people',[1] that is from the rest of the laity.

The picture is rounded off by a final chapter dealing with the funeral rites. The initiate, anointed for the spiritual combat immediately before baptism, has been faithful to death. He is interred with rejoicing at the thought of the happiness he is to enjoy for eternity. The dead body is again anointed immediately before burial, and great emphasis is laid on the fact that the body, which has been the faithful companion of the warfare of the soul, is to share in its joy and everlasting reward in the resurrection.

THE TWO HIERARCHIES

It is clear that for the pseudo-Denys there is an integral connection between the two hierarchies, the celestial and the ecclesiastical. It has been assumed (p. 10) that the one forms a continuation of the other, the ecclesiastical hierarchy being attached, as it were, to the lower end of the celestial and forming a regular series of steps with it. This is the general interpretation of the commentators, and at first sight it seems that this is how the author envisaged the connection. It does, however, entail a number of problems that must inevitably occur to the reader sooner or later, should he be inclined to delve a little more deeply. It is such problems that have led critics to assert that in such a scheme there is logically no room for the Incarnation. This seems to me to betray a fundamental misunderstanding of the author's whole system—but there are difficulties that need examining.

It appears, for instance, that in such a gradation all men must be lower than all angels; yet there is a constant tradition in the Church that some men may be higher than some angels. St. Thomas, for instance, held this.[2] Further, such a continuous

---

[1] P. 183 below.

[2] Cf. S. Th. I, Q. 117, 2 ad 3; Q. 108, 8 o; *Sent. Disp.* II, dist. 9, Q. 1 ad 1; cf. p. 126, n. 2 below. For the sake of the non-Catholic reader it may be useful to say that St. Thomas Aquinas is not considered to be infallible, and there

series would seem to make the sacraments of the ecclesiastical hierarchy lower than the lowest of the degrees of the celestial hierarchy; but we know for certain that the Holy Eucharist, for instance, contains the real presence of Christ, who is not merely a manifestation of God such as the angels are in their varying degrees, but God by substantial (hypostatic) union, God in the most complete and literal sense of the word, infinitely transcending, that is, the highest order of angels.

The alternative to this arrangement is to regard the ecclesiastical hierarchy as parallel to the celestial. An argument for this might be based on the fact that our hierarchy is proportioned to the celestial and reflects it in all its parts. In particular, we shall see, for example (p. 132), that the clergy surrounding and contemplating the holy oil at its consecration are compared to the seraphim surrounding the throne of God in motionless contemplation. It would be possible to explain the author's system on these lines; but I do not believe that this is what he had in mind. I think we can best understand his meaning (remembering that he makes no distinction between a natural and supernatural state of man: cf. p. 12 and p. 19, n. 5) by considering the opinion of St. Thomas already referred to on the question of the relative position of angels and men in the hierarchies. What St. Thomas says, in brief, is that men are by nature lower than the angels, but that they may by grace be higher.

Now it is clear that in the author's view men are by nature lower than the angels, and that in the order of being, the flow of the 'illuminative cascade', they come after angels; their

---

are questions, especially of physical science, where he is demonstrably wrong. He had, however, one of the greatest minds of all time, he is a most reliable witness to the Christian tradition, and his *summa* of theology is without parallel among Christian theological works, more particularly for the manner in which it expounds the Christian tradition in terms of the new scientific knowledge of his day. It is thus convenient to refer to it as an exposition of the Christian tradition and also because it is the system officially approved as the basis of the theological course in Catholic colleges. This does not mean, of course, that students are compelled to accept his views on disputed points, and the opposite opinions are also expounded; but his opinion is always at least worth very careful consideration. The questions he poses may at times be a little startling: the first reference above comes under the heading: Whether Men Can Teach the Angels.

INTRODUCTION

hierarchy is seen as a continuation of the lower end of the hierarchy of angels. Had there been no Fall (though such speculation is foreign to the mind of the author), this presumably is the line along which the whole of man's being, nature and grace, natural and supernatural, would have been communicated. In that case we can only conclude that all men, in every respect and for always, would have been a little lower than all angels.[1] As it is, in consequence of the *felix culpa* of the Fall,[2] redeemed man has not only regained the degree of grace corresponding to his place below the angels; through communion with Christ in the sacraments a measure of grace equal to that of the whole hierarchy of angels, and more besides, is now open to him—in theory, at least; in fact, it will always be limited, in our author's phrase, 'according to the merits of each'; but it is within man's reach. He remains man, by nature lower than the angels, still obliged to receive spiritual realities in material, sensible form, but what he now receives of these may be immeasurably more than would have been transmitted along the regular line of the hierarchies, had his connection with this never been severed.

I suggested (p. 20) that Christ by his incarnation might be considered to have 'by-passed' the celestial hierarchy. That is one way of describing it. Since, however, Christ, as God, is also the actual *being* of the celestial hierarchy, its members are, in their varying degrees, more or less inadequate manifestations of him, it might be more correct to say that he has carried this, and indeed heaven itself, into the ecclesiastical hierarchy with him: 'The holy city, the new Jerusalem, coming down out of heaven (Apoc. xxi, 2).' Or again, since the purpose of the Incarnation is to lead men back to union with God through incorporation, recapitulation, into Christ, it might also be described as a taking up of the ecclesiastical hierarchy into the celestial. This, in fact, is how St. Thomas sees it in one passage of his writings;[3] as the hierarchy of the Law was taken up into that of the Church, finding in this its fulfilment, so the hierarchy

[1] The angels could not, in such a scheme, have transmitted a higher degree of being, natural or supernatural, than they themselves possessed.

[2] The daring phrase of the *Exsultet*, the salutation of the Paschal Candle by the deacon at the Paschal Vigil commemorating the central act of the Redemption: '—how truly necessary the sin of Adam—how happy a fault that earned so great a Redeemer'.

[3] Cf. p. 30, n. 2 and p. 142 below.

of the Church is being taken up into that of heaven, and in the final consummation he envisages its members as distributed among those of the celestial hierarchy, forming with them one single unity.

Our present author would, I think, prefer to see them as but different aspects of a single movement which is, at one and the same time—or, better, outside time—a going out from God and a return to him. It would, then, I suggest, fit better into this author's scheme to regard the hierarchies as neither joined, so that one is the continuation of the other, nor as parallel, but rather as interpenetrating, the one living in the other.[1]

If I may be allowed to repeat, since this is so vital a point, man retains his nature of man. He may receive now a degree of spiritual life higher than that of some of the angels, while remaining inferior to them in the manner of his receiving it; it has to come through the material, visible forms of the sacraments, administered by a visible Church. Man sees it further reflected in his own material form and in that of the world in which he lives. Perhaps that makes it sound as though man is, after all, inferior to all the angels, but it is not really so: shall we say he is different? In order to see the matter in its true proportion it may help to consider again the fact of the Incarnation, since it is through participation in the life of Christ on the planes of both nature and grace that we attain to this salvation.

Christ himself, in his human nature, was not only, as he himself said, less than the Father ('The Father is greater than I', John xiv, 28), but, as the author of Hebs. ii, 9 says, even 'a little lower than the angels'; as we do, he received his human nature by that line of transmission. We thus have the apparently paradoxical situation of Christ who, as God (more precisely as the second person of the Trinity, the Logos), *is* the being of the celestial hierarchy, receiving as man human nature by way of

[1] I think it would be possible in this view of things to see Prof. Hoyle's 'expanding universe' and 'continuous creation' (not excluding a more extended meaning: man's assisted journey into space and his probings of the ultimate constitution of matter and of the deeper recesses of the human spirit), as the external reflection, the 'imitation', of our author's progress up the hierarchy towards its source, the complement of this in the world below the line of the ecclesiastical hierarchy. Perhaps this is the significance of Père Teilhard de Chardin's 'omega point'; I have not had the opportunity of studying the works of this writer. But I write subject to correction.

that hierarchy, ministered to by angels, and in some respects subject to them and even to men.[1] The height of the paradox is reached in the fact of the human birth. Not only is he, as the Logos, the source of the being of the mother from whom he received his human birth; she was also redeemed by his life, death and resurrection in such a way as to be conceived immaculate in preparation for her unique function as Mother of God, transmitting to him that life he was to sacrifice.

Paradox, it appears, at least, to what this author calls our 'divided' life and to our manner of viewing things from this plane of space and time. From his standpoint[2] it presents less difficulty. All this is but the presentation on the visible plane, in terms of the ecclesiastical hierarchy, of that which is present in its source as a single unity. The Redemption, moreover, is seen as the redemption through man of the whole of nature, of that material world which of itself tends to flow into non-entity. It is effected by the Incarnation, by Christ *In se reconcilians ima summis*.[3] It is in Christ that man may aspire to the spiritual realities that are the celestial hierarchy.

There is a dispute, aired periodically in the Catholic press and perhaps arousing in the 'holy people' some perplexity, since it is not always easy for some of the clergy to follow the line of argument: the question whether man can know God. Since our author regularly expresses the whole being of man in terms of a knowledge of God that is also a union and a possession, and, through that, a union with ourselves and everything else besides, it is clear that the question is important for our present study. One school is of the opinion that not only does man not know God, but that he is essentially unknowable;[4] the other school

---

[1] Cf. *Cel. Hier.* 181C f. '. . . he [Christ at the Incarnation] submitted obediently to the forms transmitted from God the Father by the angels . . .': i.e., the angels recorded in sacred scripture as concerned with the events of his birth, life and death. The paradox is deliberately heightened in the liturgy of the ecclesiastical hierarchy, e.g., *Senex puerum portabat, puer autem senem regebat* (the old man [Simeon] carried the boy, but the boy was ruling, guiding, the old man) (*Magnificat* antiphon at Vespers of Candlemass). Cf. too the medieval vernacular carols.

[2] Cf. p. 18, n. 2.

[3] From the Mass of the Blessed Virgin during Eastertide: 'reconciling, rejoining, in himself the lowest with the highest'.

[4] They distinguish between knowing 'that' God is and 'what' God is.

declares with equal emphasis that man can know God, and, some would add, even directly and in this world, and may adduce a long line of people through history who claim to have verified this from their own experience: 'Invisible we view thee; incomprehensible we clutch thee.' Both sides claim St. Thomas as their authority, and I think it is possible to find both views in his works, one as the complement of the other; but they are seen in their simpler, more elementary form in our author; both as true but neither as the whole truth. God is known and apprehended in all things (p. 10 above), at the same time he is utterly unknowable, for ever beyond all we can think or say of him. This, however, is vitally important, that there is for our author a direct line of communication from one to the other.[1] We know and possess God in all created things, but only if we pass on through and beyond them; if we try to stop at any one of them, then we do not really know or possess this one either, but only its most external, peripheral manifestation.[2] Finally, we have to pass beyond, out of ('ecstasy' in the fullest sense), not only all we can know or see, but even beyond ourselves, and know God 'by unknowing'. Yet it is at this point that we find, at the source of the stream of Light, both ourselves and all else—'losing our life to find it'. There is, however, this direct line, from the ecclesiastical hierarchy—or the things below it—through the celestial hierarchy (in the sense suggested above), the Divine Names (all true yet inadequate manifestations of God); in all this we know God, yet it is always something less than God that we know, serving to carry us on beyond it until finally we know him in the 'ecstasy' of the *Mystical Theology*, 'knowing through unknowing, in a union that passes all understanding' (*Div. Names*, 872A).

'Union' is perhaps the operative word here; love is, for this author, the motive power of the whole hierarchy, a desire for union with something that is for ever receding beyond all created things and even ourselves; and it is consonant with this, though it does sometimes arouse surprise in commentators, that

---

[1] Cf. p. 16, n. 1. All things may, for this author, become the point of departure of contemplation; cf., e.g., *Cel. Hier.* 141 ff., 328 ff.

[2] I think this is in essence identical with the Hindu doctrine of *maya*. The best Hindu exposition of *maya* known to the present writer is that of Ramana Maharshi (Cf. *Ramana Maharshi*, Arthur Osborne (Rider, 1954).)

though both *eros* and *agape* are used for this love, it is *eros* that is preferred. It is in such a setting that we may best understand the essence and *raison d'être* of asceticism, as the deliberate 'going out of' and beyond ourselves and material things, from the surface of the desirable towards its inner reality: 'If a man should give all the substance of his house for love, he shall despise it as nothing' (*Cant. of Cants.* viii, 7). Things and people do, in any case, inevitably retire before us, whether we will or not. The pain of parting and loss in this temporal scene is no more—and no less—than the withdrawal of things to the invisible plane towards their source. This has led one of the Fathers to say *melius est relinquere quam relinqui* (it is better to leave than to be left); it is better not to be tied too closely to persons and things in their present, transient, imperfect fashion, but rather to seek them in their perfection in their eternal source: 'they that use this world as though they used it not' (I Cor. vii, 31). Ultimately only in this way can one possess things also in their material manifestation. This I believe to be of the essence of the teaching of this author.

It is not, then, as some protagonists of one half of the truth almost seem to suggest, that 'it is better to travel hopefully than to arrive'. That is indeed true of travel on the visible plane, where we may never rest, because no sooner do we arrive than we realise immediately that we have not in fact arrived. But on the invisible plane, we are already at home, *in patria*, already arrived, where 'everyone shall call us by our name'. Those who attain to this happy state are in immediate union with God, with all that God is, and in God with all else besides. Even so, no created being can ever *comprehend* God, in the strict sense, circumscribe and include within himself all that God is. What each perceives and receives, though to the full limit of his capacity, so that he attains to complete happiness and full realisation of all his potentialities, depends upon the perfection of the instrument, to speak metaphorically, that receives it, the degree of receptivity and fidelity of reproduction of the instrument. Our measure of space and time in the ecclesiastical hierarchy is given us to perfect the instrument, and, as we shall see (p. 137), the Greek word for this, to perfect, complete, fulfil, is also the word for sacrament, the means of union with God through the Incarnation, uniting two distinct natures in one divine Person.

PSEUDO-DENYS AND PLATO

The term 'Platonist', applied to a writer by modern Catholic theologians, is commonly used in the pejorative sense, as suggesting, while not actually saying so, that he is 'not quite'; 'Neo-Platonist' is generally taken as implying a hint that he is suspect of heresy. Mgr. Knox even succeeds in conveying the impression that Plato, or at least Platonism, is somehow responsible for all the eccentricities of the whole gallery of queer types he introduces in his fascinating work of *Enthusiasm*. One hesitates to think what Plato, with his ice-cold serenity, order and balance, would have made of such a queer company. However that may be, it is, as I have said (p. 25), a fact that, whether we like it or not, the great Fathers of the Church, who first formulated her doctrine, were all 'Platonists', and the Church's liturgical worship, the external expression of her life, was from the beginning set in this mould.

In itself it matters comparatively little what system of philosophy is employed to explain, illustrate and develop Christian teaching; the choice must always be decided, at least partly, by the racial temperament and tradition of the people addressed. In fact, of the two major schools in the Graeco-Roman world it was the Platonic rather than the Aristotelian that seemed to our first Fathers in the Faith the more congenial; to some of them, in fact, it appeared as a providential framework designed to be filled in by revealed truth, or as the supreme effort of human thought awaiting its crown and fulfilment. To Maximus Confessor, for instance, Plato was no less than *Moyses Attice loquens*, 'Moses speaking in Attic Greek'.

Whatever system of philosophy we employ the ultimate mystery must remain a mystery. For our author it is, as we know, that of the transcendence and immanence of God; how God is able at one and the same time to be both utterly beyond and also the very being of all things. In his thought it is undoubtedly the supreme instance of 'mysteries beyond us', to be 'honoured by silence'.[1] For Plato the mystery is in its essence the same, the relationship between the things of the visible world, perceived by the senses, the 'particulars', and their cause, the 'universals',

---

[1] The concluding words of the *Celestial Hierarchy*. Some mysteries are beyond the understanding even of the seraphim, *Eccl. Hier.* 481B.

INTRODUCTION

which, by what I have called his primary intuition (p. 10), seen by him as a self-evident truth, lie in the invisible world, beyond the senses. I think it is legitimate to regard his whole philosophy as developed from this one central notion, an attempt to explain, to establish in both thought and action, the link between the visible and invisible worlds. It is probable that he, too, had towards the end, as Sir David Ross suggests,[1] 'an inkling of the fact that the relation is completely unique and indefinable'. In the meantime he uses language suggesting both the transcendence and immanence of the universals, the 'Ideas' or 'Forms'. There is no doubt that the Ideas are separate from the particulars: Aristotle sees this as the fundamental difference between himself and his master. At the same time the particulars receive their being from these; the relation is described as both 'imitation' and 'participation in' the ideas, yet the particulars have a separate real being of their own. In some way—this is the impression given—the Ideas are both present in and separate from the particular things. This world of eternal, changeless ideas is the proper home of the soul, which is akin to them and immortal. The later stage of his speculation was devoted especially to an examination of the relationship between the Ideas themselves; we see him trying to resolve them all into one supreme Idea that should contain all the rest. Was there, for instance, a separate Form or Idea of each thing in the visible world, even of manufactured things, an Ideal (in the philosophical sense) bed and table? He tends to suggest, as he proceeds, that one Idea in some way involves all others; and we find him trying to ascend from multiplicity to simplicity and one single Idea in which the others have their source, spoken of variously as the Good (this in the *Republic*), the One, the True, Being, and including one mysterious allusion to the Good as 'beyond being' (*Rep.* 509B). He never does, in fact, explain how the Ideas are related. They are not, of course, God, not even the Idea of the Good.[2] God is never far from his mind, and in his latest work assumes more prominence than the Ideas; but what is the

---

[1] *Plato's Theory of Ideas* (Oxford, 1951), p. 231.

[2] The Ideas are to be compared rather to the Divine Names, all the *affirmative* 'names', 'notions', 'ideas' that can be predicated of God. It is disputed among scholars whether Plato intended to identify the Idea of the Good with God.

relation of God to the Ideas he cannot, or at least does not, tell us.

If we attempt to superimpose, as it were, the hierarchies of the pseudo-Denys on Plato's world of particulars and Ideas we shall find that all the Ideas of all the things in the world of the senses are present in the lowest member of the angelic hierarchy, but in a higher synthesis, not one for each class of particular. In the metaphor of the hierarchies there is less diffusion of the Light, less 'division', less multiplicity; in the language of Plato the Forms or Ideas are already reduced in number. As we ascend the hierarchy we find a greater concentration of the Light, an increasing simplicity and unity; the Forms or Ideas are being assumed into higher Forms. At the summit of the hierarchies is God, perfect Unity and Simplicity, containing all these lower forms and existing as their separate being, yet also so far beyond all forms and ideas that there is nothing that we can either affirm or deny of him. At the apex of Plato's world of Ideas stands—at least in hope—one Idea that contains all the rest. How it arrived we do not know. It is not God,[1] any more than are the highest members of the celestial hierarchy. In either case we have an aspect of the ultimate mystery, 'completely unique and indefinable', of the immanence and transcendence of God.

My purpose is not to provide an apologia of Platonism or to provoke a new Neo-Platonism, but merely to draw attention to the salient facts. I would suggest to the reader that he would best understand this present author by accepting him, for this purpose, at his face value, as what he claims to be, and forgetting anything he may know of Neo-Platonism. Even in the case of Plato, it is best not to try to read into him Plato's attempts to explain what I have called his 'primary intuition'. Should the reader conceive a desire to read the Neo-Platonists, he might do so more profitably after the reading of this author. Some knowledge, however, of this intuition of Plato, as seen in its most graphic form in his famous simile of the Cave, may be of help. It is an intuition that all men share in some measure, and for the majority of men is undoubtedly their first approach to a real

[1] It is not certain that it is God, yet if it exists—and this Plato never succeeded in establishing—it is the source of the being of both the world of Ideas and that of the senses.

apprehension of God as distinct from a merely nominal assent and a formal practice of religion. This it is that the early Apologists and Fathers of the Church found such an admirable framework in which to explain and develop Christian doctrine. In this task they did, of course, use phrases and concepts from the later, the Neo-Platonist, development of Plato's thought, and in so doing one or another may have adopted ideas and expressions that, in a longer perspective, are seen to be an imperfect expression of the Christian revelation. It is, however, a fundamentally unsound practice to assume that because an author uses a particular phrase or concept from a pagan philosopher he is thereby committed to an acceptance of the complete philosophy. One should try rather to understand what the author meant and, in the case of an ambiguous phrase, assume that a Christian author meant it in a Christian sense. In this case, as I have suggested, it is not necessary to know anything either of Plato or the Neo-Platonists in order to understand the work we are considering here; but it does help to know what Plato was looking for. I shall attempt to present briefly the principal features of Plato's celebrated simile of the Cave[1] (*Rep.* 514A ff.).

Plato invites us to imagine a line of men imprisoned in an underground cave, chained immovably from birth (he frequently introduces such an improbable situation by some such disarming phrase as: Heaven knows if it is possible; in this case he does not). They are so fastened that they can see only the blank wall of the cave, neither themselves nor one another. Behind them runs a wall and behind the wall pass men, from time to time, carrying artefacts, vessels, figures and statues of various kinds that just overtop the wall. Behind these a fire is burning. The light of the fire throws shadows on to the blank wall of the cave, and the men seated there, seeing shadows of themselves, of one another and of the things carried behind the wall, take these to be real things: these shadows are the only reality they have ever known. This is the first stage.

They are now released and compelled to turn their heads to the fire and to the objects passing behind the wall, but they are dazzled by the light of the fire and cannot see clearly. The second stage.

[1] The opening of Bk. vii of the *Republic*.

PSEUDO-DENYS AND PLATO

They are next dragged up and out into the open, but cannot face the light of the sun and are too dazzled to see any of the things round about them. All they can look at first is the shadow of things on the ground and their reflection in water and shiny surfaces. This is the third stage of their ascent. In three subsequent stages they are able to raise their eyes from the shadows of real things to the things themselves, then to the moon and stars, and finally to the sun itself. On seeing this they come to infer that it is the sun that produces the year and the seasons, that controls, and is in a way the source of, everything in the visible sphere down to what they saw in the cave.

Plato himself provides the interpretation of this, and although scholars are not agreed on the details, the main lines are clear enough. The cave-prison represents the visible world and the fire the sun. The ascent to the upper world represents the ascent from the visible world to the intelligible world of the Ideas. This is the source of the being of the cave-world, which reflects its features on this lower level. The Sun, the last thing they are able to see, and only after great difficulty, is the Form or Idea of the Good, the source of everything below it. It is thus a question of an ascent up degrees that are degrees both of knowledge and of life and being until one reaches the source of all being, which is for the pseudo-Denys, and, as we have seen, probably also for Plato 'beyond being'.

The phrase 'Hierarchy of Ideas' is sometimes used by commentators. This is hardly accurate if it is taken to mean that Plato thought he had actually established the existence of a regular gradation of Ideas or intelligible realities; and it is obvious that they do not correspond to the members of the celestial hierarchy. Plato, as I have suggested, had an intuition of one single Idea as the source of all things, both separate, transcendent, and immanent in them. His Ideas were so many rungs of a ladder improvised to reach this; in his own terms of knowledge, so many hypotheses, accepted provisionally in order to rise to an 'unhypothetical first principle'. That there is, however, a correspondence in fundamentals is very clear, and it is with these rather than with the details of his system, which it seems he never settled to his own satisfaction, that we are concerned here. This correspondence is seen in the fact that the visible world springs, for him, from the invisible (the 'intelligible' in his own phrase) and 'imitates' it; that there is a gradation of being, degrees of reality, though this is never fully worked out, repeating the same pattern at a higher level; that one Idea in some way involves all others and reflects the being of these even down to the very lowest level of the shadows of the figures or puppets in the cave: even they receive their being from the Sun, 'imitating' it at this lowest level of being. Finally, there is the sense that, as each Idea is both present in yet separate from, transcending, its particulars, so it should be possible to trace these back to one single Idea, containing all the others yet transcending them. He seems to start with an intuition of the end and to feel that the end is already present, in a degree, in the beginning; yet, no matter how far he travels, there is still more to be seen. The fact that here, in the Cave simile and in the *Republic* in general, he places the Idea of the Good at the summit suggests that there is a fundamental urge or nisus towards this highest Idea inherent in the nature of man, attracting and drawing him out of himself and beyond the visible sphere, almost in spite of himself.

There is a practical consequence of all this, for his principal concern is a practical one, the training of leaders in the state. Once they have attained to the sight of the Good they must go down again to the Cave, each in his turn, to live with the rest and let their eyes grow accustomed again to the darkness. At first they will be dazed, unable to find their way about, liable to act awkwardly and possibly even exposing themselves to ridicule in consequence. But once their eyes are accustomed again to the darkness they will see 'a thousand times better than those who live there always'. They will recognise every image for what it is and know what it represents, since they 'have seen justice, beauty and goodness in their reality'.

There is a practical aspect of the scheme of the pseudo-Denys also, and it is particularly noteworthy today. As a counterpoise to the legend of his utter otherworldliness the reader is advised to note in the following pages his demand also for action on the lower level, the world of the senses. The 'imitation' of Christ on this level (the word is as common in this author as in Plato) is the practical criterion of progress on the invisible plane; man is so constituted that one cannot exist without the other. The visible measure of perfection is the degree to which the 'imitation' of Christ is manifested, made visible in the material world. So we shall find that it is an external sign that indicates the status and name of the highest degree of his 'holy people'. He is a *monachos* (monk) because of the *oneness* or unity into which he has drawn all the scattered elements of the world, recapitulating it into a microcosm, imitating and reproducing, at the head of this lowest level, the Unity which is the head and source of all the hierarchies; he is a *therapeutes* because all this is a *liturgy* echoing the eternal liturgy of heaven.

Finally, there are undoubtedly many to whom the contemplation of a scheme of this kind brings something of the cold remoteness of inter-stellar space, or the frozen, sleeping-beauty inviolability of a *Grecian Urn*—'for ever shalt thou love and she be ever fair'. Such are likely to turn with a sigh of relief to 'thoughts of home, comfortable fires and the voices of their children'. It is man's nature that this should be so. It is also of his higher nature to know the meaning of those urgent, imperious demands that lead some men deliberately to renounce all they love on the visible plane—'Go forth out of thy country—and come into the land that I shall shew thee.' To all men there must come at times a warning of their mortality, a 'sunset touch', reminding them that all this must pass, whether it pass in one blazing flash or from a slow decline into dissolution. At such moments it is good for a man to be conscious of the link between his present world and the invisible, recognising this as merely the lower end of a scale that reaches up to the source of all that is, that on the way he may encompass the whole cosmos, and that in the meantime his present moment is the image of eternity. For this, I suggest, is the most consoling message of this author, as I believe it to be also of his master, Plato, that nothing in fact is left behind, and nothing passes.

II
Text

1. The Ecclesiastical Hierarchy

THIS introductory chapter begins, as it ends, with a warning that what follows is a 'top secret' document, but, as with other 'top secret' documents, its distribution is a little uncertain. At first sight it might seem to be restricted only to all the baptised: it may be communicated only to those who have been made 'holy by a holy illumination' (372A), and 'illumination' is the author's regular term for baptism. The concluding paragraph of the chapter seems, however, to restrict it not only to the clergy but, among the clergy, to bishops, since the Timothy to whom the treatise is dedicated is exhorted in the most solemn terms to transmit it only to his 'peers' (377A), and this is clearly meant to be the Timothy who was the companion of St. Paul's travels, who became Bishop of Ephesus, to whom St. Paul addressed two letters.

This is to be explained, of course, by what in post-Reformation times came to be called the *disciplina arcani* ('the discipline of the secret'), the practice in the early Church of keeping secret from the profane, and only gradually revealing to the initiate, the mysteries of the Christian revelation. Certain remaining traces of this practice are well known: the division of our present Mass into two parts, the 'Mass of the Catechumens' and the 'Mass of the Faithful'; the practice of reciting the *Our Father* silently, except in the Mass, at which only the faithful were formerly present; perhaps the fact that until recently it was forbidden to translate the Mass into the vernacular. Even at this period the principal prohibition seems to have been on committing such things to writing, and in particular, as we learn from St. Basil, any information about rites to which only the initiate were admitted. The present author seems to prohibit communication by any means.

I stress this point here because it is typical of the obscurity of so much in these writings, at least in the details of its application. The author's remarks on the ordinary run of the laity in his chapter on the Mass (p. 92 below) suggest that he did not expect very much from them, but this is quite incompatible with the impression given by the profundity of the public sermons of the patristic period (unless we are to suppose that the Fathers habitually preached over the heads of their congregation), and even with what the author himself has to say elsewhere of the 'holy people' as 'enlightened' and 'contemplative'. It is in any case inconceivable that the teaching given in this treatise was not to be accessible even to the priests of the Church, that is those not bishops. We must leave the question unsolved.[1] My own guess is that the author, conscious of playing a part and with his habit of piling superlative upon superlative, is saying here and elsewhere rather more than he means to say, having forgotten the statement he first thought of. By the time of these writings (assuming the fifth, or early sixth, century) the original discipline had been considerably relaxed, if it ever was as strict as the writer suggests.

What is said here of the *Ecclesiastical Hierarchy* requires to be supplemented by the introduction to the *Celestial Hierarchy* and by the details added by the author when he returns, as he does frequently, to consider the general structure of both hierarchies: one is illustrated by the other. It is the complete picture, to be formed only from a study of the whole body of his work, that I have tried to sketch in the introduction. It may, however, still be useful to consider briefly the points he makes here; they illustrate very well his mode of thought and line of approach.

It will be obvious immediately that 'hierarchy' here is not to

---

[1] Stiglmayr considers it was for bishops only, de Gandillac for all the initiate. In a passage of the *Mystical Theology* (1000A) prohibiting the transmission of this to the uninitiate, the author expressly says that he means by 'uninitiate' those 'who are unduly attached to material things and cannot imagine anything higher', those, that is, incapable of understanding such a doctrine. (Cf. T. Campbell, *The Ecclesiastical Hierarchy (An Abstract)* (Washington, 1955), p. 27.) It is not clear that we are justified in transferring this to the 'mysteries'.

THE ECCLESIASTICAL HIERARCHY

be taken in the sense in which the word is most commonly used today, of the body of the clergy, or even of the whole body of the faithful including the clergy. Here it means the order or disposition—in a regular series of steps or stages—by which God communicates himself to man, and man, on his side, is gradually assimilated to God in his mode of knowledge and activity. In the author's own words it is 'a knowledge, activity and perfection' (369D) assimilating and uniting man to God. The corresponding definition which introduces the *Celestial Hierarchy* (but speaking of the principle of hierarchy in general) imports the essential note of order, disposition, arrangement; its purpose 'to give to creatures as far as possible the divine likeness and unite them to God' (165A). Only as the author develops his thesis do we find that this 'order' or 'disposition' by which man is assimilated to God is a series of steps, stages or degrees.

What is communicated to man in stages in order to effect this assimilation is 'Light', as we are told expressly in the first chapter of the *Celestial Hierarchy* (120B), using a metaphor to describe what is essentially indescribable; Light uncreated and transcendent, yet manifesting itself in these diverse created forms, 'coming down from the Father of Lights' (James i, 17) and returning to union with him.

'Of this hierarchy,' we learn here, 'the Trinity as the single source of all things is the life-giving source and essence' (373C). Here the dominant motif is heard. The Trinity itself is 'wholly transcendent', completely incomprehensible to us; it is through the Word incarnate—'Jesus' is the name most commonly used by the author—that we receive the Light or, more accurately, *become* the Light, are transformed into it in our particular degree. 'Raising our eyes to the Light that Jesus is, blessed and truly God' (372B), contemplating him in his Mysteries, we become what we contemplate; we 'imitate' Jesus—this is a recurrent phrase throughout the work—and this 'imitation' (assimilation to God through reception of the Light in this particular 'shape') beginning on the invisible plane overflows into the visible plane of our activity.

The Trinity, then, and more precisely the Second Person, is the origin and invisible head of our hierarchy. Its visible head is the *Hierarch*, the Bishop (373C), on whom, as his name implies, the whole hierarchy depends,[1] the embodiment almost of the hierarchy, through whom it receives its being and expresses and realises itself. This is not incompatible with the fact that he himself is only of the second degree of the hierarchy; the sacraments, the first degree, are greater than he. Nevertheless, they require a human minister who, once initiated and consecrated, has complete control of all. He is the channel of the Light, through whom alone it flows to others, yet he himself remains, no matter how high the degree of his personal holiness, infinitely lower than the Light of which he is the channel.[2]

The bishop, in his position as visible head of the hierarchy, is already 'a man deified and divine,[3] instructed in all sacred knowledge' (373C). He receives from God all that is necessary and diffuses it through the hierarchy. It is, however, as is obvious from the context, and as M. Gilson has expressed it so graphically, more than knowledge in the usual sense that he diffuses. This 'light' or 'knowledge' is a whole life and activity, a sharing in the life of the Holy Trinity. It is necessary to emphasise this point, for it is of the essence of the author's teaching and may serve as a valuable corrective to a certain degree of false emphasis in theological manuals; it is a point on which, paradoxical as this may sound, the author is in fact less 'otherworldly' than most.

Even in Mr. Sheed's so eminently practical summary of pure theology adapted to the needs of the ordinary man (*Theology and Sanity*), it is assumed that the life of heaven can be conceived only in terms of 'thought' and 'knowledge'. These are admittedly the best words we have to describe the spiritual possession of a thing, so that God himself can be defined by us only as *intellectio suipsius*, as 'thought' or simple spiritual act; sheer thought if you will, but a thought which, as the origin and source of all being, generates the Word through whom all

[1] *Hierarch:* Head, President, Administrator of the Sacred; High Priest; commonly used here for Bishop.

[2] For the question of the efficacy of the sacraments as not dependent on the holiness of the minister cf. p. 126, n. 2 and p. 176.

[3] θεῖος: I translate this word throughout as 'divine'. This is what the author means quite literally, with the qualifications we have seen. Radically it means 'of divine race or origin'. The author has another word for 'godlike'. All such words, 'divine', 'deified', 'resembling God', are, as I hope is already evident, attempts to express the same thing.

THE ECCLESIASTICAL HIERARCHY

created things receive their being. The spiritual is, as we have seen, not only the higher reality but also *contains* all that is in all the degrees of reality below it: the material world to which we are so attached is just the lowest in the scale. The contemplation of God in his 'mysteries' then, which we receive through the hierarchy, through the ministry of the bishop, is not just thought *about* God, it is 'thought' that *is* God, God's thought or contemplation of himself communicated to us as our being; his 'thought' overflowing into what seems to us the more real, solid and tangible body and its material surroundings. It is the continually recurring refrain of this author, alleged to be so ruthlessly otherworldly, that it is of the nature of man, in contrast with the beings of the celestial hierarchy, to receive and possess the higher, the spiritual, realities through the lower that we call material. It is of the essence of the 'sacraments', to which all this argument is leading, to present the higher spiritual realities under a material form.

God is, then, Light, and those admitted to the Light through the rite of baptism are the 'Enlightened', the *illuminati*. God may also be described as Love, again inadequately as are all names for God, but as suggesting the power which impels him to give and communicate himself—to create—as, on our side, it is our 'love and desire of the Beautiful which draws us to him—unifying and deifying our life, our habits and dispositions' (372B).[1] Our being is thus both 'loved' and 'loving', a reflection of God's love for himself; we reflect in this way the Love which is the third person of the Trinity, as the mutual perfect communication of one with the other. But it is the metaphor of light which the author finds most convenient for his present purpose. As the light of the natural world of the senses comes, bringing sight, life, warmth and growth, so God in the unseen, supernatural world diffuses the light which he is through the hierarchies of angels and men. The illumination of each is progressive, an advance to a higher degree of knowledge, reality and activity in accordance with his capacity until he is all light, resembling as

---

[1] We shall see (p. 171) that the external mark of the highest degree of the laity, the monk, is precisely this unity in his life. The following sentence here is reminiscent of the declaration of Aelred of Rievaulx that in coming to the monastery his one desire was 'to love and be loved'; perhaps a remark unique in monastic history.

far as possible God himself, deiform. 'Enlightened by the knowledge of the things we contemplate—we shall take on the form of Light' (372B). In other words, what we see *is* light in this particular shape, and through seeing it we become light.¹

Our author continues by emphasising the fact that it is one *single* power, God himself, identified explicitly, as we have seen, with 'Jesus', who is operative throughout the hierarchies, both celestial and ecclesiastical, 'transcendent', 'beyond all being', and at the same time the very being of all created things; one light we may say in descending degrees of brightness, modified according to the capacity of each to receive it, remembering that this modification also *is* the capacity to receive it.

'This indeed—according to the teaching of theology—is how Jesus works (372A). He himself is the Intelligence which is the very life of God and beyond all being; he is the source and being of all hierarchy, the source of all holiness and all divine activity; he is supreme power. To the happy beings superior to us [i.e. the angels] he gives an altogether clearer and more immaterial (lit. more intellectual) light, making them as far as possible like the light that he himself is.' He does the same for us 'through the sacred gift of the priesthood', whose function is, as we shall see, to present this light under sensible signs and symbols, 'giving a unity and a divine character to our lives', so that we approximate to and 'imitate' the celestial hierarchy.

Having treated of the celestial hierarchy in a previous work, he finds it convenient to describe the ecclesiastical hierarchy here by comparing it with that. As with the celestial hierarchy so here, 'they who hold a higher place are able on the one hand to receive hidden knowledge of divine things, in proportion to their nature and position, and attain to deification. On the other hand they can transmit to those beneath them, according

¹ Similarly for Augustine, what is seen is not a thing illumined by the Light but the Light itself. For Plato the Idea of the Good is both the being of the particulars and the light in which they are seen. In the following pages we shall find 'contemplation of and communion in' the sacraments as a phrase constantly recurring. It is for all practical purposes a hendiadys; contemplation is communion, becoming what we contemplate. More precisely it is God in the form of Christ, his life and activity both visible and invisible, into which we are initiated; hence the importance of the 'imitation' of Christ in external actions. This, too, is a theme we shall find recurring in the treatise.

THE ECCLESIASTICAL HIERARCHY

to the merit of each, a part of this deification they have received from God himself. As for those in an inferior position, on the one hand they obey those who have more power than they, and on the other hand they urge on their own inferiors. These last are themselves not content merely to progress; so far as possible they too lead others. Thus, thanks to this divine harmony in the hierarchy, each order is able to participate to the fullest extent of its powers in him who is truly beautiful, wise and good' (372D–373A). What is transmitted is the same in both cases; the form in which it is transmitted is different.

'As we have already recalled, the beings, the orders, superior to us are incorporeal; their hierarchy belongs to the spiritual order and transcends our world' (373A). These, the members of the celestial hierarchy, enjoy 'an intellectual intuition of divine truth'. In the human hierarchy, on the contrary, 'a multiplication of sensible symbols, adapted to the needs of our nature' is necessary to raise us 'through the hierarchy to the union of deification', 'sensible images' through which we may 'rise to divine contemplation' (373B).

'The blessed deity, then (376B), who is by nature the source of all deification, and whose divine goodness deifies the deified, has given to every being endowed with reason and intelligence the gift of the hierarchy to ensure his salvation and deification. To those who enjoy peace and happiness in the world beyond the gift was given in a more immaterial and spiritual form, for it is not from outside that God moves them towards the divine but in a spiritual way, illuminating them from within in a more divine manner through a pure immaterial light. As for us, this gift that the heavenly beings have received as one, without modification, has been transmitted to us by sacred scripture in a manner adapted to our powers, divided under a variety of symbols.'

'So,' he says, 'the substance[1] of our human hierarchy is the scriptures received from God', and he goes on to add that he includes under 'scriptures' tradition, 'all that these holy men in a less material way, in a manner more nearly approaching that of the celestial hierarchy, have transmitted to our teachers from mind to mind, in a corporeal manner since they did speak, but immaterial in so far as they did not write' (376C).

[1] Οὐσία: 'das Wesen' (Stiglmayr); 'l'essentiel' (de Gandillac); 'very essence' (Campbell, op. cit., p. 4).

THE ECCLESIASTICAL HIERARCHY

To the present writer, at least, the above paragraph presents a difficulty: In what sense can the Scriptures be described as the 'substance', the 'essence' of our hierarchy? What we shall find in the following pages is not the exegesis of sacred scripture, at least not in the commonly accepted sense, not a course in 'catechetics'; we shall not find the hierarchy presented as an institution devoted simply, or even primarily, to the 'ministry of the word' in the usual sense of the term. What we are going to get is nothing less than the theology of the sacraments presented in the author's own distinctive manner. One has to resist the temptation to translate 'based on sacred scripture', and leave it at that; yet this is not what the author says, and it becomes quite clear on reflection that this is not at all what he means, granted that this meaning is not excluded. It is not evident what the contemporary translators understand, or mean us to understand, by this phrase: 'very essence', 'l'essentiel', 'das Wesen'. Do they intend it to mean simply that the ecclesiastical hierarchy uses sacred scripture so largely in her public worship, so clothing her rites and ceremonies with its language, that it may be described as the very stuff of which her liturgy is made? I think a careful consideration will show that the author's true meaning would include this, as it would include exegesis and 'catechetics', the imparting of knowledge of sacred things—both in the fullest, most real sense—but all from the author's own special viewpoint. I suggest that the author means, in fact, simply what he says, that sacred scripture is, in the most literal sense, the 'substance' of the ecclesiastical hierarchy, that the Light that is manifested in sacred scripture culminates and is brought to a simple unity in this hierarchy, where man is able to communicate and enter into union with it. He sees the Scriptures as a collection of partial, limited, 'divided' manifestations of the Light culminating in Christ—'God, who at sundry times and in divers manners spoke in times past to the fathers by the prophets, last of all in these days has spoken to us by his son . . .' (Hebr. i, 1). Yet even this manifestation, of God in the fullest, most complete sense, is divided up over a series of words and actions of the earthly life of Christ, and not even all those are contained in the gospels (cf. conclusion of St. John's Gospel).

For this author the scriptures are λόγια, the word he most

commonly uses, a number of oracular utterances containing a hidden meaning, a hidden content. They are not so much a continuous historical narrative as a series of historical manifestations of the Light in more or less inadequate material forms, reaching their fulfilment and climax in the comparatively few words and actions of the historical life of Christ; then, in reverse, so to speak, on the way back to the Father, recapitulated in the simplest, most fleeting and transient of all material forms in the synaxis through the words of Institution (cf. p. 109). It is, in fact, not only the historical event but also its description in sacred scripture that is a vehicle of the Light; the author's criterion (above) would even seem to make the record higher, because more immaterial, than the event itself, record of the words and acts of Christ, as 'less material', more resembling the manner of the celestial hierarchy, than their actual historical event. The recapitulation of all this in the synaxis would then be the most perfect mode; the 'Word of God' in this extended, 'divided', fragmentary form, summed up in the Word Incarnate, and achieving its final unity (in this world of sensible symbols) in the Sacrament of Unity. Within this context should be considered the assumption of the Old Testament into the New (pp. 22 and 142).

But this requires the hierarchy, and the exposition of the divine economy of the transmission of the Light through the hierarchy is the purpose of this present treatise. Others may consider sacred scripture from without, speculate on it and acquire rational, discursive knowledge (cf. p. 67); and they will, they do, reach contradictory conclusions about it. The other, 'mystical knowledge', which is not only knowledge but also possession of its substance, its hidden content, requires an initiation through the hierarchy. This initiation will be effected by applying the Light of sacred scripture gradually to the catechumen, described (p. 100 below) as forming him, as it were, in the darkness of the womb, bringing him to birth into the light of day through the rite of 'Illumination' and finally to union in the synaxis. It is this inner reality, the hidden 'substance' or 'essence' of the Scriptures, that is the 'substance' of the human hierarchy.

It is not, then, sufficient to distribute the Scriptures to as wide a circle as possible in the belief that they will serve as the vehicle of salvation to men without more ado. They will not do this without, as our author would say, 'the gift of the hierarchy'. At the moment of his consecration we shall see (p. 157 below) the book of the Scriptures being placed on the head of the bishop in order to signify that we receive the Light contained under these 'sensible symbols' only through him. Given the divine institution of the hierarchy, then the Light is present still under the same words and actions of Scripture, the same 'sensible symbols', wholly present, but directed to this or that particular effect by the hierarch who is himself directed by the Light itself. As we read the same words of sacred scripture and contemplate the same actions, within the system of the hierarchy, through the ministration of the hierarch, what they signify is still present; they form still the channel through which the Light is communicated to us.

But, of course, there are degrees in this reception: it is of the essence of hierarchy. The major part of the pages that follow will consist in an explanation of the deeper meaning of the symbols, an unveiling of the higher spiritual reality contained in them, under which the Light is presented in the 'mysteries', the sacraments, a 'contemplation' of, or penetration through, the external signs more and more deeply into the Light they contain. Standing at the lower rung of the symbols we are expected to soar in contemplation up the whole vista of hierarchies, ecclesiastical and celestial, until we become Light itself—in accordance with our capacity: that is the reason why this document is 'top secret', to be communicated to men only in proportion to their capacity to receive it.

In consequence, the Light is presented under 'symbols' that are indeed 'sensible' but are of such a kind that they do not immediately disclose their full content to everyone, only to each in accordance with his capacity. Their true meaning is revealed only in the context of the 'mysteries', the sacraments, and then only to those who have been prepared to receive it, each in his own degree. To this end, in the words of the author, use is made of 'sacred symbols' rather than of 'formulas openly intelligible', conveying their content only to the initiate, 'for not everyone is holy and, as Scripture says (I Cor. viii, 7), not all have the same understanding' (376C). It would be 'sacrilege' to admit one to a degree of knowledge of and participation in the divine

THE ECCLESIASTICAL HIERARCHY

beyond his merit and capacity. The regulation of this is the concern of 'the heads of our hierarchy'.

'Having themselves received from God the fullness of his gift they have been charged by divine goodness with the task of diffusing it beyond them. In their ardent desire, then, to raise spiritually their subordinates to the deification which they themselves have received it has been necessary for them to transmit to us through sensible images heavenly secrets, through a great variety of formulas a mystery that is one, unique. In doing this they have been obliged to bring down the divine to human level and materialise the immaterial. They have, both in their writings and oral teaching, reduced to our capacity what is beyond all being. This indeed is what our sacred laws prescribe, not only because of those outside the Church, for whom it would be sacrilege to have access to our symbols, but also because our hierarchy does, as I have said, work through symbols, in this being proportioned to our nature, and is obliged to depend on sensible signs in order to raise us to realities beyond the senses' (377A).

This ascent of man to deification is not, of course, effected without effort on his part. It is repeatedly stated that this is granted 'according to the merit' of each and, more explicitly, that in order to attain to 'the presence of God himself uniting us to him' there is first necessary the total and irrevocable renunciation of all that forms an obstacle to it. It is necessary 'to have only that knowledge of things that gives to them their being,[1] to contemplate and know truth, to share so far as that is

---

[1] This is what the Greek says: 'knowledge of things by which ($\tilde{\eta}$) they are, exist'; it is in accordance with the author's teaching that participation in the Light is both knowledge and being, and it is what is required by his argument here. Both Stiglmayr and de Gandillac tend to tone this down, each in in his own way: Stiglmayr, 'die Kentnisse der Dinge nach ihren eigentlichen Sein', and de Gandillac, 'il ne faut plus connaître des êtres que Celui qui les rend véritablement êtres'.

It is the whole Light that is present at each stage of the hierarchies, present even in the smallest act of each individual, and in each historical manifestation recorded in Scripture (cf. p. 92, n. 1, and p. 14, n. 1); it is the form, the 'sensible symbol', that is fragmentary, 'divided', in the sense that no created form can be an adequate expression of it. Even the human form and activity of Christ (p. 115) has this 'divided' character. If it should be asked how, then, Christ incarnate differs from any other manifestation, the answer is that he is both the whole of the Light and all its manifestations;

possible by a perfect deifying union in him who is unity itself, to feast on that sacred vision which nourishes the mind and deifies all who rise towards it' (376A). It is no inconsiderable demand. How complete and utter this renunciation must be we learn from the author's *Mystical Theology* (cf. p. 95).

A word must be said here about the phrase 'according to the merit of each', or 'capacity of each', which occurs so frequently, recalling the classical Greek horror of *hybris*, that man may try to go too far and in so doing rush to his own destruction. Man can never become God without qualification; he *is* God, but only within the limits of his capacity. If he tries to come closer to the Light than his capacity warrants, he will be blinded by it: there will always be something beyond him. 'Merit' in this context, though it is indeed merit—the need for personal effort and its reward is stated over and over again—yet has a different emphasis here than in Latin theology. Light is given according to capacity, capacity varies with 'merit', and 'merit' follows effort; but all these—effort, merit, capacity—are simply aspects of the Light which is given: even free-will to accept or refuse the Light is an aspect of it (cf. p. 12, n. 3). The difference is, of course, one of emphasis; both are saying the same thing, but western theology tends to stress rather the effort of man, eastern, as here, rather the grace of God. It has been suggested that 'merit' in a context such as this is conceived as simply an increase of co-operation, of that unity between God offering and man accepting in which their wills become one. The distinction is a subtle one, and the average western reader will probably come closer to the thought of the Greek if in his reading he substitutes for 'merit' 'grace'.

Similarly 'deification', a term so common in Greek theology, is always slightly suspect to the Latin as suggestive of pantheism, or as implying such an ultimate union of man with God as to transcend any distinction and entail a complete loss of indi-

---

standing both at the head and source of the hierarchy and also at its lowest level he encompasses them all. He is both transcendent, infinitely incomprehensible God and also immanent in all these manifestations. This is of vital moment for meeting the assertion of the Hindu, when he says, with our author, that 'all things are God', and even 'are equally God', although for him there is nothing unique about the incarnation of Christ. Cf. *In Search of a Yogi* (Routledge and Kegan Paul, 1962), pp. 136 f. and 203.

vidual identity. The saving clause 'in the manner proper to each', 'according to the merits of each', 'in so far as it is lawful' is never absent from the author's mind. 'Our deification is,' in his own words, 'to become like God and be united to him *as far as we are able*' (376A). It is a large qualification.

This introductory chapter closes, as I have said, with a repetition of the warning that its teaching should be passed on only to those who have already reached this deification or union with God, an exhortation to Timothy 'not to transmit any of this teaching on the hierarchies except to teachers who have reached deification and are your equals', and to exact a similar promise from them.

2. Mystery of Illumination[1]

IN accordance with a method observed consistently throughout the treatise our author divides his chapter into three sections: (i) introductory: approach to the mystery; preliminary ideas; (ii) what is seen by the bodily eyes; description of the rite; (iii) *contemplation* of the mystery; unveiling of the inner reality, penetrating to the Light, the 'substance' or 'essence' of the rite.[2]

The principal point of this introductory section is clear enough: illumination, baptism, is a rebirth, a birth into the life of God himself; it is in fact already 'deification'—'to be deified is to be born of God'[3] (392B). The line of reasoning that leads to this conclusion is not quite so easy to follow. Briefly it seems to be this.

'The particular object of our hierarchy is to make us like God and unite us to him as far as possible' (392A). This is effected only by love or charity shown in a faithful observance of the commandments 'for it is written: He who loves me will keep my words and my father will love him, and we will come to him and make our abode with him.' Love or Charity, as we have seen (p. 51), is the universal unitive force both within the Trinity

---

[1] I have preferred to keep the author's own title: Illumination. It thus provides a link with the classical purgative, illuminative and unitive ways, and also suggests a certain connection with the Hindu and Buddhist 'enlightenment'. The author does also use the word 'baptism', but more frequently describes it as 'birth from God', or the 'birth of God [in the soul]' the effect of the Light.

[2] For a fuller discussion of the significance of this 'contemplation' cf. the relevant section of the chapter, p. 67 below.

[3] This ($\theta\epsilon o\gamma\epsilon\nu\epsilon\sigma\iota a$) may equally well be translated 'the birth of God in the soul', the coming of the Light as the being of the soul. The word itself does not in fact mean '*re*-birth' and, as we have seen, in the mind of the author birth and 'rebirth'—regeneration through baptism—are seen rather as one continuous process, a movement from becoming to true being.

and in created being, and the idea of love is closely linked with that of fire, heat, warmth, and further to birth, life and growth. The connection between light and fire is obvious, and so we find in the *Celestial Hierarchy* (328D) that the highest order of spirits, at the very point where the Light flows into creation, the 'burning seraphim', are characterised precisely by fire, the ardour of their love: they are light, which is also a burning fire. In Greek theology this is in fact a favourite description of the assimilating and unifying power of that Love which is the presence of God: a fire that transforms the soul as fire transforms metal, to such a degree that the metal, while remaining metal, takes on all the qualities of fire and is indistinguishable from it; one may say *is* fire while still metal. Here, therefore, the Light is also a Fire which is to transform the aspirant.

The liturgy of Pentecost, celebrating the Holy Spirit, the third person who *is* the mutual love of the other two, to whom is 'appropriated' especially[1] the function of perfection through the process of assimilation and union, unites in a unique way the names and attributes of Light, Fire, Love. (The author does not say all this, but I think it is in the background of his mind.)

This observance of the commandments which is the external expression and criterion of the Love that unites us with God (and is in fact God, so that we become God, doing the works of God) begins with the reception of 'the sacred words and actions' of the Church conferring the sacrament of illumination or baptism, by which we are 'deified', 'are born of God' (392B).

A certain obscurity in the text, giving a first impression of something of a vicious circle—we show our love of God by observing the commandments, but Love (God, the Light) does not come to us until we do observe the commandments—is explained once we realise that both the new life which begins at baptism, shown in the observance of the commandments and the *acceptance* of the beginning, the beginning of the beginning as it were, are equally the effects of love, a reception of the Light in

[1] All the activity of God external to himself is the work of all three persons of the Trinity, but one particular type of operation, the external form that we see, may be considered as typical of one rather than another, so by 'appropriation' is said to be the work of that person.

some degree.[1] In fact, we shall find in the second section of this chapter that the prospective Christian in making his first tentative approaches to the Church is already 'inflamed with love' of the supernatural (393B). He has already received sufficient light to bring him to this beginning, this degree of 'observance of the commandments' which consists in his petition for 'illumination', his acceptance of baptism.

This then, illumination, the 'birth of God' within us, is the essential beginning, 'for no one is able to understand, still less to put into practice, the truths received from God unless it has first been given to him to live by the life of God. Is it not true that on the human plane we first have to exist before exercising our [human] faculties?' (392B).

The author is now ready to begin his description and 'contemplation' of the rites by which we are 'born of God', but first he repeats his warning: 'Above all let no one outside the Church [lit. profane] assist at this. For as it is dangerous for weak eyes to gaze at the rays of the sun, so it is not possible without sin to approach mysteries beyond one.' He gives three instances from the Old Testament of men who sinned in this way, and their punishment.

DESCRIPTION OF THE RITE

It is perhaps not without significance for an age anxious to restore the layman to his full share in the life of the Church that it is apparently considered normal here that the first approach of a prospective convert should be not to one of the clergy, but simply to 'one of the initiate', that is to a layman (the laity are distinguished from the clergy as the 'initiate' from the 'initiators'). The simple statement here may be telescoping and giving formal expression to a whole series of preparatory negotiations, still there is no doubt that in the author's mind this would both psychologically and hierarchically be the correct

[1] It is, of course, traditional Catholic teaching that the illumination of baptism is not the 'first grace' (in this author's terminology the 'first Light') received (cf. Denzinger, *Enchiridion Symbolorum et Definitionum*, (Herder, 1928), pp. 1377 ff. and 1522). Before that there are innumerable fitful gleams of the Light, sufficient to lead on to this permanent illumination. Indeed, in this author's scheme of things every single thing in creation, and all men's experience in this world, is a vehicle of the Light. Cf. p. 161 below.

approach to the Light: at the point of its widest diffusion, its greatest dilution in the lay initiate. His further advance, to the source of the Light, will be by way of the deacon (also called the 'minister' or 'assistant'), the priest (or 'sacrificer') and the bishop (or 'hierarch', also called the 'high priest').[1]

The motive power of his approach? Again 'moved by love', which we have seen to be another name for God; Latin theologians would probably say by 'grace', thus emphasising the gratuitousness of this gift by God of himself to man: 'inflamed by love of the things beyond this world' (393B).

Only after much hesitation and mental struggle ('anguish' is the word used) does the initiate undertake to help him and escorts him to 'him who has received his name from the hierarchy', i.e. the *hierarch* or bishop. The reason for the hesitation and 'mental anguish' is clear; it seems that by proposing such a man for membership of the Church the sponsor undertakes a very real measure of responsibility for his future conduct. He will be the sponsor or 'godparent' of the man, his name being entered in the register together with that of the catechumen.

It is not stated explicitly how the convert was brought to this first step, but a preceding paragraph introduces the section with the person of the bishop, here called the high priest. It seems to be implied that the grace (love) that has brought the prospective convert so far flows from him and, more particularly, from his preaching and teaching, whether by himself or through others. He has 'announced the good tidings' (the *evangel* or gospel) to all, that God 'in his love for men has condescended to come to us and, by uniting us to him, to assimilate to himself, as fire does, all those whom he admits to union, according to their degree of aptitude for receiving deification. 'For as many as received him, he gave them power to be made the sons of God, to them that believe in his name, who are born not of blood, nor of the will of the flesh, nor of the will of man, but of God' (John i, 12–13)' (393A). The bishop, it seems, however devious the minor channels, is himself the main source and (on the visible plane) the origin of the movement. The rite described here has,

[1] The *Syriac Didascalia*, describing a Christian community of the third century, states explicitly that the proper channel of approach for the transaction of business is through the deacon: the bishop should not be approached directly.

of course, been preceded by a long course of instruction and probation.

In order to make it easier for the reader to follow the interpretation which is to follow in the next, the third section, I shall divide under separate headings the stages of the rite. This practice will be followed in succeeding chapters.

(1) *Approach and Enrolment among the Initiate* (393C)

The bishop, having received the two (the catechumen and his sponsor) 'with the joy with which the good shepherd receives the lost sheep', assembles in the church all the members of the hierarchy 'to co-operate in the salvation of the man': He begins by 'singing with all his clergy a hymn from sacred scripture'; presumably a psalm, but here and throughout the author is careful not to commit to writing any of the actual words of the rites he describes. Then, after kissing the altar, he turns towards the man who has taken position before him, and asks formally why he has come.

The aspirant, 'filled', we are again told, 'with the love of God', replies in accordance with the instruction and prompting of his sponsor. He confesses 'his wickedness, his ignorance of true Beauty, his entire lack of divine life', and asks to be allowed 'through the ministry of the bishop to participate in God and the mysteries of God'. The bishop replies that this will require a total dedication of self, tells him 'the rules of life in God', and asks if he is prepared to live in accordance with these rules. The answer of the aspirant being affirmative, the bishop imposes hands on him, makes on him the sign of the cross,[1] and instructs the priests to enter his name, together with that of his sponsor, in the register.

(2) *Stripping; Abjuration of the Prince of Darkness; Turning to the Light* (396B)

After the recital of a prayer by the bishop and other clergy the aspirant is stripped of his clothes by the deacons. He is then turned with his face to the west, with his hands extended in the same direction in a gesture of abjuration, and made to breathe

[1] Literally, 'seals' him. The metaphor is from the branding of an animal with the mark of its owner, suggesting here the relationship of a sheep to the Good Shepherd: the candidate is marked as belonging to Christ.

out[1] three times in rejection of Satan. He repeats after the bishop three times a form of abjuration. He is then turned to the east, with eyes raised and hands extended to heaven in token of 'submission to Christ and the teachings revealed by God'.

(3) *Anointing* (396C)

The aspirant is now required to make a threefold profession of faith. The bishop then recites a prayer, blesses him and again imposes hands. He is next 'completely' unclothed by the deacons (apparently he had retained some garment until this point) while the priests bring the holy oil for the anointing.

The bishop begins the anointing with a threefold sign of the cross. He then leaves to the priests the task of anointing the whole body of the man while he himself proceeds to the blessing of the baptismal font (lit. 'mother of adoption of children'). The water is blessed by prayer and three infusions of holy oil in the form of a cross. Each time the oil is poured in the bishop sings 'the sacred hymn with which the prophets were inspired by the Spirit of God'.[2]

(4) *Baptism* (396C–D)

The bishop now gives instructions for the man to be brought to him in the baptistery. One of the priests calls in a loud voice his name together with that of his sponsor. He is then led by the priests to the baptismal water and handed over to the bishop. The bishop, standing in a raised position, immerses the aspirant three times in the water, invoking each time the Holy Trinity ('the three persons of the divine Beatitude'), while the priests each time repeat the man's name.

(5) *Clothing with the Baptismal Robe* (396D)

The priests again take in charge the neophyte and lead him to his sponsor who assists them to clothe him in the baptismal robe. (We know from other sources, e.g. the *Syriac Didascalia*, that deaconesses performed this task of clothing and unclothing in the case of women.)

---

[1] The Greek word is forceful, implying here almost spitting upon.

[2] No clue is given to the identity of this hymn, but see p. 122 below. This is the first author known to mention the mixing of holy oil with the baptismal water. (Cf. Campbell, op. cit., p. 33.)

(6) Confirmation (396D)

The neophyte is now led again by the priests to the bishop, who administers Confirmation: 'Having signed him with the sacramental oil[1] the bishop declares him worthy to participate in the most holy Eucharist.'[2] In the present Latin rite of baptism there is an anointing of the neophyte (with chrism) immediately after the actual baptism, but this is not the anointing of confirmation. It does seem that the anointing referred to here is our sacrament of confirmation, but there is no agreement among the authorities. In the following section (p. 82) we shall find that the effects attributed to this anointing are those of the sacrament of confirmation.

The section ends, as it begins, with the person of the 'high priest', the bishop or hierarch. 'Having descended to realities of the lower order [i.e. the sensible signs and symbols of the sacramental rite] he rises again to return to the contemplation of the higher [i.e. spiritual] realities. So he contrives never in any case or in any way to be carried away by things foreign to his proper function [i.e. that of receiving spiritual realities and translating them into sensible, material signs adapted to the capacity of his subordinates], never ceasing to converse with divine realities and dwelling constantly under the inspiration of the divine spirit' (397A).

The bishop must never, that is, allow himself to become so involved in the lower, external activity as to lose contact with the higher, invisible order which is its source. Pope Gregory the Great, the spokesman of the western tradition, has the same teaching: that the pastor must never become too involved in external affairs, but must remain 'suspended in contemplation' between God and his people,[3] as the channel, mediator and

---

[1] Literally, 'the oil that does the work of God' (θεουργικωτάτῳ), assuming that the superlative form is not to be pressed, for the author is more than usually fond of superlatives.

[2] 'Eucharist'. Literally 'thanksgiving', the name given to the Mass because of the words that introduce the central part, the so-called 'Eucharistic Prayer': 'Let us give thanks to the Lord our God'. There can be little doubt that the Mass is intended here. Possibly the author uses this name at this point, instead of his usual 'synaxis', because of its aptness: this is *par excellence* the neophyte's thanksgiving. Cf. p. 85 below.

[3] *De Cura Pastorali.*

interpreter between the two planes. The second encyclical letter of the late Pope (John xxiii) stressed the same point, the danger of 'over-activity' on the part of the clergy.

It is interesting to note in passing, before we reach the chapter dealing explicitly with the orders of clergy, how this principle of hierarchy works out here in practice. Not only do the subordinate clergy derive all their powers from the bishop, here we see him actively presiding over the function, delegating to the *deacons* the stripping of the catechumen, after he himself has signed him with the cross, beginning the anointing that precedes the actual baptism and leaving it to the *priests* to continue. It is the *priests* who are instructed to bring the man to the font, and while the bishop performs the actual immersion they co-operate in pronouncing the words or 'form'. After the baptism it is the *priests* who clothe the neophyte (assisted by the sponsor) in the baptismal robe, and again conduct him to the *bishop*; but it is the latter who confers the final anointing of confirmation. The division of functions in this case is not very clear, and of course it must not be supposed from the scheme exhibited here that priest and deacon have not the power to perform one or other of these functions alone—but even then their power will flow from the bishop. The author's primary purpose here is to demonstrate the neophyte's gradual ascent to the Light given at each stage through the ministrations of the hierarchy, the deacon (purgation), priest (illumination), bishop (perfection and union); and even the lowest, purgation—as we have seen and shall see more fully later—implies some measure of the highest; union. It is in fact the beginning of the influx of Light.

CONTEMPLATION

The author now proceeds to what is generally described as an 'interpretation of the symbolism' of the foregoing section, but is in reality far more than that. It forms always the largest section of each chapter. The traditional use of this term 'contemplation' to describe it is at first sight puzzling. We have already seen (p. 60) something of the author's general use of the word, but it may be useful to consider it a little more closely in this context, since it bears on the central theme of his teaching. It is not the 'fruits' of his contemplation, his 'thoughts' on the rite, but apparently 'contemplation' itself that he is passing on.

Perhaps his own word, 'theory' ($\theta\epsilon\omega\rho\acute{\iota}a$), would render his meaning best, if we took the English word in its original literal sense of seeing more than is evident at first sight, the sense in which we may ask, seeing a puzzling or mysterious operation in progress, what is the meaning of it, what does it signify, what is the 'theory' behind it: What is the big idea? For our author this 'theory' or 'contemplation' is in fact an enhanced degree of 'sight', or 'seeing', whereby we can 'see' the invisible spiritual reality present in the 'sensible signs' of the sacramental rite. We both see them and see through them. Our sight of the 'signs' or symbols is simply the lowest degree of a sight that travels on through them to unimaginable heights, through ever-increasing degrees of clarity and splendour until it reaches God himself 'in so far as that is allowed', that is, in accordance with the capacity of the contemplative.

But this special power of sight is possible only to the initiate; hence the 'secret' character of these pages. It is precisely this faculty of 'sight', a 'seeing that is believing' or faith,[1] that is given in the rite of initiation or illumination. And this 'sight' is, as we have seen (p. 52), also a communion with and possession of what is contemplated, the beginning of an increasing degree of possession, which is itself also the increasing capacity of the soul for it, until its final irrevocable possession in the degree reached at death. We must, however, always bear in mind that for this author all 'seeing' is in its measure a sight of God, since all things are made in the same pattern on their own plane of being in a series descending from God himself; and this 'sight', faithfully followed, will lead to the initiation by which man will be able by 'theory' or 'contemplation' to see through these to the invisible world. We shall see the force of this later.

St. Augustine's experience of his approach to the Light, as

[1] For St. Thomas, interpreting the Christian tradition, 'contemplation' is simply the normal development of the 'faith' that is infused at baptism. Before Illumination the rites are seen only from outside; afterwards they are seen from inside, and then only, for the first time, is the full significance of the external form recognised. This includes indeed full recognition for the first time of the true significance of the whole world of the senses. Incidentally, it is not uncommon for adults after baptism to remark, concerning the more difficult teachings of the Church: But it's all so perfectly obvious.

described in his *Confessions*, follows closely that of the catechumen described in this chapter, continued into the sphere of 'contemplation'. Fr. S. Pinckaers, O.P.,[1] demonstrates excellently this progress towards the Light, or acceptance of the Light, as the central point of Augustine's conversion. This Light, after his 'returning into himself' from the world of the senses, makes him see 'that there is something to see that he is not yet capable of seeing' (Conf. vii, 10). Fr. Pinckaers regards this as the critical moment of his life, which was to make his whole life a 'seeking', contemplative, 'speculative', a desire to 'see' more, all there was to see. The gradual ability habitually to see more is, for our author, a progress up the hierarchy.

The word Augustine uses for this kind of 'seeing' is *speculatio*, *speculari*, 'speculation', meaning the same thing as our author's 'contemplation', but it is a more significant rendering of the Greek θεωρία, 'theory', especially in the context of the sacramental rites. For Augustine, as for the pseudo-Denys, it is 'a seeing of the soul which sees the *being* of a thing as distinguished from its appearances'. It is more even than the *being* of a thing; it is also in its measure a sight of God. As with the pseudo-Denys, 'what he sees [by this 'speculation'] is Light, not an object illuminated by Light different from it', and the qualities of this Light he recapitulates as: *aeterna veritas, et vera caritas, et cara aeternitas*.

Augustine's 'speculation' (*speculatio, speculari*, for St. Thomas essentially equivalent to 'contemplation') conveys better the meaning of our author from its original association with the contemplation of a public spectacle in a theatre or arena, as well as including the act of contemplating a thing in the mind. In the rites of the hierarchy the initiate both contemplates the 'sensible signs', the symbols of the spectacle, with his bodily eyes, and with the 'eyes of his soul' contemplates—according to his capacity—the spiritual realities they contain. It is generally known that drama in England had its origin in the dramatic character of the Church's liturgical worship, the unfolding of the 'mysteries' of the life of Christ under the form of a 'spectacle', a great dramatic pageant during the course of the year. Themes were embellished, added to, became gradually more

[1] 'Signification du Terme "Spéculatif",' *Nouv. Rev. Théolog.*, Louvain, July–August 1959.

secular in character, moved from the chancel of the church to its steps, on to the market-place, and eventually to the yard of the inn and its own 'temple'. This devolution is the reverse of the process by which Augustine and our catechumen make their way to the source of the Light. Moreover, in their 'contemplation' or 'speculation' of the liturgical mysteries they are not merely passive spectators, but are carried on through the symbols to become part of the spectacle, seized by it and transformed by it. But at whatever stage they catch their first glimpse of the Light, in the market-place or in the village inn, it may be followed up and traced back to this point.

The measure of the reality of this 'hierarchic' principle, for the tradition of which Augustine and the pseudo-Denys are typical spokesmen, may be gauged from Augustine's consideration towards the end of his *De Civitate Dei*,[1] of the question whether in the resurrection body we shall be able to see God with our bodily eyes. He apparently considers that we shall be able to do this, and his conclusion would seem to follow logically from his notion of 'contemplation' or 'speculation'. Such a seeing is simply the lowest end of one continuous power of sight which begins with 'sensible signs' and ends in God.

Before considering in detail the stages of the initiation described in the preceding section the author makes a few general remarks from which we learn (397A):

(*a*) This rite is 'symbolic of being born of God'. By this author means not that any single part of the rite portrays in a material image the birth of Christ in the soul as, for instance, immersion in the water is said explicitly to be a figure of participation in the death of Christ, but only that this birth is the effect produced under this whole complex of 'sensible signs'. 'Illumination' is in any case the central fact symbolised, the coming of the Light to the initiate, the Light which is God.

(*b*) It 'reflects in the mirror of natural things adapted to human faculties the mysteries contemplated in God'.

(*c*) It 'inculcates precepts of holy living'; at the same time the physical purification in the water 'teaches the aspirant in a more material manner' to purify himself from all wickedness and to 'live a life virtuous and entirely in God'.

[1] xxii, 29, already referred to above, p. 16.

MYSTERY OF ILLUMINATION

(*d*) The hope is expressed that this ceremony will impress on the 'uninitiate' the distinction between the profane and the initiate and between the different degrees of the hierarchy. 'As for us, we must raise our eyes to the Source of all initiation', to 'the truths of which our rites are only the sensible expression, to the invisible realities of which they are the visible images. As we have shown already in our treatise *On the Sensible and the Spiritual*[1] the sacred symbols are indeed the sensible signs of spiritual mysteries. They show the way and lead towards these; while the spiritual realities are the source and knowledge of all the sensible symbols in the hierarchy' (397C). He now proceeds to establish the bishop in his proper role before introducing the catechumen.

As we have been told already (p. 63) that 'he announces the good tidings of salvation' to all, so here we learn that 'he pours generously on all souls the luminous rays of his teaching', being 'always disposed to enlighten all who come to him' without regard to their former transgressions. In accordance, of course, with their capacity: 'He dispenses the light of the hierarchy to all who come to him—in accordance with the aptitude of each for receiving the divine mysteries' (400B).[2]

In this he is 'imitating' (in the sense of reproducing and presenting in material form) the goodness of God who, 'while remaining constantly the same and unchanged in himself, dispenses generously to all who contemplate him with the eyes of the soul gracious rays of his own light. It may happen, however, that in virtue of their free will souls reject the Light in the mind,[3] that their love of evil compels them to close the eyes of the mind so that they are no longer able to receive illumination. But it is in vain that they try to escape the Light which is offered unceasingly to their sight; far from abandoning them at all, it still shines even on eyes closed to it. As befits its goodness, it leaps in pursuit when they turn away from it. It may happen also that some exceed the reasonable limits of their sight and, in

---

[1] This treatise is not known to exist. The reference is probably part of the author's literary device.

[2] It is worth noting that here again the teaching and the Light of the hierarchy are identified. It is simply the Light, God himself, who is transmitted under all these material forms.

[3] Perhaps the 'sin against the Light', destructive of mental integrity and ultimately involving corruption of the whole personality.

their audacity, aspire to contemplate directly rays of Light that exceed their power of sight. In this case the Light will not act contrary to its nature of light; it is the soul rather which, presenting itself while imperfect to absolute Perfection, will not only not attain to realities that remain beyond it but will even find itself frustrated, through its presumption, in the degree of Light that is within its capacity. Nevertheless, it remains true, as I have said, that the divine light in its goodness never ceases to offer itself to the eyes of the soul. It is their business to seize it, for it is always there and always ready to give itself' (400A).

This passage, which I have quoted in full because of its importance in the author's scheme, is so nicely logical and clear that one is left speculating on the possible fate of the countless numbers of those who seem to live on the whole good lives 'according to their lights', yet never get as far as the rite of illumination. Among these are many who, so far as one can judge, spend themselves in a complete devotion to the service of God and their neighbour, to whom we of the 'initiate' can only look up in awe and say: 'You're a better man than I am.' The author has nothing to say on the question; nothing has been revealed, so there is nothing for him to 'transmit' from Scripture and tradition; and all his teaching is, he claims, derived from this source. It is, in any case, outside the scope of his work, which is simply to plot the course established by God to bring men to salvation. The light is offered; accepted and followed it will lead inevitably to 'illumination' and initiation into the hierarchy: it is as simple as that. The author does not, of course, explicitly exclude those who do not reach the stage of 'illumination' in the sense intended here, but I think there is no doubt that he considers this the one channel of the light. But have not those who have perceived the faintest stray gleam of the Light that streams in its fulness down through the hierarchies already established some contact or line of communication with the source, no matter how slight? I think that something like this could be argued plausibly to come within the logic of the author's scheme, and that a single gleam of light, not altogether rejected, could serve as the end of a golden string to draw one to the full light, even though he should not in the space of this life progress as far as the visible body of the hierarchy.

It is, of course, the unanimous teaching of modern Catholic

theologians that those outside the visible body of the Church who 'follow their lights' and really live in accordance with their conscience will reach salvation. This accords with the teaching of Augustine, speaking of this very rite of initiation, that although there is no salvation outside the Church, yet 'many who seem to be without [the Catholic Church] are in reality within, and many who seem to be within yet are really without'. In our own day the same thought is echoed in the encyclical *Mystici Corporis Christi* of Pope Pius XII.

We may now consider in the author's 'contemplation' how the neophyte presented here has in fact found his way to the Light. I have divided the section to correspond with the divisions of the preceding section.

(1) *Approach and Enrolment* (400B–C): *Manner of approach to the Bishop symbolic of the ascent of the aspirant through the hierarchy to union with the Divinity*

It is evident that the events of the aspirant's approach as described in the corresponding paragraph of the preceding section have been telescoped. A considerable period of instruction and testing, both of knowledge and of moral stamina, must have elapsed between the first tentative contact with one of the initiate and the final, formal approach to the bishop at the actual rite of initiation. The author's purpose is simply to bring into relief the essential *stages* of the approach, and he arranges his matter accordingly.

'The modest bearing of the aspirant, his confession of sin, the fact that he approaches the bishop through a sponsor (400C)' (and, as we have seen, though it is not repeated explicitly here, progressively through deacon and priest) symbolise his 'orderly ascent' to the 'Summit' of the hierarchy. 'To one who proceeds in this way the divine Beatitude grants a share in himself, imprints on him the impression of his own light, making him divine and receiving him into the communion of those who have merited deification and constitute the assembly of the saints. This is symbolised by the sign of the cross [the 'seal'] imprinted on the aspirant by the bishop, and by the registration effected by the priests who thus enrol the neophyte among the saved' (400D).

His 'orderly ascent' is thus by degrees—through purgation

and illumination to union (but each stage containing something of all three, each in effect an increasing degree of union)—led on by the Light: 'His knowledge not yet being sufficient for union with and participation in divine Perfection, he will not experience a spontaneous desire for it; gradually, however, through the mediation of those who have advanced further than he, he will advance to a higher level, then, through the mediation of those who belong to this higher level, to the rank of the first of all, and will then, being perfect, reach the divine Summit' (400C).

His progress from his first point of contact with the hierarchy is here delineated clearly enough, at least in outline; what we should like to know a little more about is the process that led him to this critical step in approaching his sponsor. At first sight, as with so much in these treatises, the only reference to this, the sentence preceding the passage last quoted, is obscure and baffling. The one fact that does emerge clearly from it is that the first stage in his conversion is a movement of introversion, a turning away from the things of the material, sensible world and a concentration within himself on the intelligible, spiritual and invisible, already a step up the hierarchy of created being, the γνῶθι σεαυτόν ('Know thyself') of the Greek oracle, to be supplemented by the *noverim me, noverim te* of Augustine. It is in fact already the beginning of the ascent up the scale of reality towards the Light (in a way, as we have seen, the 'beginning of the beginning'). Through consideration 'of his own nature he will come to know himself at his source and this [i.e. movement of introversion] he will receive as the first of the sacred gifts that will be born in him from his ascent towards the Light' (400C).

The explanation of how this happens, how a man is led from a study of external things to a stage at which he finds already within himself the beginning of a light which, followed faithfully, will lead him to Illumination, is suggested by the rest of the sentence, the opening words, in fact, of the paragraph, the statement that 'the Divinity is the source of the sacred disposition which permits holy spirits to know themselves' (400B). This can refer only to the central idea of the author that God is present to every created being as its very essence, present to a 'mind' or spirit especially as the knowledge by which it knows itself, knowledge which *is* itself, so that a knowledge of itself is also knowledge—admittedly inadequate, yet filling the whole capacity of knowledge and being of the creature—of God himself. By entering into himself the prospective neophyte is thus entering into God. This is the notion we find repeated in varying forms in the classic mystical writings, that at the centre, the 'source' of his being, every man, if he is willing to abstract himself sufficiently from external things, will come to a point at which his being takes its origin, the point of contact with God, experienced as an obscure awareness of God as the One and the All, the source and origin of all things. The acceptance of this, of the Light that has spoken to him in all created things and is now inviting him further to a perfection and fulfilment of his being[1] which will consist in a union with the Light of such a degree that, while retaining his distinct personality, he yet becomes Light, is apparently what the author describes as 'the first of the sacred gifts'. It is the beginning of a process of acceptance leading to the rite of illumination. It is also the beginning of the process of recapitulation, the leading back of the material world to its source.

(2) *Stripping of the aspirant and turning from west to east symbolises rejection of all that could hinder his union with the One* (401 A–B)

Union with the One, spoken of in terms of Light, is the end to which all the activity of the hierarchy is directed. In consequence, the stripping suggests to our author the forcible stripping from the aspirant of his former life, withdrawing from him 'all attachment to things here below',[2] from all that could keep him divided in his affections and hinder his union with the One. Similarly, his turning from west to east is seen as a turning away from the darkness of sin and ignorance to become one with the Light. For 'it is impossible to share at one and the same time in things that are opposed one to the other: he who enters into communion with the One can no longer live a divided life,

[1] As we have seen, man was elected from the beginning and, though fallen from grace, still retains a radical potentiality for all he has lost. Modern theologians would distinguish here between 'actual' (transient) grace, leading if accepted to the bestowal of 'habitual' (permanent) grace through baptism.

[2] This stripping is still a regular feature of the monastic 'clothing', the rite of entry into the monastic state, accompanied by an invocation on 'putting off the old man'.

at least if he is anxious for a secure participation in the One. He must resist firmly all the attacks of whatever might dissolve the unity' (401A). (This began already, as we saw, with the movement of introversion.)

'Placing him with his face to the west, barefoot and naked, and hands outstretched to abjure all intercourse with the darkness of evil' symbolises particularly by the breathing out, the expulsion, of 'all that in his past conduct was at variance', the 'total abjuration of every principle contrary to conformity with God' (401B).

'Having become thus strong and free from all affection for sin, he is turned towards the east to show that after repudiating all evil he will be able to receive and contemplate the divine Light in its perfect purity.' He is now 'wholly unified', at least in intention; in place of being divided and distracted among the things 'here below', he rises through them to their true being in God: 'his promise is received of tending with all his power towards the One' (401B).

Both movements are necessary, we are told; and the reminder is by no means strange when one considers that the negative aspect, the avoiding of evil, too often plays the dominant and even almost exclusive role in Christian life. But 'it is not enough to renounce all evil. It is necessary also to show an inflexible valour, to resist boldly and unceasingly all laxity, never ceasing to desire with holy love the True, and tending continually and constantly towards it with all one's power, striving always to rise to the highest perfections that come from the divinity' (401C).

(3) *Anointing of the body with oil summons the aspirant to the sacred warfare under the direction and leadership of Christ* (401C)

The images in this passage are, in fact, all taken from the world of sport rather than of warfare, the author inspired perhaps by his master's own image of them 'that run in the race' (1 Cor. ix, 24). Here Christ appears as the trainer at a kind of celestial Olympic Games, and the oil of the anointing is a massage that prepares the limbs of the athlete for the contest.

It is noted that the bishop 'whose life is conformed to that of God' (here especially to God's way of doing things in his employment of a hierarchy in his bestowal of the Light) begins the anointing himself (God is the source of all light and being), 'but it is the priests who complete the sacred task of anointing'. In this way they 'summon the initiate to the sacred contests he is henceforth to undertake under the direction of Christ'. It is not stated, but since the oil of the anointing is, as we shall see later (p. 121), a symbol of Christ himself, conveying the Light that *is* God, it is in a way God himself who is being rubbed into the limbs of the spiritual athlete, in whose power they are henceforth to act, and by whose influence they are taken up and united to the divinity. 'It is he [Christ] who as God organises the combat, as Wise makes the rules, as the Beautiful makes worthy provision for the prize for the victors. But, a mystery still more sublime, he has come down himself into the arena with the combatants to defend their liberty and ensure for them the victory over the forces of death and damnation' (404A). The initiate, therefore 'in the firm hope of winning a glorious reward in the ranks of a company commanded by a good commander and leader, will march in the footsteps of him who, in his goodness, was the first of the athletes, so striving in imitation of God himself'.

The combat is to the death, death to all that could hinder his entry to true, everlasting life through union with God. It leads therefore logically to the next step, to baptism. 'Having overcome in this way all the actions and all the creatures that form an obstacle to his deification, in dying to sin by baptism he can be said to share mystically in the very death of Christ' (404A).

It is important to notice that here and throughout the treatise the author speaks regularly of the effect of these rites in the perfect or 'completed' tense. Here, for instance, the aspirant has not only been anointed for the struggle; he has already completed it, is dead to the world, and this is now to be presented in the 'sensible sign' of immersion in the water. The fact is that these rites are—considered *as signs*, in their material aspect—partial, imperfect symbols of the reception of the Light and its effects. *What* is received is received on a plane beyond space and time, yet considering our nature it has to be presented to us extended in time and spread out over such a succession of rites or symbolic actions. It is to be further extended over the whole course of the initiate's life.[1] 'This *is* his life', at its point of entry into this world, the seal of the life of Christ applied to him, to be projected into the shape of his words and actions. He will be given a sufficiency of time on this earthly plane to assimilate it—or for it to assimilate him, for this rather is the author's way of looking at it. The initiate, on the completion of this rite (which in the author's view still remains to be completed by communion in the Holy Eucharist (p. 84), will live simultaneously in time and eternity, and his whole being will consist in the reception of the Light transformed through him into the stuff of his earthly conversation. He has already entered in Christ into the mystery of redemption, 'the mystery which was kept secret from eternity' (Rom. xvi, 25). He has become part of the mystery of God himself, *immotus in se permanens*, remaining motionless in himself while proceeding outside himself to the creation, redemption and conservation of the universe. It is, then, this ontological view, *sub specie aeternitatis*, seen from the viewpoint of eternity, perfected in its beginning, that we must remember as the author's in this and similar passages. But our catechumen is standing naked waiting for immersion in the water of baptism.

(4) *Immersion in the water symbolic of his sharing in the death of Christ* (404B)

The turning of the aspirant from the darkness of sin—an action momentary here, to be extended over his whole life—and his conversion to the Light, are different aspects of one single process, the coming of Light to the soul: Illumination. (Purgation, illumination, union are, as we saw, all aspects of one action, all containing some degree of the others.) But the Light is God himself, and, more precisely, the Word incarnate, Christ. The aspirant's rejection of darkness is the effect in him of the Light which was, so to speak, diffracted into, took the shape of, the combat of Christ against sin, culminating in his death and the resurrection which was his permanent irrevocable passage (*phase* or *transitus*) from death to life. The initiation of the aspirant is therefore his initiation or inclusion into this activity

[1] This, illustrating a principle valid throughout the author's work, is of importance in considering the 'state of perfection' of the bishop and the monk. Cf. p. 175 below.

of Christ, the overcoming of sin to the death. From a different viewpoint it is the flowing into him of the Light in this particular 'shape' or 'pattern', conforming his life to the pattern of Christ. So 'in dying to sin by baptism it can be said that mystically [not, of course, figuratively, metaphorically or by a poetic fancy, but really, in the way described; through the 'mystery' or sacrament] he shares in the very death of Christ' (404A).

This death is symbolised by the immersion of the aspirant in the water, his 'burial' in it, and this *descent* into the grave was sometimes given additional emphasis by siting the font below ground level so that one descended by steps. This may possibly be the significance of the description of the bishop as standing at a higher level (p. 65). The *threefold* immersion conforms him to the burial of Christ for (part of) three days: 'he is able to imitate mystically the death of Jesus, the Source of Life, during the three days and three nights [sic![1]] of his entombment' (404B).

It is useful to note that while for St. Paul, his putative master, it is both the death *and* resurrection (the emergence from the water) that are symbolised here, this author makes no explicit mention here of the resurrection; for him it is the *disappearance* of soul and body, their passage from the visible to the invisible plane that seems to constitute the essential note of the symbolism. (The disappearance of Our Lord from sight took place, of course, in the Ascension, the complement of the Resurrection; but he does not allude to that either.) 'Observe carefully how fitting are the symbols in which the sacred mysteries are expressed. In our view death is not sheer annihilation, as others imagine,[2] but a separation of parts, which draws the soul into the invisible world since, deprived of the body, it can no longer be perceived by us, while the body, hidden beneath the earth where it undergoes another change which modifies its corporal shape, loses all human appearance. It is with good reason, therefore, that the initiate is entirely immersed in the water as a

[1] Odd as it may seem, this is quite accurate according to the Jewish manner of reckoning. The new day begins at sunset of the previous evening and any part of a day may be considered as a day and night. Cf. Christ's own statement that he would be 'three days and three nights' in the tomb (Matt. xii, 40). Cyril of Jerusalem and Gregory of Nazianzen use a similar expression.

[2] For heterodox views of death cf. p. 187 below.

figure of death, and of that burial where all figure and form is lost' (404B).

It seems therefore that for him death, as signified by this rite, is not so much the temporary separation of soul and body as the withdrawal of both from the visible world. The soul, which is in any case of its nature invisible, is now in 'a world invisible to us', the body, the limbs that have been informed through the anointing with the life of Christ, is buried in the earth 'where all figure and form is lost'. But it still exists, for 'death is not sheer annihilation'. Where has it gone? To the invisible plane, where there is 'no more death—Behold I make all things new' (Apoc. xxi, 4–5). It has changed only; more accurately it has now reached the state to which it was destined even before its appearance in this world, 'chosen and raised up in Christ before the foundation of the world' (Eph. i–ii). The mortal has 'put on immortality,' the corruptible 'incorruption' (1 Cor. xv).[1]

This is what the author seems to envisage as taking place in baptism. It is effected in time; the least moment of time, projected forth into time and space by these symbolic rites out of the eternity in which it is effected in God. It is extended over the longer time of the life of the individual until it reaches its term, completed and decisive, in his physical death. St. Paul's use of the phrase 'destroying death' is seen in such a context to have a more than merely rhetorical and figurative significance. This 'mystic' death, fulfilled in baptism, is always present as the source of being—the death which is life, the 'opening of the gates'[2] to the eternal, 'supernatural' life to which the 'natural' life of this world is leading, as in its degree its reflection and symbol. In the interval, while man is living simultaneously in time and eternity, his 'time' has to continue (allowance being made for the mysterious state we call purgatory) until the two are perfectly synchronised as they are intended to be in God's design; the neophyte's earthly life perfectly reflecting in its limited degree the light of eternity. This is the

[1] For an interesting discussion of this question in connection with the assumption of the Blessed Virgin into heaven, in which a distinction is made between *Leib* and *Körper*, σῶμα and σάρξ, cf. D. Victor Warnach, *Liturgie und Mönchtum* (Maria Laach, 1951), Heft viii, p. 44.

[2] In the Easter Collect. Cf. p. 20 above.

point at which the 'body of sin' is exchanged for the 'spiritual body'.

To many people there must seem to be a certain confusion of thought in sacred scripture, repeated here, between the phrase 'dying to sin' and actual physical death. We do, it is evident, die to sin, as to everything else, with physical death, but that *could* be through no desire of our own, and it is not quite the point here. We 'die to sin' when we turn away from and renounce it as we have seen our neophyte do; but the movement is not completed until the moment of literal, physical death, when the 'death to sin' has been extended over the whole period of our lives. This is the point of view in which the two—death in the literal sense and death to sin—are reconciled. Death as the consequence of sin is, in any case, inevitable, whether we die to sin in will and intention or not; but it has no power, since our fall from grace and separation from God, to procure for us life beyond this world. This can be effected only by an influx of the Light through Christ, more specifically through the extension into us of the action of Christ, which was at the same time death to sin and physical death; for this action had as its complement the passage into the invisible world of eternity. It is this that is effected by 'sharing mystically in the very death of Christ' in baptism.

In this context his physical death is thus the final step of his passage in Christ up the hierarchy from the visible to the invisible plane, the last irrevocable stage of his turning towards the Light. Does this mean that with his passage from the visible world, and the burial of the body 'where all figure and form are lost', he is to lose for ever this world and his own body, at least in their 'material' form? On the contrary, it is only the present form of a world separated from God by sin that is lost and disappears. Formerly this was rather a world always in process of 'becoming', a temporary appearance or series of appearances that he possessed rather than real 'being', something that always eluded his grasp, slipped away whenever he attempted to restrain it. He has now attained to the Light, of which these are some of the shadows cast. The figure and form therefore of its earthly limitations are shed, while the 'real' body (more accurately the man who is essentially 'body-soul', the Light in this form) has passed in Christ beyond such limitations, from a world and body that is 'becoming', a transient, fleeting reflection of 'being', to being itself.¹

(5) *Clothing of the neophyte in a bright, shining garment symbolic of the Light which is God now present in him and shining forth in his life* (404C)

'The initiate is then clothed in shining garments. Through his courage and his godlike insensibility to all that belongs to the world opposed to God, and the strong tendency of his will towards the One, all that was disorder in him is reduced to order, what was unformed takes shape, and his life now shines with full light.'

This is the white robe that we know was worn throughout Easter Week at the public services of the Church by the neophytes who had been baptised at the Easter Vigil, and was worn for the last time on the Saturday, for that reason called *sabbatum in albis* (Saturday in white robes). The custom still continues in the practice of placing on the head of a child after baptism at least a white cloth with the appropriate exhortation.

(6) *The anointing—'ineffable—I leave to others—'* (404C)

'The consecration with oil gives the initiate an agreeably sweet smell, for the holy rite of the birth of Christ in him unites him to the spirit of God. But this anointing, with its action in perfuming and making perfect on the spiritual plane, is beyond human description [ineffable]. I leave the task of contemplating it to those who have merited to enter into communion on the spiritual plane in a holy and divine manner with the spirit of God.'

This anointing is, as we have seen, almost certainly the anointing of what we now know as Confirmation. We shall learn (p. 136) that 'it perfects [or 'completes'; cf. the lit. meaning of *confirm*: strengthen, ratify, bring to completion] the grace of the birth of God in us', and 'in the initiation in which we are born of God we receive the infusion of the Holy Spirit by the anointing with the holy oils'. This is connected in the same passage with the fact that Christ himself after baptism, as re-

---

¹ It is presumably clear to the reader that the author does not say all this; it is an attempt of the present writer to interpret the author's thought, to suggest what is implicit in what he does say.

corded in Scripture, received 'the consecration of the Holy Spirit'. The symbolism seen in this second anointing is therefore, unlike the 'massage' of the first, to be sought in the perfume (added to the oil). The perfume, as we shall see later (p. 121), diffuses its sweetness unseen and intangible[1]; such is the action of the Holy Spirit. Expressed in terms of 'being born of God' it seems to be comparable to baptism as adult life is to infancy, but it must be confessed that owing to the author's treatment of the whole process as one single rite, this is not brought out very explicitly here. However, in spite of his description of this anointing as 'ineffable', we shall find him elaborating his theme at very considerable length in the chapter on holy oil.

In the meantime, 'all these rites having been performed, the bishop invites him whose initiation is now completed to a celebration of the most holy Eucharist, and so admits him to communion in the mysteries which are to make him perfect' (404D).

It is characteristic that after the exuberance of language in which we were told that the initiate has turned from this world, even died to it, been united to the One and made perfect, we now learn that all—or nearly all—still remains to be done, that all this has simply 'admitted him to communion in the mysteries that which are *to make him perfect*'. This is partly to be explained by the fact already noted (p. 77) that all created perfection is relative, yet every degree of being is also a degree of perfection, even before the creature's final perfection is achieved. The author's viewpoint is a point beyond space and time. From this point of view he sees the final perfection of the individual as it is on the spiritual plane, already completed and ready for delivery, so to speak; but because of the exigencies of a human nature with its roots beyond, yet extended into, space and time, it has to be extended into the series of 'sensible signs' of the mysteries, and still further through these into the events of his earthly life. On this plane he has a lifetime still to work his way through; on the other plane he is already 'completed', in St. Paul's phrase 'dead and his life hid with Christ in God': the mysteries are the line of communication between the two, the Jacob's ladder.

The fact is that in the world of phenomena and 'sensible

---

[1] In fact, there is scarcely any perceptible smell to the mixture of balsam and oil in the Latin rite. The Greeks do, however, today at least, add other perfumes, using as many as forty, one understands.

signs' all that has happened is literally, as the name commonly given implies, a beginning, 'initiation', entrance, admittance to communion with the source of Light. Here, in the Eucharist which the neophyte is now approaching, we have pre-eminently the very Light itself, while the other sacraments or mysteries are rather partial applications of the Light to particular effects. These others are 'incomplete', he says[1] without this. The effects already symbolised are in fact accomplished by his union with and communion in the Light through the Holy Eucharist. If we find even later that he is still not perfect, that need not dismay us; his union with the Light, the unity effected in his life, is to be diffused over the space of his whole life—that is the reason of his earthly existence. The term of the process will be his perfect conformity through Christ with that 'idea' or image of him in God which is the source of his being.

The author's teaching that baptism is 'incomplete', in its above sense, without communion in the Holy Eucharist is, of course, in the Catholic tradition as expounded by, for example, St. Thomas, who holds[2] that baptism produces its effect only on reception of Holy Communion, at least in desire. Such a desire could, of course, be implicitly included in a desire to fulfil the will of God in all things.

[1] More precisely what he says is that 'participation in the other sacraments is not fully accomplished except through this' (424D). This follows logically from his theory of the line of descent of the Light and the fact that it is always leading on to something higher. All this is more evident in the original Greek where the same word is used for 'making perfect', 'completing', a person, and bestowing a sacrament on him. Cf. p. 137 below where this question is discussed more fully.

[2] S. Th. III, Q. 73, 3 c, ad 1, and Q. 79, 1 ad 1.

3. Mystery of the Synaxis or Communion

THE Mass, the Holy Eucharist, is most often called by our author the *Synaxis* (lit. bringing together, assembling, assembly). He also uses the word *Koinonia* (lit. a sharing in one common being or mode of being, usually translated as communion or community), but whereas he uses this also in the general sense of any communion or community, he confines his use of synaxis to the union or communion effected through the mysteries (sacraments). *Eucharist* in the pseudo-Denys most often has its literal meaning of thanksgiving; but he does also use it, though rarely, as a synonym for Mass or synaxis, as, apparently, in the final paragraph of the preceding chapter.

This word synaxis has, however, for our author a sense different from that in which it is commonly used in early Christian literature, of an assembly, congregation, communion of the whole Church or *Ecclesia* to perform its central, most solemn act of worship, thought he does see it as including this. For him it means primarily and essentially the *assembling*, or better *reassembling*, of all the powers of soul and body, their 'unification'—an expression he is very attached to; and it includes, of course, in his scheme of things the taking up into man of the world in which he lives (p. 114)—and their union with God. Had he lived in a machine age he might have envisaged it in terms of an 'assembly line', bringing together numberless scattered heterogeneous elements and bits and pieces and uniting them into a wonderful, and perhaps terrible, machine capable of penetrating beyond this world unknown distances into outer space.[1] Even this is a view of it from, so to speak, the receiving end; essentially it is an inpouring of the Light in its fulness, and the reassembling of all the scattered elements of man's world and their reunion with the Light is simply the effect of this influx.

Since synaxis is a term unfamiliar to the average reader, I shall generally use the word Eucharist, except where the author clearly wishes to emphasise the literal meaning of synaxis. 'Communion', suitable in some ways, might seem to lend support to a tendency in modern Catholic practice—it is hardly more than a tendency and is already being corrected by papal directives—to forget that (in the words of the *Catechism of Christian Doctrine*) 'the Holy Eucharist is not only a sacrament it is also a sacrifice', something more than the 'reception of Holy Communion'. For the author it is indeed just that: reception of, union with, the Light; with a significance, however, strange to modern pious ears, though familiar enough to his contemporaries. For him it is the communion or union of the initiate with the Light presented through the Mystery of the Holy Eucharist in the pattern and shape, so to speak, of the life and activity of Christ which had its climax in his death, resurrection and passage beyond the limits of the visible world. Through this union or communion the life of Christ is continued, flows into, the initiate. That is from one aspect; from another it is a taking up of the initiate into the life of Christ, into the Light in this form, the main lines and features reproduced in all with an infinite variety of accidental detail in the individual.

The author begins by drawing attention to the peculiar preeminence of this mystery or sacrament as shown in the name given to it of synaxis or communion, although 'synaxis', or 'bringing into union with God', is 'a character common to all the sacraments'. 'All sacramental activity deifies our divided and distracted lives, bringing unity into them and reassembling into conformity with God everything that is separated from him, and so making us enter into communion and union with the

[1] This is fully in the tradition of the primitive Church. Cf. the beautiful Offertory prayer of the *Didache*, Chapter IX: '. . . as [the grains of wheat of] this bread were scattered over the hills and are now brought into one, so may thy holy Church be brought back from the ends of the earth into thy kingdom'.

MYSTERY OF THE SYNAXIS OR COMMUNION

One' (424C). Later Christian tradition, too is in accord with this conception in regarding the Eucharist as especially the 'Sacrament of Unity'.[1]

We have seen already (p. 85) how in the author's scheme this 'synaxis' or 'reassembling' involves literally reuniting one's whole world with God: man is conceived as conveying his world with him in his return to union. This unity is shown also—or should be shown—in the external organisation of life by which all is made to serve more or less directly to union with God. This restored unity is seen in its perfection in the microcosm that is the monastic community, where everything is made deliberately and systematically to serve this one end of union with the One, thus forming a small local manifestation of the Church as a whole. It is this 'unity' in his life which, as we shall see (p. 171), constitutes the monk in the state of perfection.

This unity and union then is *par excellence* the effect of this sacrament, and 'participation in the other sacraments of the hierarchy is not fully accomplished except through this' (424D). It is presumably in this sense that we are to understand the further statement (425A) that 'each of the [other] sacraments of the hierarchy is imperfect ($\mathring{a}\tau\epsilon\lambda\acute{\eta}s$) in this sense that it does not achieve our union with the One'. The others, that is, lead us to the union which is achieved through the synaxis, lead us *to* 'synaxis'.[2] Nor is this really contradicted by the fact that it will be said expressly later of the 'Sacrament of Unction' that its 'dignity is equal and its power identical with those of the mysteries of the synaxis' (476C). It is God, the Light, as we have already noticed (p. 52), present and operative in all, but producing this or that limited effect; in the union of the synaxis there is no limitation other than the capacity of the individual who receives the Light. The distinction would thus seem to be simply that traditional in Eastern theology, between the operations of God and God himself; a distinction, that is, only in its effects on us. We are 'enlightened' by the other

[1] So for St. Thomas (S. Th. III, Q. 67, 2 c), supporting this by I Cor. x, 17, it is the *sacramentum ecclesiasticae unitatis*.

[2] In the descending scale they come down from the Unity which is Christ in the synaxis, and in the ascending scale they return into him. For the question of the difference in dignity of the sacraments, cf. p. 121, below.

sacraments; the synaxis is our union with the very source of the Light.[1] In support of this our author points to the fact that the Holy Eucharist is in fact celebrated as the central point of each rite with, as its consummation (the author does not expressly say this, but we know that in fact it was at this date the rule for all who assisted), the 'reception of holy communion'. 'For it is almost impossible for any of the sacraments to be celebrated without the most holy Eucharist effecting, by its divine activity at the chief point of each rite, the spiritual unification of him who receives the sacrament, dispensing to him from God its mysterious power of bringing him to perfection and so effecting his entry into communion with God' (425A).

Generally speaking, this tradition does still persist today. In the author's time the Eucharist (with reception of holy communion as an almost integral part for all) regularly followed immediately baptism and confirmation. Today, when children are baptised in infancy, they regularly communicate as soon as they reach the use of reason, are old enough to know what they are receiving. Adults commonly communicate at Mass the morning after their baptism or, in the recently revised discipline, possibly on the same day. Holy Orders are conferred at various points in the actual celebration of the Eucharist. Religious professions take place during the celebration. The holy oils for anointings are consecrated during the celebration of the Eucharist, and anointing of the sick is regularly accompanied by reception of holy communion as *viaticum*.

'Thus the priests in their wisdom have done well in giving to the synaxis a name which does signify the very essence of its operation' (425A).

He sums this all up by comparing the name of *synaxis* with that of *illumination* 'which produces in us the birth of God': Since it is the first to bring *Light*, the *beginning* of all illumination, we call it by this name, though in fact all the sacraments do transmit divine illumination'. So—it is implied though not stated here again explicitly—all the sacraments bring a measure of unity, are leading to union with the One, with the Light, but the synaxis is so called because it offers the completion and perfection of the unity to which the others have led.

---

[1] With the qualification we have seen on p. 28, that every stage is a degree of union.

MYSTERY OF THE SYNAXIS OR COMMUNION

DESCRIPTION OF THE RITE

The author now proceeds as before to a summary description of the rite of the Holy Eucharist or Mass. For the sake of clarity the principal parts of this will again be tabulated in order and the same numbers be used when we pass to the 'contemplation' of the mystery.

(1) *Prayers at foot of altar and incensing of altar and congregation*

'The bishop, having finished the prayers at the foot of the altar of divine sacrifice, begins by incensing the altar, then passes [with the incense] round the whole congregation' (425B).

(2) *Chant*

'Returning to the altar of divine sacrifice he begins the sacred chant of the Psalms, and all the orders of the Church [i.e. clergy and laity in their various degrees] accompany his voice in this holy psalmody' (425B).

(3) *Epistle and Gospel*

'Immediately after this the assistant clergy read aloud from the books of the sacred scriptures' (425C).

The reference is clearly to the reading (or singing) of epistle and gospel, the epistle probably being preceded by the reading of one or more 'lessons' from the Old Testament. It would be unprofitable to attempt to determine precisely who these 'assistant clergy' are; it most probably means simply the deacons. The word I have translated as 'assistant clergy' is λειτουργοί or 'liturgist', an indeterminate word denoting anyone engaged in a public work or duty, but commonly used by this author to denote the deacon. We shall see later that only bishop, priest and deacon are reckoned in the order of clergy; there is no reference to 'minor orders' or to a subdeacon. The difficulty in interpretation arises, of course, from the impossibility of knowing how much of the picture presented here is to be taken as belonging to the first century, and how much to the fifth century, in which the author was probably writing. The third-century *Syriac Didascalia* directs that the portions of sacred scripture shall be read by a *lector*, 'if one is available', and we know that in some places it was the custom from the second century on to employ a lector for this duty.[1] However in this same *Didascalia* we find one of the deacons acting as *porter* or doorkeeper. In Rome, during the pontificate of Cornelius (d. 253), we learn from Eusebius that there were already 46 priests, 7 deacons, 7 subdeacons, 42 acolytes and 52 clerics of lower order.[2] I shall accordingly translate this word simply as 'ministers' or 'assistant clergy', so leaving the question open, except in places where it is quite evidently restricted to deacons.

(4) *Dismissal of:* (a) *Catechumens;* (b) *Possessed;* (c) *Penitents*

'There remain only those who are worthy of contemplation of and communion in the divine mysteries' (425C).

Admission to the Holy Eucharist is, as we have seen, the final stage of the neophyte's initiation. He is now capable of that contemplation of the mystery which, penetrating beyond the external signs to the inner content, gives him a 'knowledge' that is at the same time possession, participation; so that, as we saw (p. 52), 'contemplation of' and 'communion in' are in such a context practically synonymous terms.

(5) *Singing of the Creed*

It is commonly assumed that what the author calls 'the hymn of the catholic faith'[3] sung at this point by 'the whole congregation' is the symbol or creed. If, as scholars generally agree, the creed was introduced into the Mass in the year 476, this treatise could not have been written before that date. Those who, principally in an attempt to establish the identity of the author, would make the date of composition the late fourth or even late third century hold that the *Gloria in excelsis* is referred to here. A full discussion of the question would be beyond the scope of this work, but the author's later description of this hymn (p. 109) makes it reasonably certain that he is referring to the creed.

[1] Cf. 'A Third Century Christian Community', *Clergy Review*, January 1956. The tradition which preferred a child for the reading of the Scriptures, in the belief that the age of innocence would interpose less obstacle between the Word of God and its hearers, would form a less 'opaque' channel of the Light, is altogether according to the mind of our present author.

[2] Cf. Jungmann, *Missarum Sollemnia* (Herder, 1949), Vol. I, p. 263.

[3] Lit. 'catholic', 'universal' hymn, which may mean simply a hymn summarising the whole history of the works of God. The general meaning is in either case the same.

MYSTERY OF THE SYNAXIS OR COMMUNION

In the meantime 'some of the ministers remain at the door of the church to ensure that they remain closed'.

(6) *Offertory*

'The other ministers,' we are told, 'fulfil a duty corresponding to their order', a phrase that suggests the existence of orders of clergy below that of deacon; but nothing more is said of them, except that 'the highest in dignity [clearly the deacons] assist the priests to place on the altar of divine sacrifice the sacred bread and the chalice for consecration'.[1]

(7) *Offertory Prayer and Kiss of Peace*

'All present exchange the ritual kiss of peace.' This is followed immediately by (and is closely connected with):

(8) *Reading of the Diptychs or Lists of Saints*

(9) *Lavabo*

'The bishop and priests having washed their hands in water, the bishop takes his place at the centre of the altar surrounded by only the priests and those highest in dignity among the ministers [i.e. the deacons]' (425D).

(10) *Preface and Consecration*

'The bishop praises the holy works of God, then accomplishes the divine mysteries and exposes to view through the sacred symbols the works he has just praised' (425D).[2]

(11) *Communion*

'Having shewn in these symbols[3] the gifts of the work of God,

---

[1] It is worth noting, as an instance of the mentality already remarked (p. 77), that the bread for the offertory is already 'sacred'. (It is, of course, literally that, in the most literal sense of 'sacred', i.e. 'set apart'.)

[2] Καὶ τὰς ἱερὰς θεουργίας ὁ ἱεράρχης ὑμνήσας ἱερουργεῖ τὰ θειότατα καὶ ὑπ' ὄψιν ἄγει τὰ ὑμνημένα διὰ τῶν ἱερῶς προκειμένων συμβόλων. There seems no doubt that the third of these three clauses is intended as an extension and interpretation of the second: what has been 'accomplished' is precisely the 'works of God' that have been 'praised', summarily enumerated; and this 'accomplishment' is the presentation of this to view (for the contemplation and communion of the congregation) under these forms or symbols. Cf. p. 59.

[3] ὑποδείξας: ' The word has the connotation of showing 'secretly', by indication, indirectly, and seems an obvious reference to the first half of the same sentence (above), the showing forth of the redemptive work of God in this 'secret', 'mystical' manner in the Mystery.

he himself approaches to holy communion in them and invites the others to do so' (425D).

(12) *Prayer after Communion*

'Having received and distributed holy communion[1] he concludes the ceremony with an act of thanksgiving' (428A).

The section ends with a reminder similar to that in the corresponding section of the chapter on Illumination. The bishop must condescend to the nature of men by presenting the invisible mysteries in visible form, yet he himself must remain always in contemplation of these in their invisible source: 'While the mass of the people give their attention to the symbols, he does not cease, under the inspiration of the Holy Spirit, to raise his mind to the sacred source of the sacramental rite. This he does by contemplation on the spiritual plane in accordance with the principle of the hierarchy, in that habitual purity befitting a life lived wholly in God.'

One hopes that 'the mass of the people', too, do in fact penetrate a little beyond the external signs of the sacraments they receive, and we shall find (p. 180) that the author expects they will. It is a question of degree, and this essential feature of hierarchy, function and degree is what he especially wishes to emphasise. A minimum of penetration beyond the outward signs is clearly essential, but the minimum is not very much. The initiate must know at least that he is entering into communion with God and his redemptive work present under this symbol, but it is not necessary—though it is desirable—that he should realise the full implications of this. It is of the essence of the Church's liturgical worship—recapitulated under this symbol and receiving its wider diffraction in the whole complex of words and actions that surrounds the central action—that it offers a revelation and possession of God within the grasp of the smallest child who has attained to the use of reason, while at the same time it opens up to the mystic and proficient ever-advancing vistas of deeper meaning and experience in proportion to his growing capacity; a capacity that is itself produced by the object of his contemplation, transforming the beholder into that which he sees.

[1] Note that he is here fulfilling his essential function as 'hierarch', head of the hierarchy; receiving the Light and transmitting it to others. We shall find the notion developed in the 'contemplation' which follows.

MYSTERY OF THE SYNAXIS OR COMMUNION

CONTEMPLATION[1]

As in the chapter on Illumination, this section begins with some general remarks addressed to the 'imperfect', apparently identified here with the 'newly initiate' (428A). They are presumably included among the 'mass of the people' of the preceding section.

We have already seen that the 'perfect' and 'imperfect' in any given passage are to be identified only by reference to the context. All are 'imperfect' from one point of view; from another all have some degree of perfection—it is all a matter of degree, and in the last analysis there is only one Perfect, one Good. Our neophyte has now been admitted to 'the mysteries that are to make him perfect' (p. 83): we discover here that he is nevertheless still imperfect. He has apparently been placed in communion with the source of his perfection, but this has not yet produced its full effect, been extended over the full measure of the space and time that have been allotted him.

'Speaking on the level' (428A) of such, he suggests that the more superficial penetration of the symbols may be within their grasp, though of course they will be incapable of following him to the higher levels. So the singing and the readings from the scriptures will 'teach them the precepts for a virtuous life' (428B), and in particular how 'to purify themselves from all that could dissolve their union with God'. Sharing, at peace with one another, in the same sacred food in holy communion will teach them 'to bring unity into their way of life[2] by living wholly in God' (428B) and, (such apparently is the thought) produce unity among themselves. The fact that this rite is the *commemoration* of the Last Supper, that there Our Lord said with reference to Judas: 'You are not all clean' (John, xiii, 11), and that here are excluded all who 'present themselves in impurity without being reconciled with him', will impress on these newly initiate that in approaching the sacred mysteries 'they are

[1] At this point the author apostrophises his 'fellow-bishop Timothy', the companion of St. Paul's travels, to whom the treatise is dedicated, as 'Pretty Boy'. It is not for the uninitiate to speculate just how bishops do address one another in private, but one may doubt if this is the usual mode.

[2] We have seen already, and shall see later in detail (p. 171), that unity is the measure of the degree of perfection. The monk is of the 'perfect' in the order of the laity because of the perfect 'unity' of his life.

assimilated to them and enter into communion with them' (428B).

Such signs 'will suffice to nourish the imperfect. We, however, must rise from effects to their cause and, through the light that Jesus will dispense to us, we shall be able to contemplate adequately the spiritual realities in which is reflected clearly the blessed goodness of the originals which are beyond understanding. Do you yourself, O holy Sacrament, most divine of all the sacraments, raise the veils that conceal and enclose you with their symbols; reveal yourself clearly to our sight and fill the eyes of our mind with an unveiled unifying light' (428C).

He then proceeds to his customary—in this instance exceptionally lengthy—'contemplation'. Having paused at the 'entrance to the temple', the more external aspects of the mystery, he now proceeds to 'penetrate within it' in order to 'unveil the spiritual nature' of the symbols (428D).[1]

We shall again separate this 'contemplation' into paragraphs corresponding with the numbers of the last section.

(1) *The bishop diffusing the sweet perfume of the incense among the people, then returning to the altar: a symbol of God advancing to communicate himself to men and return with them to unity, yet remaining immovable and unchanged in himself, suffering no diminution*

'The blessed Deity who transcends all being, although in his divine goodness he advances to communicate himself to those who receive him, yet never departs from a state that remains stable and immovable, an essential stability and immobility. And although he gives light to all who are in his image, in their own degree, he remains in himself truly distinct and unchanged.[2] The same is true of the holy sacrament of the Eucharist; while it remains in its source single, simple and undivided, it yet multi-

---

[1] The imagery seems to be taken from the practice in the mystery religions of introducing the initiate gradually into the temple, where a statue or picture of the god was unveiled before him, shining upon and possessing him. Here the liturgical rites are the veils of the mystery; we are now about to see what is concealed beneath them, so that it may shine forth, enlighten and possess the initiate.

[2] Cf. the hymn of none in the Roman rite: *Rerum, Deus, Tenax Vigor,/ Immotus in te permanens* . . . (O Strength and Stay, upholding all creation,/ Who ever dost thyself unmoved abide . . .).

MYSTERY OF THE SYNAXIS OR COMMUNION

plies itself for love of men under a variety of holy symbols; it is extended over the whole of those figures that represent the deity. But in returning to its own unity it brings back into unity all these various symbols, so conferring unity on all who approach it with reverence' (429A).

The thought seems to be that all that has come out from God, focused with ever-increasing sharpness in the Old Testament, receiving full clarity and final definition in Christ, is now present in the Eucharist as a single unity. It is from the Eucharist that the Light manifested in all the moving figures of creation now comes out to man in all the activities of the ecclesiastical hierarchy and returns with them into unity. As already suggested, in the mystery of the Eucharist itself this unity, in coming out, is extended over, multiplied into, the whole complex of rites with which the central act and sign is surrounded, the rites in each single celebration and extended further over the whole of the liturgical year, that cycle of feasts in which, with Advent, the end is also the beginning.[1] It is not stated explicitly in this

[1] The celebration of the Eucharist is the central point of the Church's life. The 'hours' of public prayer, the 'divine office', seven times during the day and once (ideally at least) during the night, are a kind of further extension of the external clothing, the symbols, of this central act, revolving round it like so many planets round a central sun. The prayer of the week and, beyond that, of the Church's year, is a still further extension including the seasons and man's seasonal work and activity. Each celebration of the Eucharist is the 're-presentation' of the whole Work of Redemption. The seasons and feasts of the liturgical year give it a further temporal and spatial extension, throwing into particular prominence one or other aspect of that work which is present as a whole in each celebration. These feasts and seasons do, however—such is the teaching of theologians such as, e.g., Abbot Marmion—give their own special light and grace, the Light in this or that particular form and manifestation. The analogy of the operation of the Light in the sacraments in our author's scheme should be considered in this connection: the whole of the Light is present, but applied to one particular specialised activity, as it was present at each stage of the gradual unfolding of the external form of the work of redemption, its 'temporal extension', in the Old Testament. It is noteworthy at this point that all the 'symbols' of the hierarchy contain the whole Light in one or other limited aspect, as we saw that the whole Light is present at every stage of both hierarchies in a limited, particular manifestation. So here, at the very beginning of the Eucharist, the simple act of incensation is a figure and symbol of the whole, and indeed of the whole of the work of creation and redemption. It is a principle valid throughout the hierarchies. Here we see the Light brought to a unity and focused on the Point that is the Eucharist, the point at which it

treatise (see, however, p. 12 ff. above), but I think that in the author's mind this unity is conceived as further extended over the neophyte's whole life and activity, including the world outside him, that all is considered as being carried back into unity by this process. We saw (p. 74) how his conversion began with a movement of introversion, a withdrawing into himself away from the external appearances to the source of their reality; it was the first moment of a unity which seems to be conceived as finding its term here, the neophyte's whole world taken up into the unity from which it sprang. It is the function of the hierarch or bishop, himself the channel of all this, to present the double movement of going out and return in symbolic, material form, the symbol in this case being the rite of incensation.

'In the same way the bishop, as befits a man divine, transmits to his inferiors that simple [i.e. 'unified', all its infinite variety seen in one single glance, or more accurately as one single Act which is God] knowledge of the hierarchy that is proper to him. In order to do this, he uses a multitude of symbols, but he then returns, free and liberated from all lower reality, to his source in the One without having undergone any diminution, where he contemplates in clear light and in their original unity the inner nature of the sacred rites. He returns, that is, to the higher realities after his descent to those of the lower order to which his love of men inspired him' (429B).[1]

[1] The motionless activity of God is thus reflected in the bishop, and should be further reflected in all those who receive the Light from him: a going out to the activity of daily life without diminution of union with the Light (cf. below, *Washing of the Hands*), a reception of Light which is also its reflection down the scale (cf. p. 13 above).

In eastern liturgies, such as that of this author, the concept of the liturgy of the Church on earth as the reflection in the extension of space and time of the liturgy of heaven is particularly prominent. It is the liturgy of heaven, enacted before the throne of God, made present on earth with all the ceremonial of the Byzantine court that we see here, enabling man to enter ever more deeply from glory to glory into the life of heaven. This was given visible expression in the church building, in the throne of the bishop set in the apse with the drama of the liturgy unfolding before him and, as we see here, periodically proceeding out from his throne and returning to it. The

emerges from and returns into the invisible spiritual plane. Anyone who might see in this only a crafty and cunning infiltration of Neoplatonism into the pure light of the Gospel might be well advised to consider the statement of Christ, that he 'came out from God' and was now 'returning' (John xvi).

(2) *The Sacred Chant* (429C)

There follow here some general remarks on 'the sacred psalmody which accompanies almost all the mysteries of the hierarchy', in which, however, nothing is said of the actual music. The subject of the psalmody is assumed to be the books of sacred scripture, most of which are alluded to explicitly though, oddly enough, no mention is made of the Book of Psalms. Presumably this was considered unnecessary, since the word is itself contained in the expression 'psalmody'.[1] It is clear that for our author the fourth gospel holds a specially important place as 'the theological explanation of the supernatural mysteries of Jesus, intended for those who are qualified for deification'. The synoptics by comparison are considered simply to record 'the divine works of Jesus made man'.

All are expected to profit from the learning thus acquired and from the spiritual exhortations contained in them, leading to a 'life similar to that of God'. The purpose of these sacred chants is, in fact, 'to celebrate all the words and works of God, to recount all that the men of God have said of God and all they have done in his service'. Thus they form 'a complete historical poem of all the divine mysteries, giving to all who sing them reverently the right dispositions for receiving and distributing the mysteries of the hierarchy' (432A).[2]

---

[1] The 'sacred chant' at this stage plays a greater role in the Byzantine liturgy than in the Latin, though the general structure of the two is parallel. The language, however, of the author does suggest that he includes under 'sacred chant' also the extracts from sacred scripture, including epistle and gospel. The reader presumably realises that in the Latin rite too, in the sung celebration which is the norm, these passages are sung, and so may legitimately be considered as part of the 'psalmody', even though they may be sung to tones varying from melodies of some complexity down to a simple monotone.

[2] Recent popes have emphasised the didactic value of the Church's liturgy, the peculiar power of knowledge of religion acquired in this context, where it is both knowledge and being in the fullest sense that are received.

---

spirit of this was equally, of course, the spirit of the early Latin liturgy; but in the Byzantine rites it received greater external emphasis, leading the envoys of the Russian Vladimir to report, on witnessing the liturgy at Constantinople: 'We no longer knew whether we were in heaven or on earth, for it is impossible there should be such majesty and beauty on earth.'

MYSTERY OF THE SYNAXIS OR COMMUNION

(3) *Epistle and Gospel* (432A)

The sacred chant has 'prepared our souls for the mysteries we are about to celebrate'. It has brought together and 'summed up' the truths of religion through the medium of music, and in so doing has not only 'placed us in harmony with divine realities' but has also 'established harmony within ourselves and with one another, so that we form only one single homogeneous choir of holy men' (432B). The passages from sacred scripture which now follow are considered to pick out a particular theme and 'develop with more numerous and clearer illustrations and explanations what the sacred psalmody has only summarised or sketched in outline'. The whole *work of redemption* in general is celebrated, that is, then some particular aspect of it is singled out for more detailed consideration. Generally speaking, it is still the operation of the universal principle of hierarchy, the diffraction or breaking down into more and more words and 'sensible signs' of what is beyond words and even 'beyond understanding'.

The principle characteristic that is expected to strike the participant in this reading of the sacred texts—and here the dominant motif of the author is again sounded—is 'their *unity* and harmony, the origin of which is the unity of the Holy Spirit himself'.

'So there is good reason for reading publicly the New Testament after the Old. In fact it seems to me that this order, coming from God and prescribed by the hierarchy, indicates how the one has foreseen the divine works of Jesus and the other describes their realisation; how the one depicted the truth in images and the other has shown the reality present. For the events reported by the one have confirmed the authenticity of what was announced by the other, and it is in the Work of God that the Word of God finds its culmination and completion' (432B).

All this has been didactic and preparatory to the actual *re-presentation* of the 'work of God' (always with the qualification that it is nevertheless the outer fringe of this central action that is in its essence, at its source, beyond all sensible expression). This is now to be accomplished, but first must take place the:

MYSTERY OF THE SYNAXIS OR COMMUNION

(4) *Dismissal of Catechumens, Possessed and Penitents* (432C)

They are dismissed as not being at the stage of development, or alternatively, not possessing the dispositions essential for union with God; they may, however, profit by attendance at church for the chant and the readings from sacred scripture. 'They ought, in accordance with the rules of the sacred hierarchy, to hear the chant and the readings from sacred scripture. They are not, however, admitted to the celebration of the mysteries which follow, nor to the contemplation which is reserved for the perfect eyes of the perfect.' (The necessity for this dismissal will be more evident if one remembers the fact already mentioned, that at this date the actual reception of holy communion by all was in practice an integral part of attendance at the mystery.) In this the Church 'apportions to each in proportion to his merits,[1] and with a view to his salvation, the share in the mysteries proper to each, measuring and proportioning its gifts in accordance with the circumstances of each' (432C).

We shall find later (p. 179) that these 'profane', excluded from the celebration, form the lowest of the three degrees of the laity. Even within the group there is an ascending scale, from the catechumens, the lowest, to the penitents, the highest. The extremes, the catechumens who have not been admitted to initiation, and those of the penitents who are on the verge of being readmitted to communion, emerge clearly enough, but the line of division in between is blurred. The language of the author is obscure and repetitive, and the impression is given that he sees within the three degrees many classes and subdivisions—as of course, in the nature of things, must be so. It is unfortunate that he does not give us a clearer presentation, since this degree of the laity is treated at greater length here than in the later section explicitly devoted to it. His divisions are as follows, in the order of exclusion:

(a) *The Catechumens*, who 'have reached only the lowest rank for, not having received any initiation, they have no part in any sacraments of the hierarchy' (432D). Initiation, we recall, is the sacrament of 'birth from God'. This class of people is therefore here compared, in a passage not free from obscurity, to unborn

---
[1] Cf. p. 58 for the significance of 'merit' in such a context.

MYSTERY OF THE SYNAXIS OR COMMUNION

infants who are still in process of 'becoming', of coming into being. They are still being formed and developed by sacred scripture until they are ready for illumination, ready to come forth to full being, to the light of day. Should they be brought forth too soon they would not, in fact, be born to life, rather they would be 'born dead', still-born.

'Children according to the flesh, if they are born before the proper time for delivery, are imperfect and ill-formed, or abortions and still-born, and fall to the ground without having received life or having seen the light of day. It would be foolish in such a case to judge merely from the external appearance and say that because they have escaped the darkness of the mother's womb they have therefore come to the light. (The art of medicine, which knows better than any other all that concerns the body, would show indeed that for light to have effect it is necessary to have organs capable of receiving it.) The catechumens, therefore, are brought to the point of birth by the spiritual food of the Scriptures, which gives them form capable of life. Then only, when they are formed and can be born of God, is it granted to them for their salvation and in due order to enter into communion with the truths that are to enlighten them and bring them to perfection. For the present, since they are still unformed, the mysteries that bring to perfection are kept from them, because of the dignity of these mysteries and also that due care may be given to the delivery and life of the catechumens in accordance with the divine order instituted by the hierarchy' (433B).

(b) *The Possessed (Energumens)*. Nothing in the text suggests that by 'possessed', 'energoumenoi', the author has in mind 'possessed' in the strict sense in which alone the word is used today, of an indwelling of an evil spirit in a human being, living and working in him (such is the force of the Greek word) so that the acts of the person are no longer his own but those of the evil spirit in him. Such a one would clearly not be responsible for his actions, though he might be—and also might not be—responsible for admitting the evil spirit in the first place. On the other hand, I do not think the author would be aware of any distinction—except one of degree—between 'possessed' in this strict sense and all who give themselves up to the service of the devil through acting from a false and evil principle; in a greater or less degree and in matters of greater or less importance. In the author's scheme of things even material evil—including such physical disabilities as epilepsy, which was no doubt sometimes taken as a sign of possession in the strict sense—would be attributable to the entrance of evil into creation, and so ultimately to the devil. In the moral sphere, and in the case of these 'possessed' at the Eucharistic assembly the position would be clear: either Christ is living and active in them or the devil. This whole class between the catechumens and penitents had abjured Satan and turned their backs on him in the rite of illumination. They have now fallen from grace and returned to the service of Satan, some more, others less; none presumably wholeheartedly, or they would hardly be present at all at this assembly. Apparently they want to compromise, to keep a foot in both camps; or they mean well, yet fail in spite of this, almost as though they were led by a power beyond their control. They all no doubt do intend to qualify sooner or later for the class of penitents; but not just yet. The type is a familiar one in all ages, and we may imagine them praying with Augustine for 'repentance, but not yet'.

Radically then, in the author's way of looking at it, these are 'possessed' in the sense that they 'deliberately refuse to conform their lives to the divine model and adopt instead the sentiments and habits of abominable demons'. Their error consists fundamentally in 'turning away from goods that really exist, the possession of which endures beyond death and procures eternal happiness, and directing their desires and activities towards corruptible, material things and their manifold passions' (433D).

This body 'holds the second rank, above catechumens whose rank is the last. For I hardly think they are equal, he who, on the one hand, has received no initiation and participated in no divine sacrament and, on the other hand, he who has shared in some of the most holy sacraments before lapsing, by sloth or an excess of activity, into a state contrary to that effected by these sacraments. They too, however, no less than the catechumens, are prohibited from contemplating the holy mysteries and from entering into communion with them' (433B).

It is interesting to note that an 'excess of activity' may have turned them from the contemplation of 'goods that really exist',

MYSTERY OF THE SYNAXIS OR COMMUNION

and to remember that the late Pope (John XXIII) has recently warned the clergy of the danger of 'over-activity'. No one is likely to deny that excess of activity can be an anodyne, and frequently is used as an excuse for escaping from fundamental and so more exacting duties that weigh upon the conscience—or subconscience.

This class seems to shade off almost imperceptibly into that of:

(c) *The Penitents*, the highest of this whole degree and so excluded last. These are they who 'have given up a life of sin but are not yet free from evil imaginations because they have not acquired a lasting desire of God and a love without alloy (436B)—men who have not succeeded in unifying themselves completely; they who, to use the language of the Law, are not completely irreproachable nor without sin—they whom some imperfection prevents from reaching the height of conformity with the divine' (436A).

One is left speculating on the probable size of the class composed of these three groups, perhaps wondering rather uneasily what one's own position might have been; for surely if the standard of excellence demanded was exacted too literally, few could have been left within the Church to assist at the celebration of the sacred mysteries. It is, however, obvious that the author's own exuberance of language has carried him away a little. It is again all a matter of degree. We shall in fact find later that of the two degrees of the laity left in the Church only the higher, that of the monks, is expected to have 'unified itself completely', and to have reached 'the height of conformity with the divine'—and even this, of course, only within its own degree, the limits of its own being: above them are still the degrees of the clergy and, beyond them, the mysteries.

All these others are grouped together as 'profane' in the literal sense of those who must stand 'before' or 'outside' the temple, not allowed to enter, except for the former, preparatory part of the celebration. What of the still more numerous multitude who have no intention or desire of entering? Among them are they who are 'entirely deaf to the teaching concerning the holy sacraments and do not even see the visual presentations,[1] for

[1] Lit. εἰκόνας. The meaning is not clear. It is difficult to refer it to the 'sensible images' of sacred scripture seen during the first part of the Eucharist. There is an equally vague reference a little earlier (428C) to representations

they have shamelessly refused the saving initiation and the birth of God in the soul; they have rejected Scripture by these fatal words: 'We desire not the knowledge of thy ways' (Job xxi, 14). It is possible that these are people who began instruction as catechumens and failed to persevere, or were found on probation to be unsuitable, not, that is, giving reasonable promise of being able to fulfil the obligations of the Christian life. It would be unreasonable to apply such words to those who had not heard of the Church. We must, however, remember in any case that all are being pursued by the Light.

(5) *The Creed* (cf. p. 90) (436C)

'Only then do the holy priests of a holy liturgy and all those participating, turn to the contemplation of the sacramental rite and sing the universal hymn of praise in honour of the Principle, the origin and dispenser of all good, he who has instituted for us the saving sacraments by which are deified all who take part in them. This chant is sometimes called hymn of praise, sometimes symbol,[1] at other times and I think more fittingly, thanksgiving [eucharist] of the hierarchy, for it summarises all the sacred gifts we owe to God.' (The author has mentioned the institution of the sacraments; he adds here the creation, redemption and incarnation.)

Called on page 90 the 'universal, catholic hymn', it will be evident that its description here fits better the creed than the *Gloria in excelsis*. As a recapitulation of all the works of God it forms an obvious link here between all that has been recalled by the sacred chant and readings of scripture and the mystical 're-presentation' of the work of redemption which is now to follow.

[1] I.e. confession of faith, creed. It is, however, significant in the context of this treatise that the word is the same as that for the external form of the mysteries; it is a 'manifestation', 'revelation', in its degree of the invisible working of God.

---

on the 'outside' or in the 'vestibule' of the church whether to be taken literally,—impossible if this is to be the first century—or figuratively, referring to the more superficial significance of the symbols. If taken literally, of murals or mosaics at the entrance of the church—possible by the late fifth or early sixth century (the most likely date of composition)—then the passage is roughly equivalent to 'those who never darken the doors of our church'. There is no vital point at issue.

MYSTERY OF THE SYNAXIS OR COMMUNION

If the reader should find this varying use of 'eucharist' confusing—simply for 'thanksgiving' in general, occasionally of the Mass, and now here as a synonym for the creed or 'symbol'—he will find it helpful to recall the origin of its use in the context of Christian worship already referred to (p. 85); Eucharist as the name for the whole rite of what we of the West now more commonly call the Mass. The responsorial exchange between priest and people began the 'preface', leading to the prayer, or series of prayers, that had as its climax the consecration of host and chalice. The Preface and Canon of the Mass, the so-called 'Eucharistic Prayer', is itself a hymn of praise and thanksgiving for the whole work of redemption (singling out at different seasons for special mention some particular aspect of that work), in the course of which this work of redemption is accomplished and made present.[1] The creed also, as a solemn declaration of belief in God's work of creation and redemption, here detailed in a more formal manner, is to that extent also an act of praise and thanksgiving, and since this author, unlike St. Paul, does not commonly use the word eucharist of the Mass, and never restricts it to that, it is not illogical that he should use it in a general sense of any formal act of praise and thanksgiving, and therefore here of the 'symbol' or creed.

(6) *The Offertory* (437A)

'The love of God for men having been celebrated in this holy manner [i.e. by the singing of the creed], the divine bread, covered by a veil, is presented together with the 'chalice for consecration'.

The author has no comment or 'contemplation' to offer on this.

(7) *The Kiss of Peace* (437A)

Symbolic of the unity of purpose with which we must seek union with God, the source of peace and union with our fellow men.

'The Kiss of Peace is exchanged reverently, then they proceed to the reading of the diptychs.'

---

[1] Cf. the 'secret prayer' of the Mass of the Ninth Sunday after Pentecost in the Roman rite: . . . *quoties huius hostiae commemoratio celebratur opus nostrae redemptionis exercetur.*

The thought of the passage that goes on to explain the significance of this kiss of peace may seem rather involved until one remembers that unity with the Light is the effect of the Light itself, and it is union with the Light which shows itself in union with our fellow men: in a word, union with others is the external effect, not the cause, of our union with God:

'Now it is impossible to recollect oneself in order to attend to the One, or to participate in a peaceful union with the One, if a man is divided in himself. If, on the contrary, through the lights that come to us from the contemplation and knowledge of the One, we succeed in recollecting ourselves and unifying ourselves in a truly godlike manner, it will never be our lot to give way to the many irregular desires that foment among men gross and passionate dissensions. It seems to me then that it is such a life, unified and without division, that is enjoined by the sacred ceremony of the kiss of peace, establishing him who assimilates himself to God in him who is himself the source of this assimilation, and depriving him who leads a divided life from participation in the divine rites' (437B).

From the author's standpoint, that is, this act is a symbol or sensible sign of the participant's union with God. Reconciliation with one's brethren (Our Lord's injunction, Matt. v, 24) is here less the removing of an obstacle to union than an effect of union: but the two are inseparable; the nature of man is such that he must give such external expression to, sensible signs of, his internal disposition.[1]

(8) *Reading of the Diptychs or Lists of Saints*

Permanent record of their names on memorial tablets signifies their eternal dwelling with God; the reading of these at the moment of the synaxis their inseparable union with him.

'At the reading of the sacred diptychs that follows the kiss of peace are proclaimed the names of those who have led a holy life and have attained by constant effort to the perfection of virtue. We are thus encouraged and drawn by their example

[1] The gravity with which this act of unity was regarded at this period may be seen clearly in the *Syriac Didascalia*, where the deacon at this point calls out: Is anyone present with anything against his neighbour? Should the answer be in the affirmative, the sacrifice could not continue until the speaker had come forward and been reconciled by the bishop. Cf. 'A Third Century Christian Community', *Clergy Review*, January 1956.

towards a mode of life that will assure us greater happiness, towards the peace that comes from conformity to God; for the tablets proclaim, as though still living, the names of those who, theology teaches, are not dead but rather passed from death to a life wholly divine' (437B).

The inscription of names on such 'memorial tablets' is not meant to suggest that God needs any such *aide-mémoire* 'but rather to signify suitably that God honours and knows for ever those who have become perfect in conforming entirely to him. As Scripture says: 'He knows those who are his own' (2 Tim. ii, 19),[1] and: 'Precious in the sight of the Lord is the death of his saints' (Ps. cxv, 5). The death of the saints signifies here the perfection of their sanctity'[2] (437C).

The fact that the names are read 'at the very moment that are placed on the altar of sacrifice the sacred symbols by which Christ signifies and communicates himself' shows that 'they are inseparably united to him in a holy supernatural union' (437C).

It is noteworthy that the author speaks only of those who have already died in communion with the Church as being recorded on the diptychs. It may be that he is selecting his material in a way that will emphasise his point of 'union' or synaxis—only those already dead could be said to be 'inseparably' united to God. We know in fact that both living and dead were recorded on these diptychs; the names of the living might be removed,

[1] It is necessary to know the original Greek (translated literally here) in order to appreciate the full significance it has for this author: ἔγνω κύριος τοὺς ὄντας αὐτοῦ. The Latin Vulgate, and still more the Rheims English version, tend to distort the original, the latter transforming it into the Latin 'indirect question': 'The Lord knoweth who are his.' In this present scheme it has rather the same implication as in Gal. iv, 9: '... after you have known God, or rather are known by God'; the suggestion being that our knowledge (and being) are a reflection in this degree, at this stage of the hierarchy, of the knowledge that is the being of God himself. St. Gregory is in the same tradition when, in commenting on the Vision of Ezechiel (Hom. iii, bk. 1; there is a section in the Monastic Breviary for the Feast of St. Matthew), he says: 'By faith we are known by almighty God, as he himself says of his sheep: I am the good shepherd, and I know my sheep and mine know me'; the implication being that the sheep know him *because* he knows them.

[2] Presumably in the sense of p. 77, the degree of perfection of the neophyte reaching its final, irrevocable, inamissible term only with death, the conclusion of one continuous process of dying, of passage from the visible to the invisible.

should they fall into heresy, or apostatise; only when their names had been transferred from the living to the list of the dead could their position be called secure, inseparable, '*in memoria aeterna*'. It is generally realised that the two lists of saints combined with the name of pope and bishop, and the *mementos* of living and dead, in the *canon* of the Roman Missal had their origin in the diptychs.[1]

(9) *The Washing of Hands* (*Lavabo* in the Latin Rite)

(1) Symbolic of the purity with which one ought to approach the mysteries; (2) washing of the hands (the extremities) only signifies that, provided one is already firmly united to God, it is possible to proceed generously to his service in external tasks without detriment to this union.

The author produces these interpretations in the reverse of the order I have given above, presumably because in his view, as we have seen, this ministration of the sacraments is itself an instance of 'proceeding to the service of God in external tasks', a condescension from the contemplation of 'spiritual realities' to the presentation of these in 'sensible signs' as our human nature requires. Accordingly (2):

'When these rites have been completed in the way described, the bishop, facing the sacred symbols, washes his hands with water, as do also the venerable order of priests. As indeed Scripture says,[2] he who is already washed needs to wash only the extremities. Through this purification of the extremities [lit: 'extreme purification', 'carried to the extreme'] he will be able to remain in the perfect likeness of God; proceeding generously to tasks on a lower plane he will not be contained by or [unduly] implicated in them, since he is wholly united to God, and, turning back immediately to the One, his return will be pure and immaculate, preserving the fulness and integrity of his likeness to God' (440A).

---

[1] This Communion of Saints is still brought out very strikingly in the Byzantine rite by the act of placing on the paten at Mass, together with the host for consecration, also particles (cut from the one circle of bread in a preparatory rite) representing severally the Blessed Virgin, prophets, apostles, other classes of saints, and the faithful living and dead. Of these only the one for Christ is consecrated, becoming the Body of Christ; the others are placed in the chalice after the communion, thus united with the sacred elements, and are so consumed by the priest.   [2] John xiii, 10.

MYSTERY OF THE SYNAXIS OR COMMUNION

This translates an extremely difficult and involved passage. The author seems to be trying to express what I have called (p. 18) a simultaneous turning both ways, at one and the same moment facing the Light while distributing it below him. In this the bishop is simply in the 'likeness of God' who is immanent and transcendent, proceeding outside himself to the work of creation and redemption while remaining motionless in himself. The angels too, when 'sent' by God on a mission, never leave the presence of God. In other words, he is repeating and emphasising his first point in connection with the incensation. The bishop remains in contemplation while engaged in diffusing what he receives into the sensible signs of our world of space and time. The finger he has had in even such unworldly worldly affairs is no sooner inserted than it is withdrawn. Once again it is union, synaxis, that is presented in this symbol. There is a cumulative effect, and we now approach the climax.

Our author also sees this as an application of the general rule of purity required in one who is to celebrate the mysteries, 'recalling the ritual ablutions that already existed in the hierarchy of the Law. For they who take part in the celebration of the holy mysteries ought to be entirely pure from even the slightest untoward thoughts that burden the soul, and to celebrate the divine mysteries with a purity as nearly as possible equal to that of the mysteries themselves. Then will they be enlightened by a clear vision of the divine, for these supernatural rays will reflect their own brightness with a fuller and brighter radiance in mirrors made in their likeness' (440B).

The author sees an additional significance in the fact that the hands are washed 'in the presence of the sacred symbols' that are to become the body and blood of Christ. This signifies for him that all, even our most secret, thoughts are open to Christ and 'seen by him'. In consequence—such seems to be the thought—everything about us must be pure, down to the very finger-tips and our smallest action. 'Hands' in fact have become here 'finger-tips' in the desire to emphasise the 'extreme' purity (the play of words is the author's own) that is required. There is no inconsistency; although the rubrics today do speak of 'hands', in practice it is commonly only the finger-tips that are washed.

MYSTERY OF THE SYNAXIS OR COMMUNION

(10) *Preface and Consecration* (440B ff.)

All that follows here until the end of the chapter is exceptionally diffuse and repetitive, and although it would not be correct to call it also digressive, its coherence is not always immediately apparent. In consequence, it is only by careful and close reading that one is able to isolate the essential points. The divisions here given must, therefore, be rather arbitrary, but it is hoped that they will, together with introductory notes and reasonably full and literal quotations from the text, help the reader to follow the argument.

We have in fact come now to the central point of the rite, which is itself, we must remember, the summit of the whole ecclesiastical hierarchy. All that has gone before was preparatory to this, yet not merely preparatory; I think in the author's view it is rather the outer circumference, the fringe, of the veil of sensible signs in which the spiritual reality is to be presented. Indeed, I think he would see the whole of the visible creation as forming a single great variegated robe of sensible signs round this one central symbol, in which it is all carried up into the invisible world of 'spiritual realities' and united to the One from which it receives its being. For him it is the one single point of contact and synaxis, union, between the invisible and visible worlds, at which the latter receives a being which is fulfilled only by a return to unity, by 'losing itself' so far as external evidence goes. We shall find later (p. 171) that the criterion of perfection is the degree in which this cosmic unity is achieved in the soul and reflected in the external ordering of life. Various aspects of Christ's work of redemption, as revealed in sacred scripture, have been sung and heard; certain themes have been isolated for special consideration in epistle and gospel (and, though it is not mentioned here, the sermon or homily has further elaborated the main theme); a résumé of it all, a declaration of faith which is of its nature also a hymn of praise and thanksgiving, a *eucharist*, has been sung by the whole congregation: all these have been so many 'sensible signs' revealing, and in their own degree making present, what they signify. Now all that has been revealed gradually by these many diverse symbols is to be made present under the one symbol of bread and wine, and through this symbol the participant is to enter into communion with, become one with, all that has been symbolised. In all this we must not lose sight of the fact that it is ultimately a person, the Word Incarnate, with whom the communicant is thus united, in such a way as to become involved in, transplanted into, his life, being and every action, and return to heaven with him.

We shall seek in vain here for any 'Explanations of the Mass' or 'Keys to the Eucharist' such as have appeared in modern times. For our author all that was effected by the 'sensible signs' of the words and actions of God incarnate in this world is now present in the 'sensible signs' of the mysteries. These signs may be given indefinite expansion and elaboration—their ultimate expansion is no less than the whole of space and time—but in their essence they are contained in the simple central action of the synaxis. By initiation into the mysteries all that is contained in them—revealed more or less inadequately by the 'sensible signs' in which they are presented—becomes the initiate's own. For our author it is as simple as that—and as great a mystery, in both the original technical language of theology and the more common sense.

(*a*) The author introduces his 'contemplation' here by what appears to be intended as a simple statement of what happens before he goes on to develop his theme. It is simple but not easy, because being so concise, repeating almost exactly the words used in describing the rite on p. 91, it is necessary to consider carefully the exact significance of each word:

'He unites himself to the divine realities and, having sung the sacred works of God, he performs the sacred rite and makes present in visible form [lit. 'draws into sight'] the things of which he has sung the praises'.[1] His action, that is, consists essentially in making present in these 'sensible signs' the subject of the foregoing chant, praise and eucharist.

The customary rendering of the Greek ἱερουργεῖ ('he performs the sacred rite') by the word 'consecrate', as in my own headings, tends to obscure the fact that it is not simply the changing of bread and wine into the body and blood of Christ, the 'production', to express it crudely, of the sacred host in

---

[1] τοῖς θείοις ἑνοῦται καὶ τὰς ἱερὰς θεουργίας ὑμνήσας ἱερουργεῖ τὰ θειότατα, καὶ ὑπ' ὄψιν ἄγει τὰ ὑμνημένα.

MYSTERY OF THE SYNAXIS OR COMMUNION

which Christ is present in a manner only dimly apprehended; it is the whole life and activity of God become man that is here in question. In this one simple act (by a mode of action, that is, more closely resembling the one simple Act that is God) the bishop is making present in 'visible form' all that Christ, God incarnate, made present in his historical words and actions, the whole work of redemption.

That this clearly is the author's meaning is confirmed by two passages that follow (p. 115, pars. 1–2), where the same statement is made in a slightly different form: (1) 'He proceeds to their presentation [the presentation, that is, of the mysteries of which he has sung] under the form of the symbols;' (2) 'He makes visible through the symbols before him the things of which he has sung.'

The author now proceeds to explain how this works in our regard, how we benefit from it: by communicating in the rite we share in the whole life and activity of Christ which has just been portrayed in outline, and so return to union with God through Christ and his redemptive work.

(*b*) 'It is necessary to explain now, so far as we are able, what these works of God are in our regard. To speak of them is in fact beyond my power, or even to understand them clearly so as to reveal them to another. Still through the divine aid of the hierarchy we shall at least explain to the best of our ability what is effected in its liturgy in accordance with the Scriptures by the divine bishops' (440C).

There follows a brief résumé of the fall of man and of his redemption through the Incarnation, in which Christ 'united himself to our lowness without losing anything of his own nature', granting us 'as to offspring of his own to enter into communion with him and to share his own beauty', effecting 'a total transformation of our nature' (441B). (From his point of view an offering of 'Light', from our side an acceptance of it.)

'Finally he revealed to us that, in order to raise ourselves spiritually to the world beyond and to live in God, we must assimilate ourselves fully to him, so far as is in our power' (441C).

Through this rite, that is, we receive the Light: through Christ, in the 'pattern' of Christ, and our acceptance of it and our own efforts towards 'assimilation' are, as we know, also received. This assimilation is, in fact, not primarily the imitation of Christ in our daily actions; primarily it is our 'synaxis' or union with the Light through Christ, in the pattern of his life: the assimilation of our daily activity to that of Christ is a consequence of this. The activity of Christ here present becomes ours, and this is continued into the activity that is, one can only say, more directly attributable to us. We are absorbed into, drawn up the scale, as it were, into the redemptive work of Christ, and this is reflected down into our further work.

This leads us to the author's next point: Since this 'assimilation' is to be worked out over a certain space and time, it would seem to entail a certain continuation in terms of space and time of Christ present in this pattern.[1]

(c) 'But how are we to make this imitation of God a reality except by renewing ceaselessly the memory of the most holy actions of God through the sacred chants and sacred liturgy instituted by the hierarchy? As Scripture says, we do it for a commemoration of them.[2] That is why the divine bishop, standing before the altar of divine sacrifice, sings of the holy works that have been mentioned, which Jesus in his care for us accomplished for the salvation of the human race, with the consent of the Father and in the Holy Spirit, as Scripture says' (441C).

The connection in the author's mind between the 'making visible' the works of God and their 'commemoration' is not immediately evident, nor do the passages that follow help to clarify the matter in any considerable degree. The point appears to be that the 'making visible' the works of God under this symbol in the mystery is associated with a recounting of the principal features of these works because we have also to assimilate our own external activity to that of God, more precisely to that

---

[1] Cf. pp. 77 ff.

[2] The reference is apparently to Luke xxii, 19 (cf. also I Cor. xi, 24). The Greek text here in fact says: εἰς τὴν αὐτῆς ἀνάμνησιν, where αὐτῆς can refer logically only to the previous μνήμης (memory). The translators tend to render it as though it were αὐτῶν, referring to the 'works', the 'most holy actions of God'; which is what one would expect. If this is indeed the text, and the reading in the MS. is a copyist's error, then the transposition of thought is interesting: Our Lord said 'Commemorate me'; what our author sees commemorated is Christ with his whole redemptive work, or, more accurately, the whole redemptive work *in* Christ, and now in this symbol.

MYSTERY OF THE SYNAXIS OR COMMUNION

of Christ in this world.[1] This is the external shape assumed by the simple unity of the mystery in its wider extension, a shape shifting and varying in detail through the course of the Church's year. It is the pattern and the source of our activity. As the simple unity which is Christ was made visible in his historical activity, so the central act of the priest, 'making visible' the works as a whole, by his 'commemoration' gives also to the details of this activity a degree of visibility; but it is the mystery, the 'performance of the sacred rite' which gives these actions their visibility and presence, from which they come and into which they return. Indeed, it is through this that the further extension of the whole of the cosmos receives its being. The one is the visible 're-presentation' of the works of God in its most simple, most 'unified' form, at the point where it emerges from the invisible; the other is the pattern it assumes as it enters our world of space and time. The one is for us the point of unity, the other the external shape and pattern of our activity, as it was, as it is, that of Christ.

If the present use of 'commemoration' and 'memory' should seem to our modern western minds equivocal,[2] to our author it is rather a matter of degree. The acts of Christ 'commem-

[1] Cf. p. 95 above (429A). This—and indeed all the 'symbols' of this mystery indicated in the various subdivisions of this chapter—is essentially a repetition of the symbolism of the incensation, in slightly different terms: a going out from God, encompassing the whole of creation, and returning with it to unity. (Incidentally it again illustrates the principle that everything in the hierarchies contains, within its own limitations, the whole.) It is made present continually in the mystery so that man himself may enter into communion with it and so be brought back to unity.

[2] Cf. (p. 23, n. 2) the Semitic concept of 'memory' and 'commemoration', presumably the mentality Our Lord assumed when using the equivalent word at the Last Supper. Cf. also St. Augustine's view of 'memory'. Here, assuming such a tradition, the central action would be seen as the point of contact with the source and the 'commemoration' the spreading out of that into visibility in ever-widening circles until it embraces the whole cosmos. Both should be compared with the teaching of St. Thomas that the mystery of Christ, and in detail the different mysteries of his life, are the physical efficient cause of our salvation (cf., e.g., S. Th. III, Qq. 48, 50, 56, 57, and 51, 2 ad 2, and 4), and (III, Q. 8, 2) that the whole humanity of Christ flows into all men, primarily into their souls and then into their bodies. Cf. Abbot Marmion's application of this (p. 95) in the particular 'Light' or 'grace' given by the particular mysteries of the life of Christ 'commemorated' throughout the Church's year.

orated' are the acts into which the simple act of God has been, as it were, broken up, the colour taken by the single ray of light invisible in itself, visible only in its effects where it enters into our world of space and time, the visible presence of God incarnate. The words of sacred scripture 'commemorating' these acts are themselves, in their own degree, a certain 'making present or visible' the works of Christ. Now Christ, of whose activity these 'commemorations' are some of the external, visible manifestations, is to be made present in the most complete, literal sense, but under what one might call the least degree of visible manifestation, only one stage removed from the invisible and immaterial, the symbols of bread and wine. Through union with these man may pass over with them and return to union with the invisible God. It is the folding up, as it were, of man and his works into the works of Christ and through him into union with the Father. This, ultimately, is what the author means by 'assimilation' to God; man's 'imitation of Christ' in the popular sense is the reflection of this into the visible world; but man is such a unity that he cannot have one without the other. It is necessary to realise this in order to appreciate the significance of the author's next point.

(*d*) The presentation to our sight of Christ under the appearances of bread and wine is symbolic of the Incarnation whereby he became 'a being composite and visible' (444A) in all his visible words and actions. It is also a symbol of our unity with him and in him with one another: our reception, our assimilation of him, the One, in holy communion signifies the perfection with which 'we must make one with his divine life' (444B). This seems to be the gist of the author's meaning, but the passage requires very close reading.

To the modern reader it may seem remarkable that no special reference is made to the death of the cross, and we find nowhere the modern expression 'sacrifice of the cross', although there is no doubt that the Eucharist is, for our author, a sacrifice. The sacrifice of Christ, his death on the cross, does indeed form the centre and climax of the work of Christ; but it is not the whole of it, and it is the whole that the author sees presented here. For him what is primarily symbolised by the consecration of the bread and wine is union, communion, synaxis, this 'coming out' of Christ from the Father into the visible, material

MYSTERY OF THE SYNAXIS OR COMMUNION

world, the communication of himself to men, and his return to unity taking men with him. The sacrifice of the cross is simply the central act of the drama by which he effected this.

In the author's own words: 'Having thus sung the praises of the mysteries, and having entered with the eyes of the soul into their contemplation, the bishop proceeds to their presentation under the form of the symbols in accordance with the divine institution of God himself. That is why, having sung the praises of the divine actions, he apologises modestly and in the manner befitting a bishop for serving as an instrument of a liturgy that is beyond him. In his reverence he first cries: 'It is you who have said: Do this for a commemoration of me' (441D).

'He then prays that he may be worthy of the dignity of fulfilling, in imitation of God, this divine action of accomplishing the divine mysteries and distributing them faithfully. He prays also that all who participate may take part without sacrilege. He then accomplishes the most divine mysteries, and makes visible [lit. 'draws into sight'] through the symbols before him in the sacred rite the mysteries of which he has sung [lit. 'the things he has sung'] (444A).

We must never forget that it is primarily 'Light' that is distributed, light in the 'shape' of Christ taking a visible form in the 'mysteries' of his earthly life. It is necessary to recall this in order to appreciate the significance of the passage that follows: it is the movement out from the simple and invisible to the 'composite and visible' that is stressed, a movement first to visibility, then to *two* separate elements, further into the division necessary for distribution to the communicants; a movement outwards that is also a drawing into unity, since the whole remains wholly present after the division in the part that each receives. It is the synaxis. In the author's own words:

'The bread was covered and undivided: he uncovers it and divides it into many parts. Similarly he shares the single chalice, thus multiplying and distributing symbolically the One, that which constitutes the most holy act of the whole liturgy' (444A). [The bishop has, in fact, fulfilled his own distinctive function of receiving the Light, giving it a visible form, and diffusing it to those beneath him.]

'In his goodness, in his love for men, the simple and hidden unity of Jesus, the Word, who is perfect God, has in fact become

MYSTERY OF THE SYNAXIS OR COMMUNION

through the incarnation, without undergoing any change, a reality composite and visible. He has admitted us generously to unifying communion with himself, binding our lowness to his infinite, divine stability, on condition however that we adhere to him as members adhere to the whole body by that conformity with the divine which consists in a life without sin ... it is necessary that we fix our gaze on the divine life of God incarnate, that we take as model his holy impeccability and so tend to that perfect purity which consists in a permanent deification. Only on this condition, and in the manner suited to us, will he grant us to assimilate ourselves to him and to enjoy communion with him' (444B). [in a word all is given, including our own efforts, yet none the less they remain our efforts.]

'Such are the teachings revealed by the bishop in fulfilling the rites of the holy liturgy, when he makes visible publicly the offerings that were before veiled;[1] when he divides into many parts their original unity; when by the perfect unity of the sacrament which he distributes to the souls who receive it he admits to perfect communion with it all those who take part in it. In presenting Jesus to our eyes he shows us in a sensible manner and as in an image that which forms the actual life of our soul. He reveals to us how Christ himself came out of the secret sanctuary of the Godhead to take, for love of man, the form of man, to become totally incarnate without any confusion of substance; how he descended without loss of his natural unity to the level of our divisibility; how the actions inspired by his love for us bestow on the human race the power of communion with him and his blessings,[2] on condition however that we make one with his divine life and imitate him as much as is in our power, that we become sufficiently perfect to enter truly into communion with God and with the divine mysteries' (444D).

(11) *Communion and Thanksgiving* ('*Postcommunion*') (444D)

It will be immediately obvious that my own division here into a section headed 'Communion' is a purely arbitrary one, since our author has already considered 'communion' as simply one

[1] This seems to be a literal unveiling of the symbols, covered before that with a veil (as they still are in Eastern rites, even when exhibited for the adoration of the faithful), not the 'making visible' that is the central act of the mystery.

[2] Cf. St. Thomas above, p. 113, n. 2.

MYSTERY OF THE SYNAXIS OR COMMUNION

aspect of that central act of the rite which has been headed 'Consecration'. In fact, for him, as we saw at the beginning, the whole rite is essentially 'communion', 'union', synaxis. The division is intended to be useful as indicating the structure of the rite as identical in essentials with contemporary rites. The passage that follows is in fact, in the author's rambling style, little more than a repetition from a slightly different angle of what he has said in the preceding section; but serving to recall also the central thesis of his whole work: the 'universal rule' of the transmission of Light through a hierarchy.

'Having himself received holy communion and distributed it to those present, the bishop concludes the ceremony with an act of thanksgiving which he sings together with the whole congregation. It is indeed proper first to receive before giving, and participation in the mysteries always precedes their distribution. Such in fact is the universal rule and order of procedure in the works of God.'

'The holy pontiff begins by himself participating fully in the divine gifts which it is his duty to distribute to others; only then is he in a position to distribute them. The same rules apply for the conduct of a life really divine: anyone who is so misled as to claim to teach sanctity before he has acquired the habit of practising it is wicked and completely at variance with our holy institutions. Just as with the light of the sun; it is the most tenuous and transparent substances that are filled first with the light that flows into them, and only then, having become in a way suns themselves, do they transmit to those that come after them all the light with which they are overflowing. So one ought always to avoid the presumption of shewing to another the ways of God if he has not yet reached a perfect, lasting deification himself, if the inspiration and choice of God have not called him to the office of head' (445A).

(12) *Conclusion* (445B)

'All the sacred degrees, then, assembled according to their place in the hierarchy, after they have communicated in the divine mysteries end the ceremony with an act of thanksgiving, each of them acknowledging the graces divine activity produces in him according to his capacity. He who has taken no part in the divine mysteries and has made no recognition of them at

MYSTERY OF THE SYNAXIS OR COMMUNION

all will naturally be unable to give thanks, although of themselves the infinite gifts of God do deserve to have thanks given for them. But, as I have said,[1] it is because these men are inclined to evil and have refused to consider the gifts of God, that their wickedness has made them insensible of the unceasing thanks that should be given for this divine operation: "Taste and See," says Scripture.[2] For it is through initiation into the mysteries of God that the initiate will recognise the immensity of the graces received. By participating in them men will discover their sublimity; their grandeur will be revealed only to those who contemplate them. Then only will they too be able to praise and give thanks for these beneficent gifts of God that come down from beyond heaven itself' (445C).

Since whole classes of persons have been physically excluded from the rite, it may seem a little unkind to blame them for not taking part in it. It might seem even more unreasonable to our way of thinking to class as 'wicked' the immeasurably greater number of those who have never heard of the mysteries, who are, in the technical phrase, in 'invincible ignorance'—'How shall they believe him of whom they have not heard?' (Rom. x, 14). Yet this is, as we have seen (p. 72), in the author's line of thought. The Light is present for all to see; if only they open their eyes to it, it will lead them by way of the catechumenate and illumination to union, synaxis.

[1] Cf. p. 103. [2] Ps. xxxiii, 9.

4. Mystery of the Sacrament of Unction

THE author treats here of the consecration of the holy oil and of its use. Only one oil seems to be in question, and it apparently corresponds to the chrism of our present Latin rite, since it is said to be mixed with perfume.[1] Moreover 'Mystery of the Sacrament of Unction', assuming that this is indeed the author's own heading, seems to be a general term for the ceremony of anointing in all rites in which holy oil is used, not all of them sacraments in the strict sense in which the word is used today; in fact, it is used 'for the most sacred rites of the liturgy in almost all the functions of the hierarchy' (473A).

There is, however, no enumeration of the rites in which the oil is used. We have already learned that it is used in the rite of initiation, and in the following pages it seems reasonably certain that one of the anointings mentioned in initiation is that of the Sacrament of Confirmation. There is no reference to its use in the conferring of Holy Order, or for the Anointing of the Sick, in modern times known as Extreme Unction (the Last Anointing). The last anointing for this author (quite distinct, of course, from the sacrament of that name) is the anointing of the dead body in preparation for burial, as part of the funeral rites (p. 198). In the author's view it is, as we saw, one of the threefold system of sacraments which does in fact cover our seven sacraments, with the exception that there is no mention of matrimony.

---

[1] Two other oils are used in the present Latin rite, one especially for the anointing of the sick. It is not, however, certain that one of the other two might not be valid for the same purpose.

MYSTERY OF THE SACRAMENT OF UNCTION

The chapter dealing with this is the most obscure and shapeless of the whole treatise. Possibly the author had a foreboding of this when he declared (p. 82) that the mode of operation of the holy oil, being on the spiritual plane, was 'beyond human description', 'ineffable'. It may be, however, that this very obscurity and formlessness is the reader's best clue to its understanding. One thing is clear, that in the author's mind this sacrament has the purpose of 'bringing to perfection', to 'completion', to 'maturity and fulfilment'; all that is implied in our modern phrase of 'confirmation'. If there were any doubt of this, we are told right at the end, almost as a recapitulation of the whole (p. 137), that it is most fitting that this mystery especially should be called the *sacrament* of the holy oil. We shall see in its appropriate place the full significance for him of the word traditionally translated by 'sacrament'; it is completion, fulfilment. This mystery brings the initiate to the point of fulfilment, but there it leaves him; it is in the synaxis that he finds his fulfilment, in union through Christ with all that is. Up to that point his movement, through the operation of this sacrament, his completion and approach to maturity, is precisely a movement away from transient, material phenomena towards their source, a progress beyond all 'shape' and form towards that which is beyond all creation; a passage from the visible to the invisible. Accordingly, 'invisibility', 'formlessness', is the dominant note throughout the chapter, providing the thread—so it seems to the present writer—of the discussion that is to follow. In the oil it is the fragrance that receives special emphasis, invisible and untouchable; perhaps the most elusive of all material symbols. In the rite of consecration it is the veil covering the oil that is dwelt on at greatest length; it symbolises the seraphim brooding in motionless, ceaseless contemplation over the All-Holy, motionless, yet the immediate channel of all the being and activity of the whole line of hierarchies that stretches away beneath it. Yet they effectively cover and conceal the Mystery. So far is the initiate brought by this sacrament. Remembering the imagery of the pagan mysteries (p. 94), again reflected here, though not explicitly developed along this line, in initiation the neophyte is brought into the temple; this present sacrament places him before the god concealed beneath the veils; it is in the synaxis that the veils are removed—even the veils that are the seraphim—and the initiate enters into immediate, direct contemplation of and union with the ultimate Reality beneath.

In this connection it is important to note that it is for this author 'Jesus', the Word incarnate, who is here adored by the seraphim, and that 'this sacrament has the same dignity and power as the mystery of the synaxis' (476C). It is Christ, wholly present and operative; one might almost say it *is* the synaxis, but still veiled, it remains for the veil to be removed, opening the way to immediate union. Accordingly, 'almost the same ceremonies [as in the synaxis] are used in the consecration of the oil'. These ceremonies of the consecration are taken as symbolic of the effects of anointing in whatever connection it may be performed. As already noted, the Light tends here to become a Perfume, a Fragrance, diffused through the hierarchy in decreasing degrees of intensity the further we are from its source. More particularly it is the sanctifying action of the Holy Spirit that is signified by this effusion of perfumed oil. As on Christ, after baptism, the Holy Spirit descended in visible form, so on us after baptism are poured out the gifts of the Holy Spirit[1] in the visible form of the holy oil (484C).

It is Catholic teaching, defined as *de fide* by the Council of Trent, that the sacraments are not equal in dignity. It might be argued plausibly that this need not exclude the possibility of two of the seven being equal. Nevertheless, it seems certain that the author's statement that unction has 'the same dignity and power' as the synaxis is not intended without qualification. It must be considered in conjunction with his apostrophe earlier of the Eucharist (428C, p. 94 above) as 'most divine of all the sacraments', and with the fact that in his scheme baptism and unction are shown clearly as leading up to the Eucharist as to their completion and fulfilment. It seems that the phrase is to be explained by his desire to emphasise his general principle (372C, p. 52 above) that it is God (Jesus) who is operative throughout the hierarchy, producing this or that limited effect, and that here particularly it is Jesus operative both in the synaxis and, through the invisible action of the Holy Spirit infused in unction, drawing man up into union with himself.

[1] In what is apparently the sacrament of confirmation, although, as we saw, the point is disputed by the commentators. But see p. 136 below.

MYSTERY OF THE SACRAMENT OF UNCTION

Following his regular practice, our author begins with a short introductory section, in this case very brief, and continues with a summary of the ceremony of the consecration before passing to his 'contemplation' of the details of the rite:

'So great then, is the synaxis and such the beautiful rites by which, as we have said, it raises our minds to the One and effects our communion and union with him. But there is another sacred rite of the same kind: our teachers have called it the *Sacrament of Unction*. When we have examined in detail the sacred symbols that represent it to us we shall rise by degress of contemplation through these many images to the sight of the its source in the One' (472D).

DESCRIPTION OF THE RITE

'(1) As in the celebration of the Eucharist, the orders of the imperfect[1] are dismissed as soon as the members of the hierarchy have incensed the whole church, the psalms have been sung and the sacred scriptures read. (2) The bishop then takes the holy oil and places it on the altar of divine sacrifice (4) covered by (3) a twelve-winged veil.[2] Meanwhile the whole congregation unites in singing the sacred hymn with which God himself inspired the prophets.[3] He consecrates the oil with a prayer, and (5) henceforth uses it in almost all the functions of the hierarchy' (473A).

CONTEMPLATION

Introductory

As in preceding chapters, he first passes in brief survey over the more superficial symbolism of the rite. The central theme is

---

[1] The word may mean also simply 'uninitiate' (cf. p. 137 below), but as we know from the synaxis, it includes both catechumens and those baptised but lapsed.

[2] Lit: 'with twelve wings'. We shall see below (p. 130) that they symbolise the two seraphim, each with six wings. It is presumably not twelve veils that are in question, but probably a circle of material cut up round the circumference into twelve segments, 'tails' or 'wings'. A veil of this kind, cut into four or so segments, is sometimes used for a ciborium. Stiglmayr has an interesting reference to an ancient fly-whisk, formed of an angel's head with six wings at the end of a stick, used for keeping flies away from the Eucharist and for tempering the heat.

[3] I.e. the Alleluia. Cf. p. 140 below.

MYSTERY OF THE SACRAMENT OF UNCTION

'invisibility'. The holy oil is veiled, God is hidden and invisible; so, too, the initiate must strive ever to be 'invisible', moving ever towards the 'hidden' God in his activity and with his actions aimed at nothing on the visible plane, especially not seeking the approbation of men. He must turn his gaze always towards the unseen God. By contemplation of the invisible God men will become like him, come to resemble the Invisible Fragrance, invisible in itself, visible only in its effects. Their 'contemplation' of God will involve modelling their activity on his, but their good works must be done with the intention of resembling God, particularly in his 'invisibility', in living above the visible plane.

Such seems to be the argument, but it is not easy to follow. The dominant idea is, as we saw, that all movement must be towards the invisible, but that as we approach the invisible our influence on—and in fact our possession of—the visible world increases. In this instance it is, however, expecially difficult to decide which, in the author's view, is cause and which effect, more accurately perhaps, to distinguish the relationship between cause and effect. Is, for instance, the concealing of our virtues the cause of our resemblance to the hidden God or the result of it? The question is raised in an acute form in the passage I shall quote immediately, where the argument seems to be that we can reach the fragrance of the divine beauty only by resembling it, but that we come to resemble it by reaching it and remaining in contact, 'fixing our gaze' on it.

I think the answer is to be found in the fundamental notion of the author, already discussed, that our being itself—which in this world is rather a 'becoming'—is already a reflection of the being of God in whom cause and effect are one: our activity, too, is received, the activity by which we come to a greater degree of the resemblance of God. It is a commonplace of spiritual writers that the search for God is already evidence that one has found him—in a degree, but there is more to come.[1] Similarly that the eating of spiritual food increases the appetite and the capacity: desire grows and is fulfilled. But nowhere more than in our present author is this the regular warp and woof of the writing. It is useful to recall the fact again here,

[1] Cf. Augustine's consciousness (p. 69) that 'there was something to be seen that he was not yet in a position to see'.

because the cumulative effect on the reader—whether intended or not—is to form in him a habit of mind which is in effect a constant quandary, compelling him to pose the question: Is this my act or is it not? Is this my life or is it the life of God? And he is forced to the conclusion that the answer is both Yes and No, to borrow St. Paul's words and say: Now I live, yet not I . . . In a word, the effect is to keep this fundamental fact so before him that it becomes an habitual way of regarding this world, to transport him in mind to the invisible world, to the 'hidden God', where his 'life is hid with Christ in God'.[1] And this is the whole object of the author's writing.

But let us see his own words, not easily translated:

'The spiritual lesson to which this rite of the blessing of the holy oil raises us is, I think, this: it shows us that the good odour of the sanctity of virtuous men is hidden in their souls enjoining on the saints not to display, in a vain desire of glory, the beauty and good odour of their resemblance to the hidden God. This hidden divine beauty, whose perfume surpasses all the mind can think of, does in fact elude all profanation. It discloses itself to the minds of those only who are able to perceive it; for it is its nature to be reflected in our souls only through images that resemble it and which, like it, are incorruptible. Now the resemblance effected by this imitation of God produces a true image of its model only if the soul fixes its gaze on that spiritual and fragrant Beauty; in this way alone is it able to imprint and reproduce in itself the fairest image of this beauty.

Just as on the plane of sensible images, if the artist keeps his eyes constantly fixed on the original, without allowing himself to be distracted by any [other] visible object, not dividing his attention in any way, then he will produce a complete double,

---

[1] Strictly speaking, God is more myself than I myself am, and closer to me than I am to myself; my actions are his before they are mine and set my own in motion. It is in this spirit that Benedict tells his monks that before they call upon God he will say: 'Behold I am here'; and Bernard, in the same tradition, that however early they rose for the night office, it would be Christ himself who had awakened them and they would find him already waiting in the cold darkness of the monastic choir. It is a consoling thought and worth a little 'contemplation', the initiate, down to the very spring of his being and activity, cradled and enfolded in the being of God.

so to speak, of whatever object he intends to copy. In this way alone does he arrive at a true resemblance, in which the original is seen in its image and the two are present the one in the other, with the sole qualification that they remain in their essential being distinct. So too in the case of those who love the divine beauty, forming its image in their souls: diligent and constant contemplation of this hidden, fragrant beauty enables them to attain to an exact copy of the original, to perfect conformity with God.

With good reason therefore do these divine artists fashion the power of their souls on the model of a Virtue spiritual, transcendent and fragrant. In practising the virtues required for the imitation of God their aim is not at all to make themselves, in the words of Scripture, a spectacle to men,[1] but rather their attention is given to the hidden character of the mysteries veiled by the Church in this manner.

In accordance with their state they love and desire only what is truly beautiful and good, not vain appearances that the thoughtless mass of men praise. Able to distinguish, like God, between true beauty and evil, they are truly the divine images of that infinitely divine Sweetness which, concealing within itself true fragrance, is not concerned with specious counterfeits which seduce the majority of men, but is content to impress its authentic stamp on the souls that are true likenesses of itself' (476A).

As in the case of Illumination, he has first considered the more obvious, the surface significance of the symbol—to lead to the invisible. He now proposes to penetrate more deeply into the invisible itself; but how far men will be able to follow depends upon their ability to move habitually on the invisible plane.

'But to continue our examination. Having considered the external organisation of this magnificent sacred ceremony let us now turn our eyes to its deeper [lit. more divine] beauty; let us[2] consider it in itself, freed from its veils, shining with a beautifying radiance and imparting to us the fulness of that perfume

[1] '. . . the greater treason, to do the right deed for the wrong reason' (T. S. Eliot's Beckett).

[2] I.e. bishop and clergy alone, not the laity, as is clear from the next passage quoted.

which can be perceived only by men with the ability to receive it'[1] (476B).

In order to reach this Light, which is also an invisible Fragrance, men have to become 'invisible' (ἀθέατοι, 476A) in both active and passive sense, 'unseeing' and 'unseen'. The difference in degree in 'invisibility' is shown by the veiling of the oil: the bishop and his immediate assistants at the summit of the hierarchy see it unveiled, the others see only the veil.

In case such an *embarras* of veils as we have here should also serve to obscure the author's meaning in some degree, it may be useful to notice at this point that: (1) The sacramental symbols are themselves 'veils' in the figurative sense. These the author removes in his 'contemplation', so that the Light concealed beneath may stream out and enlighten the initiate. (2) The veil in the literal sense, here covering the figurative 'veil' that is the symbol itself. This signifies for the author that there must be degrees in the unveiling, the communication, of what lies beneath the veil of the symbols. He alone (with his assistant clergy) sees it unveiled, and tempers it to the capacity of those below.

(3) The bishop with his assistants are therefore themselves a veil: (*a*) literally, in the sense that they stand round the holy oil, concealing it from the people; (*b*) figuratively, they are the twelve-winged veil that in the ecclesiastical hierarchy fills the role of the seraphim in the celestial hierarchy, surrounding the Divinity. As these receive the Light and Fragrance immediately at its point of entry into creation and distribute it to those below, so the bishop and clergy in our hierarchy see and receive it immediately and distribute it.

'Those who surround the bishop have the right to assist fully at the consecration of the holy oil. They are not prohibited from sharing in it or contemplating it. Rather is this sacrament made present to their sight, for they are capable of contemplating what is beyond the reach of the ordinary people.[2] On the other

---

[1] The confusion of metaphor is the author's. As in the previous passage, Fragrance stamps a mark or seal on the soul distinguishing it from counterfeit coin, so here it reverts to its original quality of light; yet it still imparts a fragrance to those who contemplate it.

[2] They alone are allowed to see the oil unveiled, because only they are capable of seeing immediately the spiritual reality beneath it. The rest receive it through them. It is not that the others will not see the Light, that

hand it is their duty to conceal the sight of this from the multitude and to exclude them in accordance with the laws of the hierarchy; for though the rays that stream from the most holy mysteries enlighten divine men in all purity and without intermediary because they live on the spiritual plane; though these mysteries diffuse their sweet perfume openly over the minds of these divine men, yet their fragrance is not shed in the same way over those who remain on a lower plane. Accordingly, so that it may escape all profanation from those who do not live in conformity with God, these who contemplate the secrets of the

---

they will not come into immediate contact with it (cf. p. 14) and even be 'filled unto all the fulness of God' (Eph. iii, 19); this they do in the synaxis. What the author is concerned to illustrate here is the mode of operation of the hierarchy. This is the ladder of ascent, the machinery, if you will, by which they are raised and established in union. He is not considering the *ultimate* disposition of the members of the hierarchy; what we have here is simply one 'still', so to speak, from a moving picture. Some of the imperfect and uninitiate are to be clergy and bishops; the bishop himself has had to be raised in the hierarchy through the assistance of others. There will, it is certain, remain degrees of perfection in heaven, and it is certain that the *character* of the priesthood will remain; but it does not follow that, once they have been raised to union in the synaxis, lower degrees in the manner of operation of the hierarchy may not have a greater capacity for the Light, and in consequence enjoy for all eternity a higher and a fuller life. The author does not consider the matter, but this seems to be implicit in his conception of the assumption of the hierarchy of the Law into the ecclesiastical and the ecclesiastical into the celestial (cf. p. 22, n. 1 and p. 141 f.). The alternative would lead to some odd conclusions; it would seem, for instance, to make the patriarchs and prophets of the Old Testament for ever inferior to all the clergy of the New Law.

This is not incompatible with what is considered on p. 176, of the power of the priesthood involving also a personal sanctity. This (assuming that the mind of the author has been interpreted correctly) was given for the purpose of the ministry. Once the initiate has been established permanently and (with his death) inamissibly in union, synaxis, it will have filled its purpose. Meanwhile it seems a demonstrable fact that in this transient world there is no necessary proportion between position in the hierarchy and personal sanctity, and even—given that it is always received through this line of communication—between order in the hierarchy and the amount of Light that may be transmitted to others. Nevertheless, in assessing degrees of sanctity it is necessary to tread very warily. It is extremely difficult to gauge the radical, essential goodness of a man—one may easily be misled by passing aberrations or by the minor failings that are often the most irritating to others—and it is impossible to know his final state.

spiritual order cover the oil with winged veils, veils not without value to those of the inferior orders for, if these are well disposed, they will serve to raise them spiritually according to the measure of their merits' (476C).

It may strike the reader as a little odd in the paragraphs that are to follow that it is assistance at the consecration of the oil that seems to be in question rather than the reception of the sacrament of unction. The truth seems to be that the ceremonies described and interpreted here symbolise the effect that will be produced when the sacrament is received. The same reverence is shown here to the oils as to the sacred species in the synaxis or Eucharist, and the author himself says explicitly that the rites for the consecration of these are almost identical. In the case of the Eucharist participation in the sacrament normally follows immediately; in the latter case this is normally delayed. But the measure of what is received is decided by (or decides) the ability of the recipient to penetrate beyond the veil of the 'hidden', 'secret' reality.[1]

(1) *Rite of Consecration*
Significance and effect of actions similar to those of the Eucharist.

(*a*) The diffusing of incense first round the altar, then round the whole church and its congregation, finally the return to the altar, with which this rite begins as in the Eucharist, is symbolic of the manner in which 'the gifts of God are communicated to all the saints according to their individual merits, without suffering in themselves any diminution or modification' (476D).

(*b*) So, too, the singing and recitation of passages of Scripture, as in the Eucharist, will produce the dispositions necessary for the reception of these gifts, 'cause to arise in the souls of the imperfect the life-giving sonship of God' (477A). But what they receive will not stop with themselves; 'once they have received the habitual faculty and power' of 'living in conformity with God', as they progress themselves so what they have received will be transmitted to others. How this will happen the author does not fully explain; his purpose is to illustrate simply the *principle* of grace like a perfume through the hierarchy, an unseen fragrance.

[1] Remembering, however, that it is precisely the purpose of the sacrament to *give* this perception.

MYSTERY OF THE SACRAMENT OF UNCTION

A moment's reflection, however, will suggest that in the context such a transmission is inevitable and necessary, as each member rises in the hierarchy and each act and thought of the individual serves as a more diaphanous vehicle of the Light.

Here as elsewhere we are faced with the difficulty of distinguishing the various classes present at this part of the ceremony. It is evident, however, that they will be the same as those present at the first part of the Eucharist, catechumens and penitents, initiate, perfect. In this instance the difficulty is increased by the corruption of the text, probably arising from successive attempts by the copyists to make sense of what they could not understand. The author's only point here is that this part of the rite will produce its effect in proportion to the dispositions of those who assist at it.

(*c*) Exclusion of catechumens and penitents after the above preliminary rites has the same significance as their exclusion after the first part of the Eucharist.

'What more need we say? Is it not true that in consecrating the oils the same rites are followed as for the Eucharist? Here too, as already recalled, are excluded from all share in the mysteries the orders not yet fully purified whom we have already enumerated. Is it not true also that this mystery is presented only in symbols to the sight of the holy people, that only those perfectly holy can, through their elevation to a higher degree contemplate it in the hierarchy without an intermediary, and participate in its consecration? All this we have said more than once, and I think it superfluous to return to it instead of pursuing our path and considering the divine spectacle of the bishop when he covers the holy oil with twelve wings, then consecrates it' (477C).

(2) *The perfume mixed with the oil* symbolises the spiritual gifts imparted to the soul by it. By analogy with material perfumes that require the sense of smell in the percipient—keenness of the sense of smell varies with individuals, and some have no sense of smell—these gifts are received only in proportion as the soul is adapted to receive them, is turned to and is like God.

'Let us then conclude our explanation by saying that the holy oil is mixed with fragrant substances and that in consequence it possesses a number of aromatic properties that bring fragrance to those who come in contact with it in the measure that the perfume has reached them. We learn from this that the transcendent fragrance of Jesus, our Lord, pours out its spiritual gifts on the powers of our souls, filling them with delight. The perception of sensible perfumes is pleasant and causes great delight in that organ in us capable of perceiving scents, provided it is sound and adapted to the perfume it receives. Similarly, one could say by analogy that the powers of the soul, provided no inclination to evil comes to corrupt them and they keep the power of discernment proper to them, also become capable of receiving the perfumes of the deity. They are filled with a holy happiness and nourished with a divine manna—this through the action of God, and in the measure that the soul responds to his graces by turning to him.

'Thus the composition of the holy oil, giving in some degree form to that which is without form, shews us in a figurative manner that Jesus is the rich source of divine fragrance. He himself, in the measure proper to the deity, diffuses into souls that have reached the greatest likeness to God divine fragrance that captivates them and disposes them to receive the sacred gifts and enjoy a spiritual nourishment; each receiving the fragrant effusions according to the part he takes in the divine mysteries' (480A).

(3) *The 'twelve-winged veil'* that covers the holy oil symbolises the seraphim, the highest order of created beings who, being closest to God and giving him their undivided attention, receive the first and fullest effusion of his grace. Through them it is transmitted to the lower orders.

It is obvious that what follows now is intended as a development of the theme with which the preceding paragraph concluded, the measure of fragrance received by each 'according to the part he takes in the divine mysteries'. It is a cardinal principle of the author's work that the ecclesiastical hierarchy is the earthly counterpart of the celestial hierarchy, modelled on it in every way. But not only is the ecclesiastical the counterpart of the celestial and its reflection in material, visible terms, it also contains all that is in the celestial—in the visibile, material terms of the mysteries, as is required by our nature. It is God surrounded by the seraphim and the whole subordinate hierarchy of heavenly spirits (every higher degree contains all that is in all

MYSTERY OF THE SACRAMENT OF UNCTION

the lower (p. 11)) who is dispensed through the mysteries by the ministry of the bishop. It is significant, too, in this context that for our author it is not just 'God' in general but specifically 'Jesus' (the incarnate Word, through whom all created beings receive their being) who is surrounded and adored by the seraphim. The author therefore illustrates the dispensation of Light in the ecclesiastical hierarchy by reference to the celestial, which he has already discussed in an earlier treatise.

The symbolism of the seraphim is dwelt on in considerable detail and, it must be admitted, with some incoherence. I shall attempt to disengage the principal points of the argument.

(i) The twelve-winged veil with which the holy oil is covered at its consecration symbolises the adoring seraphim, who remain always in the immediate presence of God.

'Now it is clear, it seems to me, that the beings who are superior to us [i.e. the angels, as is clear from the Greek] because they are more divine receive the stream of sweet odours nearer to their source, so to speak.[1] For them there is a clearer flow and they, in their more perfect transparency, receive it better.[2] Over their receptive powers its waves flow generously and penetrate them superabundantly. To spirits inferior and less receptive the Source of these perfumes conceals and refuses itself because it surpasses their capacity, for it dispenses its fragrant gifts proportioned to the recipients and in accordance with the harmony and measure proper to the hierarchy.

[1] There seems to be a lack of logical sequence here. The author's argument requires him to say that as the angels receive more or less fragrance in proportion to their distance from the source, so, too, it is with men. Instead he says that the angels receive more than men because they are closer to the source. This is not, moreover, in accordance with his own thesis. It is not a question of ascending up the scale of the ecclesiastical hierarchy until we reach the lowest rung of the celestial, then continuing our ascent of that. Rather is it that we receive through the ecclesiastical hierarchy all that is in the celestial, but in the material form of these symbols. Cf. (ii) following and p. 30 ff.

[2] The author's original symbol, it will be recalled, is light, penetrating more or less diaphanous material which tempers and diffuses its brightness as it proceeds down the scale. Here the Light has become a stream of Fragrance, which yet, by a mixture of metaphor, retains the properties of light. It does, however, illustrate aptly the author's concept of the One operative throughout the mysteries, yet producing this or that particular limited effect.

'Thus, the twelve wings signify the order of the seraphim that occupies so high a rank at the head of the holy beings superior to us, who remain seated close to Jesus. They are devoted, so far as they lawfully can be, to the contemplation of him, to receiving reverently within the infinitely pure receptacle of their souls the fulness of his divine gifts, repeating (to use here terms from the world of sense) with a voice that never ceases their well-known hymn of praise.[1] For these beings above us are unwearying in their knowledge, unfailing in their love of God, and their sublimity places them also completely above sin and forgetfulness. Their unceasing cry signifies, I think, that they know and understand divine truths with full attention and complete gratitude, perfectly and immutably' (480C).

(ii) To these correspond in the ecclesiastical hierarchy the bishop and clergy.

'As for the incorporeal qualities of the seraphim, such as described by sacred scripture, I think we considered them sufficiently when we expounded the order of the hierarchies that live beyond the skies and that we made them sufficiently clear to the eyes of your soul. But, since the clergy standing round the bishop[2] present to us now an epitome of this sublime order, let us contemplate once again with perfectly spiritual eyes the splendour of their perfect likeness to God' (480D).

(iii) Interpretation of the symbolic physical attributes assigned to the seraphim by sacred scripture (because these will illustrate the qualities of their counterparts in the ecclesiastical hierarchy, the clergy).

---

[1] Presumably the *trisagion* ('holy, holy, holy') of Is. vi, 3.

[2] It is not quite clear whether the clergy with the bishop represent the seraphim, or whether the clergy surround the bishop as the seraphim conceal God (Is. vi, 2). The point is not vital. What the author is concerned to stress here is the fact that the bishop receives the Light immediately and then gives it this material form adapted to the needs of those below him, just as the seraphim receive it and temper it to their subordinates (not, of course, in material form). In this bishop and clergy act as one body. Thus too, like the seraphim, they form a veil between the Light and those below them. His additional point is that it is the Word, incarnate in human form, and present in the material form of the holy oil, who is adored—by the seraphim in their hierarchy and by the clergy in our own: One adored by both.

MYSTERY OF THE SACRAMENT OF UNCTION

(a) 'Their infinite number of eyes[1] and their many feet symbolise to my mind their eminent power of contemplation in the presence of the divine illumination, and the perpetual movement and vast reach of their understanding of divine things' (481A).

(b) 'The six wings spoken of by Scripture do not for me signify a definite sacred number, as certain scholars teach. They show rather that in what concerns the highest existence and the highest order of beings who live near God all the spiritual powers by which they are like God, whether first, middle or last in order, possess the same ability to rise, and all enjoy the same liberty and belong to the world beyond this.[2] This is the reason why, when the Scriptures in their wisdom describe these wings in their sacred allegories, they place them on the upper part of the body, on the middle part and at the feet, indicating that the seraphim have wings all over and that they thus possess in the highest degree the power of rising towards true Being.'

(c) 'From the fact that they hide their faces and feet [beneath their wings] and use for flying only the middle wings we should learn that this order, at the very summit of the highest beings of all, shields its sight from mysteries that are too high and too deep for its understanding; that it uses its middle wings to rise with all its force towards the vision of God, but submits its life to divine guidance and allows itself to be led in recognition of its own limitations' (481B).[3]

---

[1] The commentators note here that the author appears to confuse cherubim (Ez. i, 5 ff., and Apoc. iv, 7 ff.) with seraphim, adding that Clement of Alexandria does the same. Perhaps one ought, however, to remember that the higher order, the seraphim, have all the qualities of those below them, in the author's conception.

[2] They apparently have all these qualities, purification, illumination, perfection, all in one; telescoped, as it were into one union with the Light. This seems to be the meaning of the passage of the *Celestial Hierarchy* (209C) where he treats of this.

[3] Here, too, the commentators notice the inconsistency of this with the previous passage, where they are said to use *all* their wings for flying. In fact, however, he does not say that they *use* all their wings, only that they *are*, so to speak, 'all wings' all given to the upper regions, just as by another metaphor they are 'all eyes'. More serious is the fact that he seems to represent them as covering their own feet and faces, though in Is. vi, 2 it is the Lord whom they cover. It appears to be a continuation of the confusion with the cherubim.

(*d*) Their 'crying without ceasing one to another' the author sees as signifying: (1) Their perfect union and communication one with the other of the Light they receive; (2) As *arousing* the Light (the oil, the perfume) to diffuse itself beyond them; i.e. they are the first and highest in the created channel of transmission; all others receive it *through* them, through their 'crying' which, as it were, awakens and sets in motion the flow.

'The phrase of Scripture: "They cry one to the other" (Is. vi, 3) signifies to my mind that they transmit generously one to the other the fruits of their contemplation of God. We think it useful also to note that in the Hebrew text the Bible calls the most holy beings seraphim as signifying their nature; their *burning fervour* from the presence of the divine life which continually moves them.

'If it is true then, as Hebrew scholars say, that theology calls the divine seraphim "burning" and "inflaming", using a name that indicates their essential quality, this is because they possess, according to the rules of symbolism, the unfailing power of arousing the holy oil to manifest itself and diffuse its efficacious perfume' (481D).

(4) *Covering* of the holy oil with the winged veil symbolises the *adoration* of the seraphim. While manifesting himself in bodily form in the Incarnation, and continuing his activity in the visible form of the holy oil, Christ yet remains God and unchanged—the seraphim continue to adore him.

'It is the will of the Being whose perfume surpasses all understanding to reveal himself through the mediation of spirits fiery and perfectly purified, who thus call it in a supernatural manner to manifest itself. This most divine order of the beings who dwell beyond the heavens knows therefore that Jesus descended among us to sanctify us. While it understood that God in his divine ineffable goodness became man and saw him in his human form consecrated by the Father himself and by the Spirit, it also understood clearly that in all his divine actions he remained essentially unchanged as the principle and origin of all things. Accordingly, by sacred tradition, at the moment of the consecration of the holy oils they are covered with the symbol of the seraphim to reveal and to signify that Christ remains perfectly unchanged although he is fully and truly incarnate' (484A).

(5) The fact that this same holy oil is used 'for all the liturgical consecrations' indicates that God, while operating and manifesting himself in different ways in the sacraments, yet remains one and unchanged in himself.

This, it is obvious, is a development of (4) above, but with an important addition. Through Illumination and Communion the neophyte was brought to union with the One. He is now shown that the One, while proceeding outward to these varied works, remains motionless and unchanged in himself, surrounded by adoring seraphim: all these operations are in God one act, in fact they *are* God apprehended by us in this way. Similarly—it is implied, as in the case of bishops it has already been explicitly stated (p. 96)—the neophyte, while proceeding outward to the work of God in the world, must remain immovably and inseparably united to him.[1]

It will be noticed that although our author had said before (p. 122) only that the oil was used in 'nearly all' the liturgical consecrations, here he goes a little further and says it is used in 'all'. It need not affect the lesson he draws. In fact, however, he enumerates here only four uses of it, for baptism, confirmation, blessing of the font, consecration of altars, though we shall find in a later chapter that it is also used for anointing the dead (p. 198):

Baptism: 'Further, by a still more divine symbolism the holy oil is used for all the liturgical consecrations, thus shewing clearly that, according to the words of Scripture, he who performs every consecration remains identical in himself throughout all the works of his divine goodness. So the consecration with the holy oil accomplishes in us the sanctifying grace of birth from God. Similarly is to be explained, I think, the rite by which the bishop pours the holy oil in the form of a cross in the purifying baptismal font, shewing to the eye of the contemplative that Jesus consented for our deification to the humiliation of death on the cross, so raising from the abyss of death and destruction all who, in the mysterious expression of Scripture,

---

[1] Cf. the collect for Low Sunday in the Roman rite (with special reference to the neophytes baptised at the Easter Vigil): '... that as we have passed through the paschal solemnity, so we may keep it in our manner of life'.

have been baptised in his death (Rom. vi, 3), giving them rebirth in God to eternity'[1] (484B).

Confirmation: As on our Lord, present in this world in visible form while remaining God, one, indivisible, immovable, unchangeable, the Holy Ghost appeared after baptism in visible form (the appearance of a dove (John i, 32)), so he provides for us through the visible form of the holy oil (in the sacrament of confirmation after baptism) the fuller infusion of the Holy Ghost. (In the author's thought the Christian himself is, of course, a visible manifestation of Christ; so it is fitting that on him too the descent of the Holy Ghost should be in visible form.)

'We might add that when we are initiated into the sacrament by which we are born of God we receive the infusion of the Holy Spirit through anointing with the holy oil. This symbol seem to me to signify that he who for us, in his human form, received the consecration of the Holy Spirit, while preserving unchanged the essence of his divinity, himself provides for the infusion in us of the Holy Spirit' (484C).

Consecration of Altars: Signifying that through Christ comes all our sanctification. This recalls the idea with which the author began in describing the incensing of the congregation: all holiness, all being, come out from God and return to him. In Christ (*on* him), symbolised by the altar, we are offered in sacrifice and are sanctified, receiving the fruits of his sacrifice and ours. What therefore flows to us from the altar in the holy oil, as it were, is Christ in this 'pattern', as offering himself in sacrifice and as the altar on which we too offer ourselves. It is odd that the author nowhere mentions the familiar fact that the name 'Christ' itself means 'Anointed' and that by 'becoming anointed' with the holy oil we 'become Christ'; it is to this union with Christ in his sacrifice, the synaxis, that the oil brings us.

'Notice also that, in accordance with the rule of the hierarchy, the rule of the sacraments requires that holy oil be used in the

---

[1] Cf. p. 78 above, where the initiate is said to share in the death of Christ by descending into the baptismal water as Christ descended into the grave. Here we see Christ under the form of the holy oil descending into the water in which the initiate is to die and be reborn in Christ. In the Roman rite for the blessing of the water at the Easter Vigil the same is also signified still more strikingly by immersing three times in the water the paschal candle (representing the risen Christ).

consecration of an altar. This reveals to our contemplation the divine transcendent mystery of the origin, essence and perfecting power of all the action of God in us. It is in fact on Jesus himself, as our divine altar of sacrifice, that is effected the consecration and sanctification of souls, because it is in him, according to Scripture, that we are admitted to consecration and offered mystically in sacrifice. Let us regard, then, this altar of divine sacrifice in this spiritual view, for it is there that the holy victim is consecrated and sacrificed, and learn through these symbols how the holy oil consecrates this altar. The altar is in fact Jesus, sanctifying himself for us and dispensing to us the fulness of his own sanctification, dispensing to us generously as to sons of God the effects of his own sacrifice' (485A).

Two Appendices: (1) This is aptly called the *Sacrament* of Unction, as making sacred and bringing to perfection.

The point of this paragraph will be seen only if one remembers that the word used by the author, commonly translated by Latin theologians as *sacrament* (as here), is τελετή from τελεῖν: *to accomplish, fulfil, complete, make perfect* in the most general sense; used also in a restricted sense meaning *to initiate*, i.e. into the mysteries of religion in which the initiate, through communion with the god in a ritual re-enactment of the earthly life of the god, becomes possessed of his qualities and attributes. From this it comes to mean *to make sacred, sanctify*: (1) from the point of view of the god, being devoted to and delivered over to possession by him; (2) from the point of view of the effect of this on the devotee, his sanctification and deification: hence it means *to make perfect* in this final, religious sense, the last completion and fulfilment of man. It is instructive to notice the development of thought in this, of which all who used the word must have been conscious in some degree. This final stage of the union of man with God is in its most literal sense his fulfilment and accomplishment, his realisation, filling completely and perfecting his whole being. All his former experience has been, in this view, merely a *becoming*, a moving towards being in its full sense, towards his completion.

The Latin word *sacrament* used in place of it (it obviously does not translate it) retains in itself only the idea of *sacred*, of *devotion to*, being *set apart* for, and was used also of the oath by which a soldier devoted himself to military service; but in its religious use it did have the associations of the Greek τελετή. More expressive is the Latin alternative *initiation*, implying rather the *introduction* into what is promised by religion, or the actual rite which accomplishes this, ultimately, in any case, a rite by which one *enters into* the life of God.

From the circumstances of this τελετή, *sacramentum*, *initiatio* (the ritual, symbolic enactment of an activity of God, participation in which admitted the initiate into the activity signified), the words obtained their later sense of the presentation of an invisible reality in a symbolic, material form, a sense gradually restricted in technical theological language to the *sacraments* strictly so-called, but into late medieval times still used in this more general sense.

Much more common, in fact the usual word in our present author, is the Greek μυστήριον (mystery) to express the 'sacraments' in this later connotation; so in this treatise Baptism, Eucharist, Holy Oil are all 'mysteries'. This does, it is obvious, serve better to emphasise his main argument that the reality of the rite is *hidden*, to be 'seen' only by penetrating the outer form of the symbol. It is for this reason that the rite itself is 'hidden', 'secret'; even its more superficial significance is beyond the capacity of all but those who have been admitted to the inner reality through the rite of initiation.[1] This is for him, as we have

[1] Cf. the distinction of the Latin theologians between *sacramentum* and *res sacramenti*, between the material form and the inner content.

It may be useful to note here again explicitly that it is not for this author primarily a *doctrine* or *knowledge* that is hidden, but a being, a life, an experience, the whole being in fact of the creature. P. Bouyer does make this point at the end of his masterly disquisition on the history of the word 'mystic' (*La Vie Spirituelle*, Suppl. 9, May 1949, reproduced in its main lines in his chapter on the pseudo-Denys, op. cit.). Surely, however, he exaggerates in implying that there was *no* doctrine in the Greek mystery religions. Admittedly it was the *rite* that was secret, but it was secret because it was the key and the entry to what lay behind it; re-enactment of the symbolic rite admitted the initiate to contact with the god represented and opened the way to an immortal life. Belief that initiation could do this was itself a doctrine; there was indeed little knowledge of what lay beyond the gate; the vital knowledge, which was secret, was the formula, the rite for reaching it. Fundamentally this is true of our present author; the rite is secret because it is the initiation into a life, invisible, immortal, on another plane. This 'contemplation' of it is its presentation in inadequate material symbols, in words; the existence to which the rite admits is 'beyond human description' precisely because it is on another plane; knowledge of it is the

seen, a universal principle, to reach the higher reality through its lower manifestation. In the case of unction it serves his purpose to use also the alternative τελετή with its connotation of bringing to perfection or maturity, since this is for him, as also, of course, for later theologians, the distinctive effect of the rite.[1]

'So it appears to me that those responsible for our human hierarchy, having received from God understanding of these symbols, aptly call this holy liturgical rite the *sacrament* (τελετή) of unction, because of its power of *perfecting*. This amounts to calling it a "perfecting" (τελετή) of God, understanding this in a double sense; firstly because God himself as man sanctified himself[2] for us, secondly because this perfecting activity[3] is the source of all perfection and sanctification' (485A).

The sense of the passage in this context, with reference especially to the visible outpouring of the Holy Spirit upon Christ after baptism (p. 136), is clear. The Light, the Fragrance, comes to us in the 'form', the 'shape', of Christ; it is in him and through him that we receive it. It 'sanctifies' him first, is in him first. Through him it is communicated to us; it sanctifies, perfects, consecrates us in the one identical sacramental activity—Christ 'confirms', 'sanctifies', us in himself: we share in his 'confirmation'.[4]

It is then this 'perfecting' activity of Christ communicated to man, conforming and moulding man to Christ in the pattern of

---

[1] In the words of the children's catechism 'strong and perfect Christians and soldiers of Jesus Christ'.

[2] Or 'sacrificed', 'made sacred'. The context makes it clear that it includes all the meanings suggested above. The word used this time is in fact ἁγιάζεσθαι that used in John, xvii, 19, where our Lord says: '... for them do I sanctify myself, that they also may be sanctified in truth.'

[3] Or 'sacramental activity' (τελετουργία).

[4] Cf. I Cor. i, 30: 'Of him (i.e. of God) are you in Christ Jesus who of God is made unto us wisdom and justice and sanctification and redemption.'

'ignorance' of the *Mystical Theology*. In both instances it is primarily the *rite* that is secret (and even in this work, intended only for his equals, the actual 'forms', or formulas, are never given); there *can* be no *adequate* knowledge of the 'hidden', 'mystic' reality to which the rite admits. This reality, present in sacred scripture, in the sacraments, in the liturgical rites of the hierarchy (cf. p. 109), concealed, yet also in varying degrees revealed in these material symbols, is no less than the ultimate Mystery of St. Paul's epistles, Christ.

his death, resurrection and return to the Father, which brings man to his 'fulfilment', his 'perfection', his 'realisation'.

The connection of this with the author's first and principal interpretation of the rite (p. 122), the procession of Christ out from the invisible and the simple to the visible multiplicity of the created world and his return to the invisible Unity, is obvious. It paraphrases Our Lord's own description of his mission as coming out from the Father and returning to him (John xvi, 25; xvii, 4), as the word going out, and returning not empty but as having accomplished and completed ($\tau\epsilon\lambda\epsilon\iota\omega\sigma\alpha s$) all that was commanded. As seen by us, bounded by the limits of each individual's immediate horizon, it is for him a progressive withdrawal from the visible world culminating in the complete withdrawal of death through which alone man reaches his final completion and realisation.

(2) *The Alleluia*

This final paragraph seems to be in the nature of an afterthought. Our author did not tell us (on p. 122) what was the 'hymn' that was sung while the oil was being placed on the altar for consecration. Here he does so. It was *Alleluia* (Praise be to God), still a constant refrain in the liturgical worship of the Church, and in the Latin rite added to all hymns, antiphons and responsaries during Paschal-tide. It is probably also associated in the author's mind with the Jewish 'Praise' or *Hallel*, the psalms sung at the Passover feast, celebrating that passage through the waters of the Red Sea to the Promised Land which prefigured the Christian passage through the waters of baptism.

'Regarding the sacred hymn revealed to the prophets [i.e. Apoc. xix, 1–6] when God visited and inspired them, those who know Hebrew translate it thus: *Praise to God*, or *Praise the Lord*. Since all the appearances and acts of God have a symbolic meaning it is fitting to mention here this hymn which God himself revealed to the prophets, for it teaches us with equal clarity and holiness the praise that is owing to the beneficent gifts of God' (485B).

5. Mystery of the Priestly Consecration

THE introductory section of this chapter is exceptionally long, but it repays reading, for it forms, even more than other parts of the work, a synopsis of the working of the hierarchies. (As we know, it is of the essence of the author's teaching that the whole can be seen reflected in every part so that any section of his work is an epitome of the whole, in this reflecting, as he would say, the operation of God.) There are in fact three hierarchies, each is threefold, and each of the three degrees has three divisions. The ecclesiastical hierarchy, for instance, the one with which we are most familiar, is divided into: (1) the sacraments; (2) those who dispense the sacraments; and (3) those who receive them (the 'initiators' and the 'initiate'). The author will explain again in passing the three divisions of the sacraments, in accordance with their function of purifying, enlightening and perfecting (bringing, that is, to perfect union), and in doing this he will incidentally clarify some of his statements made in the chapter just concluded. All the sacraments in fact, we now learn, produce all three effects, though one effect is more particularly ascribed to a particular sacrament, and so it is throughout the hierarchies; all are degrees of movement towards or reception of the Light, are in fact degrees of Light. He will then go on to treat in detail of the special subject of this present chapter, the second main degree, division or order of the ecclesiastical hierarchy: the Clergy. In the following chapter he will discuss the third degree, the order of the initiate, the Laity, the People of God.

We said there were three hierarchies. One, the hierarchy of the Law, has in fact already passed away, though I think that in the author's mind it might be more adequately described as having been taken up, 'fulfilled', 'perfected', in the others, and in that sense still existing.[1] The hierarchy of heaven contemplates God directly, without symbols and images, that of the Law only in symbols, and those obscure and difficult to penetrate. The hierarchy of the Church stands midway between the two, contemplating indeed (in the full sense explained of receiving its being) through the medium of symbols, but able to rise through them to spiritual contemplation similar to that of the angels. The symbols of the Law, that is, established a 'line of communication' with the celestial hierarchy by way of the ecclesiastical. Modern theologians, regarding the matter rather from a juridical standpoint and speaking in terms of time, commonly explain the Jewish ritual as conferring a *claim* on the salvation which was to be effected by Christ. St. Thomas seems to see rather more in it than that. Writing rather in this earlier tradition of a 'whole', ontological view, from a standpoint outside space and time, he suggests that the Jews did, through these symbols, share in a certain way in the sacrifice of Christ, establish a contact, that is, with the hierarchy of the Church.[2]

The author will thus be repeating what he has already said several times, adding a detail here or there with an occasional seeming contradiction, yet never, in that exasperating way of his, giving us the complete picture. It is perhaps here, however, from this comparison of the three hierarchies one with the other, each with its threefold division and subdivision, that we come closest to a sketch of the whole, at least in outline. Most remarkable here is his introduction of the hierarchy of the Law and the connection he establishes between the three hierarchies. Taking as his standard the ecclesiastical hierarchy with its division into sacraments, clergy and laity, the place of the sacraments is, in the celestial hierarchy, filled, he says, by purely spiritual knowledge of God without symbols and images (bearing always in mind that this 'knowledge', 'contemplation' of God is in fact the Light itself, the whole being of the creature, and the word translated by 'sacrament' is in the Greek more accurately 'perfection' or 'fulfilling'). The place of the sacraments in the hierarchy of the Law, the 'perfection', 'fulfilment',

[1] Cf. p. 22, n. 1 above and p. 145 below.
[2] Cf., e.g., S. Th. I–II, 100, 2, c; III, 82, 1 ad 3, 62, 6, c.

given through its ritual observances; is simply a motioning onwards, or upwards, the 'advance of souls to worship in the spirit' (501C). These observances gave nothing of themselves; their whole purpose was to direct men on to what, in the language of time, was still to come in the hierarchy of the Church, to establish already the symbol to be carried on into the symbol of the Church and receive there its hidden content. The ecclesiastical hierarchy thus occupies 'a central position'.

Nevertheless, even in the hierarchy of the Law it is already light that is received through this contact with the Church, this link established by its ritual observances; a light 'proportioned to their weak sight' (501C), yet sufficient to lead men to the full light. Moreover these figures already revealed in dim outline the pattern that was to come, the pattern of Christ, 'modelled on the pattern that had been revealed to him [Moses] on Mount Sinai'. I have no doubt that this is the significance for our author of the passage to which he alludes (Ex. xxv, 40): Moses had been led into the cloud beyond the sight of ordinary mortals; what he saw there was translated into signs and figures proportioned to the understanding of his people, the prescriptions of the Law and the furnishings of the tabernacle. It is worth recalling in this context that in the author's view (basing himself as always on Scripture) the hierarchy of the Law was offered ('is' offered indeed from the author's extra-temporal standpoint) equally to the nations as to the Jews, but only the Jews accepted it. To each nation is appointed its angel to reveal and minister these first beginnings of the light.[1]

Since we know from the *Celestial Hierarchy* that there are three degrees of angels, the reader may wonder where a fourth element 'as sacrament' is to fit in, if we are to preserve the threefold division on which so much emphasis is laid. There need be no difficulty if we remember that the highest degree of angels *is* the 'sacrament', the 'perfecting', 'fulfilment' of the lower, the higher giving themselves in the most literal sense to the lower and the lower receiving this immediately; not as in the case of

---

[1] Cf. *Cel. Hier.* 260C, where the author is explaining that it was not the fault of the angels that only the Jews responded to the revelation of the angels appointed over each people. Cf. also 1092D (*Letter* viii). The author would presumably explain the religion of the nations by their deviation from, or distortion of, what had been (is being) revealed to them.

men who, in their central sphere that embraces both spiritual and material, receive a 'perfecting' that is both spiritual and material, spiritual in a material form.¹

Our author enumerates in passing the analogous divisions of the hierarchy of the Law: the priesthood (initiators), and people (initiate), and the perfection or 'sacrament' that is indicated through its obscure symbols that direct men to the sacraments of the New Law as their fulfilment. It places men at the first stage of the ascent to the apex of the heavenly hierarchy. More accurately it leads to the symbols in the hierarchy of the Church which there are not only symbols but also the spiritual realities of the hierarchy of heaven. Ascent here, at this second stage, is progress through what is external and material in the symbol to its inner spiritual reality, man in his present state being disposed to take up his abode at the visible exterior.²

I shall try to make the author's argument easier to follow by dividing it into sub-headings.

(1) *Introductory: Each hierarchy has three divisions*

'Such is the consecration of the holy oil. Having explained this it is now time for us to expound the orders of the priesthood, their functions, powers, activities and perfections, and the three orders they constitute. In this we shall try to shew the organisation of our hierarchy, how it has avoided and excluded all disorder, disharmony and confusion, how, on the contrary, it shews order, harmony and a proper differentiation in the relationships that bind together the holy orders.

'As for the threefold division of every hierarchy, it seems to me that we gave sufficient explanation of this in the case of the

¹ Cf. p. 14, n. 2. God's 'knowledge' of us is our being, a being that is in our case both spiritual and material; we and our world are God's knowledge of himself, within the limitations—indefinitely expandable—of our own particular being. It is necessary to use this terminology, implying an opposition between 'spiritual' and 'material' which is unknown to this author; rather is it a question of degrees of being, one flowing from the other.

² This progress is not, it should be needless to say, an increasing facility in interpreting the liturgical symbols; it is a growth to spiritual maturity, an infusion of Light, which is shown in visible form through the symbols in which it is given. The only criterion known to this author for assessing the degree of Light in the individual is its external manifestation in the exercise of the Christian virtues, the 'imitation of Christ'.

hierarchies already spoken of, when we said that according to our tradition every hierarchy is divided into three parts: the divine sacraments, those who live in God, understand these sacraments and initiate others into them, finally those whom they initiate' (501A).

(2) *Each of the Three Hierarchies (of heaven, the Old Law and the Church) Explained in Detail*

Emphasising that each has sacraments, or something analogous, as its highest degree, and that the hierarchy of the Church, fulfilling that of the Law, thus occupies a middle position. (This in spite of the author's confession that—preceding paragraph—he has already given 'sufficient explanation'.)

(a) *The Celestial Hierarchy:* 'Thus the hierarchy of the heavenly spirits has, in place of sacraments,[1] that knowledge of God quite without material images[2] that is proper to them and corresponds to the maximum of their powers; they have fully and completely the power of becoming like God and of imitating him as far as that is possible. The highest rank are they who illuminate and lead the others to this perfection. These live in the presence of God and generously diffuse on the orders of a lower rank, in proportion to the capacity of these, that knowledge of the divine that the Deity, absolute perfection and source of wisdom for divine souls, unceasingly bestows on them. The ranks that come after these first spirits, and rise through their mediation to illumination through this divine activity of the Deity, constitute the order of the initiate, and thus we have to call them' (501B).

(b) *The Hierarchy of the Law:* 'After this[3] celestial hierarchy the beneficent deity, suiting his gifts to our capacity and, as Scripture says, treating us as children (Gal. iv, 24), bestowed on us the hierarchy of the Law. He concealed the truth beneath obscure images, making use of representations far removed from the original, symbols difficult to understand and figures of which the meaning could be seen only with difficulty, giving to the feeble eyes that contemplated it, in order not to injure them,

---

[1] Lit. 'as τελετή', 'as its perfecting power', 'as the perfection, fulfilment, it gives'. Cf. p. 137 above.
[2] A knowledge that is, of course, their whole being. Cf. p. 144 above.
[3] In order of appearance on our stage of space and time, not of dignity.

only a light proportioned to them. In this hierarchy of the Law the sacrament ['perfection', 'fulfilment', given, cf. p. 137] is the advance of souls to worship in the spirit. The initiators into this worship are the men whom Moses himself, the first initiator and first head of the high priests of the Law, initiated into the mysteries of the tabernacle (Exod. xxvi, 30) when he wrote concerning this tabernacle for the instruction of the others the rules of the hierarchy of the Law, calling all the institutions of the priesthood copies of the model that had been revealed to him on Mount Sinai (Exod. xxv, 40). As for the initiate, these are they whom the symbols of the Law raise, according to their ability, to a more perfect initiation (501C).

(c) *The Ecclesiastical Hierarchy:* 'Now according to theology this more perfect initiation is given by our hierarchy, which is the fulfilment and end of the hierarchy of the Law. Our hierarchy is at the same time both celestial and of the Law, sharing by its central position in both the other hierarchies. It has in common with the one spiritual contemplation; like the other, it makes use of various symbols of the sensible order by means of which it rises to the divine. Like every hierarchy it is divided into three orders. It comprises first the sacraments, next a priestly body with the duty of distributing the sacred mysteries, imitating in this the operation of God himself, finally the faithful whom this priesthood leads to the holy mysteries according to the measure of their ability' (501D).

(3) *Each of these three divisions of each of the three hierarchies has a threefold division*

'As we saw in the hierarchy of the Law[1] and in that which is more divine than ours, each of the three divisions of our hierarchy is arranged in three ranks, the first, middle and last, in an order proportioned to its sacred object,[2] uniting all the elements into one harmonious and coherent whole' (504A).

---

[1] The author apparently forgets that he has not said this explicitly of the hierarchy of the Law. He said it of the celestial hierarchy, and it is, as we know, a dominant motif of his work.

[2] It is not clear whether this is an allusion of the Trinity as reflected in creatures, or no more than a general reference to the regular pattern revealed throughout the hierarchy. It is worthy of note that this pattern is further reflected in each individual member of each section of the hierarchies. In the *Celestial Hierarchy* we are told (273C) that 'every spirit,

MYSTERY OF THE PRIESTLY CONSECRATION

(4) *A general treatment of the three degrees within each of the divisions of the ecclesiastical hierarchy, before proceeding to a more detailed consideration of the three degrees of the clerical division, the proper subject of this chapter*

Nothing new is added in these three short paragraphs. It seems to be the author's intention simply to emphasise that the same pattern emerges at every level. So we are told of:

(i) *The Sacraments*: 'Now the first effect of the sacraments, manifesting the action of God in this symbolic form, is to purify the imperfect; the second is to illuminate and initiate those whom it has purified; its last, which includes and fulfils the two preceding, to perfect the initiate in the knowledge of the mysteries to which they have access' (504A).

(ii) *The Clergy*: 'Let us see now the division of functions in the ministers of the liturgy. Their first power consists in purifying the imperfect by means of the sacraments; their second in illuminating those whom they have purified; the highest of all, and intended for all who communicate in the divine light, to perfect these in that highest knowledge that is the illumination proceeding from their contemplation of the mysteries'[1] (504B).

(iii) The Laity ('initiate'): 'Finally, regarding the initiate, their first power consists in being purified; their middle virtue in receiving, once purified, the illumination which permits them to contemplate certain mysteries;[2] their final power, more

---

[1] This appears to be the meaning of the passage, though it might equally well mean: 'that comes from the contemplation of the mysteries to which illumination brings them'. Ultimately it amounts to the same: illumination is both the cause and effect of contemplation of the mysteries; a reception of Light.

[2] The author seems to have in mind here less the sacramental mysteries than the measure of penetration of the mysteries (remembering, in any case, that each of them gives all in some degree). What is received by each member will depend upon his capacity (upon his 'dispositions' in the modern term), and this should be constantly increasing. The author seems to envisage Jesus as reaching out, as it were (cf. interpretation of incensation,

---

heavenly or human, possesses in itself degrees and powers of first, middle and last order'. Tauler, in a sermon on this passage, assigns the exercise of each of these powers to the impulse of one or other of the orders of the celestial hierarchy (cf. Gandillac, op. cit., p. 223).

MYSTERY OF THE PRIESTLY CONSECRATION

divine than the others, in receiving from the illuminations given in their contemplation an irradiation of knowledge that accomplishes their perfection' (504B).

(5) *The Three Degrees in the Order of the Priesthood*

The ascending scale is an instance of a universal law valid for all created things.

'We have spoken already of the threefold power in the celebration of the sacraments; we have shown, with reference to the Scriptures, that the birth from God is a purification and illumination; that the sacraments of the synaxis and holy oil are perfect knowledge and understanding of the work of God and that by them is achieved both the unifying ascension to the Deity and holy communion with him.[1] We must now show how the priestly class comprises three harmonious orders: those who purify, those who illuminate and those who make perfect.

The law of God requires that in their ascension towards the

[1] This forms the most concise statement we have had regarding the relationship between the sacraments; the author, whether deliberately or not, has led us on step by step in the spirit of his own hierarchies, never revealing all he might say. It seems that his mystery of illumination (apparently including both baptism and confirmation) is for him even purification, illumination and perfection, each stage giving a degree of all three, as the candidate is passed on through deacon, priest and bishop, yet none of them giving anything except through the contact they establish with the Light in the synaxis. His tendency almost to identify unction and synaxis is understandable if we remember that the perfection given through unction is the work of the Holy Spirit present first in Christ in the synaxis as the one source from which it proceeds to these various tasks. The continual increase in perfection that is expected of us comes through an increase of Light, of the operation of the Holy Spirit through constant 'commemoration' (p. 112 above) of the work of Jesus, and an ever-closer union with this in two directions—into the invisible world and outwards into external activity. Since the author's purpose is primarily to demonstrate the 'hierarchy', the manner of communication of the Light, he does not use the idea of the Eucharist as the 'food' or nourishment bringing the soul to maturity and perfection, though the very nature of bread and wine, Our Lord's own utterances and the circumstances, proximate and remote, of its institution, might lead one to expect it. That the thought is implicit in his connection of unction and synaxis is clear.

---

pp. 94 and 120), from the synaxis through the invisible operation of the Holy Spirit (infused in unction) and drawing up the initiate into increasingly closer union with himself, ever more deeply into his own life.

supreme light the members of a lower rank pass by means of the higher. Do we not see in the sensible order that the simplest of created things approach first those with which they have most affinity and then, by means of these, act on the others according to their specific nature? It is not unfitting, then, if the Author of all harmony, visible and invisible, permits the rays that reveal the actions of God to penetrate first to those who have reached the nearest likeness to God, and that it is through the medium of these, souls more transparent and better disposed by nature to receive and transmit the light, that he distributes his illuminations to lower beings in proportion to their aptitude.

It is the function, then, of those who contemplate God first to reveal to those who hold the second rank, without jealousy and in due measure, the divine spectacles into which they have themselves been initiated. To initiate others into the mysteries of the hierarchy, this is the role of those who have received the fulness of knowledge of the divine secret of all that concerns their hierarchy and to whom has been given the sacramental power of initiation. In fine, to communicate the sacraments to those who merit them, such is the function of those who possess knowledge of and perfect participation in the consecrations of the priesthood' (505A).

(i) 'The divine order of bishops is, then, the first of those who contemplate God, who is himself the first and the last, for in him all the ordering of the human hierarchy finds its completion and fulfilment. Just as we see that every hierarchy has its end in Jesus, so each hierarchy has its own bishop [lit. *hierarch*, head of the hierarchy] as its particular end. The power of the order of bishops extends through all the stages of the organisation, and through each of the sacred orders it accomplishes the particular mysteries of its hierarchy.[1] But it is to bishops only in preference to members of the other orders [i.e. the subordinate clergy], that divine law gives as their special function the most divine acts of the sacred ministry. The rites, in fact, through which they perfect the faithful are images of the divine power, and it is this that

[1] The powers of the subordinate clergy, that is, are contained in the bishop, and communicated by him to them. So it is, in a sense, the bishop himself who is operative in all the functions of the hierarchy, even when they are performed by his subordinates—this in the visible hierarchy; at the last remove it is Christ himself who is operative throughout.

gives all their effect to all the divine symbols and sacred institutions. It is indeed the duty of priests to administer[1] some of the sacraments; a priest, however, cannot confer the sacrament of birth from God [i.e. baptism] without the holy oil[2] nor celebrate the mysteries of the synaxis unless the symbols of the synaxis are placed on the altar of sacrifice. One might go further: he himself could not be a priest before consecration by the bishop had conferred the dignity on him. Divine institution has reserved to the sacramental powers of bishops both the ordination of the clergy, the blessing of the holy oil and the consecration of[3] the altar' (505C).

'Thus the order of bishops is that which enjoys the fulness of the power of administering the sacraments. It has the privilege of fulfilling every sacramental consecration of the hierarchy. It is the order which reveals the sacred mysteries and expounds the properties and powers of each' (505C).

(ii) 'The order of priests, whose function is illumination, conducts the initiate to initiation into the sacraments in subordination to the divine order of bishops. In communion with the bishop it exercises the functions proper to its sacred ministry:[4] in the exercise of these functions it reveals the work of God through the sacred symbols[5] and those who present them-

[1] In the technical phrase, translating literally the Greek, 'perfect', 'confect'.

[2] If the actual baptism is meant here, then the use of the holy oil is not essential to its validity; but he has made his point: the subordination of the other ministers to the bishop, who alone may consecrate the oil. This seems to be the point also of the reference to the altar; the Eucharist may be celebrated only on a duly consecrated altar, and for this consecration oil blessed by the bishop is necessary. In fact, this consecrated altar is not essential to the validity of the Mass; but again he has made his point.

[3] This is not in fact correct of the consecration of the altar, at least today, even if we take 'divine institution' to mean no more in this context than an ecclesiastical regulation. Still, in fact altars commonly still are consecrated by bishops, or by prelates such as abbots, and this is really all that is required by his argument.

[4] We have seen this happening literally in the account of illumination, the rite of initiation.

[5] 'Reveals' literally in presenting it to the initiate in the form of the sacramental symbols, and concurrently instructing them in rational language concerning the 'mystic', 'hidden' reality they receive in it. There is no opposition, as we have seen (p. 19, n. 2), in the author's mind between these two kinds of 'knowledge', 'mystical' and rational; the rational is simply a lower degree of the other.

MYSTERY OF THE PRIESTLY CONSECRATION

selves it perfects sufficiently to permit them to contemplate this work of God and to communicate in the sacraments. It is to the bishop, however, that are referred all who aspire to a deeper knowledge of the rites they contemplate'[1] (508A).

(iii) 'Finally the order of deacons ['ministers', λειτουργόι] is charged with the duty of purifying and sifting those who do not bear in them the resemblance of the divine, before they can approach the rites of the priests. They purify those who present themselves; they sanctify them, separating them from participation in evil, and prepare them for initiation and communion in the sacraments.[2] That is why, in the course of the ceremony in which they are born of God, it is the deacons who strip them of their former garments, who loose the shoes from their feet, who place them facing the west for the abjuration, then turn them round to face the east; because their order and their power is in purification. It is they who invite the aspirant to reject the errors of his former life, who show him in what darkness he has lived hitherto, who teach him to leave the darkness and turn towards the light.

Thus the function of the order of deacons is purification, since it raises the purified in such a way as to make them worthy of illumination by the rites of the priests; because it frees the imperfect from all their sins; because, like a midwife, it brings to birth in them the lights and purifying lessons of the Scriptures;[3] because, finally, it excludes the unworthy so that only those suitable remain for the priest. This is why it is the custom of the hierarchy to place this order in charge of the doors of the church, showing by this that before aspirants have access to the sacred mysteries, they must submit to complete purification. Certain people with the power of purification have been charged precisely with the task of initiating them, to see that they enter with holiness into communion with the mysteries,

[1] In a word, they are brought increasingly closer to the Light through deacon, priest and bishop until final union with it in the synaxis.

[2] Receiving the Light from Christ through the line of bishop and priest, the task to which they apply it at this first stage is purification.

[3] A different metaphor (cf. p. 100): The deacon develops the unborn baby until it is ready for birth, the priest assists it to the light of day, the bishop brings it to maturity (though in fact the metaphor is not developed as far as the bishop when it is first used).

and so to introduce into the sanctuary only the immaculate'[1] (508B).

(6) *Every higher order in the hierarchy contains all in the degrees below it (so, for instance, the bishop possesses the power not only of making perfect but also of illuminating and purifying)*

Still the distinction of functions is observed as being a figure and symbol, an expression in material terms, of the action of God himself, who first purifies, then enlightens and finally perfects through conformity and union with himself. (At the same time we must also remember that lower degrees are for their part degrees of *all* that is above them in the scale, and ultimately images of God himself. So purification is already a degree of union, with all that this implies of 'contemplation', 'mystical' knowledge and experience, a reception of light which purifies by enlightening, and each stage that is left behind on the way to final definitive perfection is the final perfection of one in a lower degree.)

'We have shewn that the order of bishops is charged with the duty of consecrating and making perfect; that the order of priests illuminates souls and brings them to the light; finally that the task of deacons is to purify and to discriminate. It is clear, nevertheless, that it is not the sole function of the order of bishops to consecrate, but that equally it enlightens and purifies. Similarly the order of priests unites to the power of enlightenment that also of purifying.[2] For though it is impossible for the inferior to encroach on the functions of superiors, apart from the fact that such presumption would be sacrilege for them, superior powers, on the other hand, possess, apart from their own proper knowledge,[3] also the sacred knowledge of the ranks inferior to their own sacramental function. It is none the less

---

[1] Those, that is, who have now proved their ability to lead a sinless life and are ready for the definitive 'perfection' of baptism.

[2] May it be noted again that the author is describing in each case simply the office distinctive of each grade of clergy. The priest, for instance, celebrates the Eucharist, and the deacon, though he cannot celebrate, may administer holy communion.

[3] It is worth noting here a further example of the principle evident throughout the work, that 'knowledge' is taken again as equivalent to the whole sacramental power of the clergy, to the Light which descends into the human hierarchy and is transmitted through it in these material forms.

true that since the distinctions in the priestly order present under the form of material symbols the working of God and shew an order of illumination corresponding to the harmonious order and distinction of the divine activity, they have been arranged in a hierarchy of three degrees (first, middle and last) according to their function. They reflect then, as I have just said, the order and distinction in the mode of operation of God.

'The Deity, however, first purifies the souls into which it penetrates. Then it enlightens them. Once they are enlightened it brings them to final perfection in their likeness to God. It can, then, be easily understood why the hierarchy, being constituted according to the likeness of God, is divided into distinct orders and powers; to shew clearly that the operations of God maintain a firm order and distinction.

'Having thus expounded to the best of our ability the orders of the priesthood with their functions, powers and activities, let us now learn, in as far as we shall be able, of their consecration' (509A).

DESCRIPTION OF THE RITE

The description of the actual rite is very brief and it is likely that the author is giving the bare essentials. (1) Common to all the ordinands is the fact that: (*a*) they kneel before the altar; (*b*) the bishop imposes hands; (*c*) makes the sign of the cross on them; (*d*) makes a public proclamation; (*e*) followed by the kiss of peace. We shall find in the 'contemplation' that a celebration of the Eucharist concludes the rite, but the fact is not mentioned in this section, descriptive of the ceremony. (2) Variations peculiar to the different degrees are that: (*a*) on the head of the bishop alone is placed the book of sacred scripture; (*b*) both he and the priest kneel on both knees; (*c*) the deacon kneels on only one knee. (3) The significance of the kneeling is developed in two additional paragraphs.

'On each of those he consecrates the bishop makes the sign of the cross. In the case of each of them he then proceeds to a public proclamation[1] and ritual kiss, all the clergy present

[1] Apparently, from the description which follows (p. 155), a solemn pronouncement to the people on the nature of the office of the priesthood, made in the present Latin rite at the beginning of the ceremony, after which

following the consecrating bishop in embracing him who has just been consecrated to one of the priestly orders we have just spoken of'[1] (509C).

CONTEMPLATION

After the very long introduction to this chapter the symbolic interpretation of the rite is proportionately brief. The author considers first the rites common to all three priestly orders, then those peculiar to each.

(1) *Rites Common to all Three*

(a) *Significance of the Presentation of the Ordinand and his Kneeling before the Altar.* 'The presentation and kneeling before the altar teach all those who receive the priestly consecration to submit their lives entirely to God who is the origin of every sacrament [or, 'of all consecration, perfecting'], to offer to him a soul entirely pure and holy, as far as possible like his own and worthy of that divine Altar,[2] perfectly holy and sacred, which consecrates to the priesthood the souls that have received the form of God within them' (509D).

(b) *The Imposition of Hands.* (The central, essential part of the rite. There is no mention of the prayer which applies this action to its specific effect, the consecration of bishop, priest or deacon.) 'The imposition of hands by the bishop indicates that it is under the protection of him who is the source of every sacrament that those to be consecrated, like children dutifully subject to their father, receive the qualities and powers of the priesthood. At the same time they are liberated from the powers opposed to

---

[1] In present usage we speak of the 'consecration' of a bishop and the 'ordination' of lower clergy, but since this author uses the one general term, most nearly rendered by 'consecration' in this context, I have retained this where it expresses better the author's conception of degrees of the one rite.

[2] In the tradition of the Fathers, Christ is Priest, Victim and Altar—the Altar on which, in which, all our offerings are made, on which alone they are acceptable. The exhortation (above) before ordination in the present Latin rite states expressly that the altar represents Christ; accordingly, it is vested and receives a solemn genuflection or profound bow, even when the Sacrament is not reserved on it.

---

the ordinand is officially 'called' (*vocation*) by the archdeacon to ordination. Here this proclamation seems to take place after the ordination, possibly with an official formal intimation of the ordination of the candidate.

them. This rite teaches them also to fulfil all the functions of the priesthood as under the orders of God, in all acts of their lives considering him as their head' (512A).

(c) *The Sign of the Cross.* (There is no mention of anointing here, though we know (p. 122) that the holy oil is used for 'almost all the ceremonies of the hierarchy'. In the present Latin rite the hands of the priest are anointed in the form of a cross, the hands of the deacon are not anointed and those of the bishop have been consecrated already when he received the priesthood. It is likely that there was an anointing here, but it is not mentioned because the author is dealing with ceremonies common to all three.)

'The sign of the cross signifies the renunciation of all carnal desires, a life consecrated to the imitation of God, constantly directed towards the divine life of Jesus incarnate, of him who, being without sin, humbled himself to crucifixion and death, of him who marks all who imitate him with this sign of the cross that symbolises his own innocence' (512B).

(d) *The Proclamation.* 'The proclamation by the bishop of the ordination and of the ordinands signifies mystically that the consecrator, in his love of God, is the interpreter of the divine choice. It is only in virtue of the grace he himself has received that he calls the ordinands to ordination; it is God himself who moves him in all the ordinations he performs in the hierarchy. In the case of Moses, the founder of the hierarchy of the Law, although Aaron was his brother and he knew him to be the friend of God and worthy of the priesthood, yet he did not confer on him this dignity until God had ordered him to grant it. It was then licit for him to confer through the hierarchy the fulness of the priesthood in the name of God, who is the source of every sacrament (Ex. xxix, 4). So, too, the divine founder of our hierarchy (for it is Jesus who, in his infinite love for us, assumes also that function) refused to glorify himself, as Scripture says, for it was another who said to him: "Thou art a priest for ever according to the order of Melchisedech" (Ps. cix, 4). Moreover, when he conferred ordination on his disciples, although as God he was in the hierarchy the source of every sacrament, we see him referring his act of consecration to his Father and the Holy Ghost, since he said to his disciples, as witness sacred scripture: "That they should not depart from

Jerusalem but should wait for the promise of the Father, which you have heard by my mouth and in accordance with which you shall be baptised with the Holy Ghost" (Acts, i, 4). So also the chief of the apostles, having gathered round him ten bishops, his peers, in order to ordain to the priesthood a twelfth disciple, left prudently to the Deity the task of choosing, saying: "Shew us which thou hast chosen" (Acts, i, 24); and it was he whom the divine lot designated who was taken into the community of the twelve. But what was this divine lot that fell, by divine interposition, on Matthias? There are numerous explanations of this, which I find far from satisfactory. I will, therefore, say what I think about it. It seems to me that Scripture understands by 'lot' some grace of God [i.e. charism] which manifested to the college of bishops him whom divine choice had designated. For it is not on his own initiative that the bishop should perform consecrations to the priesthood, it is under divine impulse, directed by heaven through the hierarchy, that he must fulfil these sacred rites'[1] (513A).

(e) *The Ritual Embrace.* 'The kiss that concludes the priestly consecration also has a sacred significance, for not only all those assisting, who are endowed with the dignity of the sacred office, but also the consecrating bishop himself, kiss the ordinand. When indeed a soul, through qualities and abilities worthy of the sacred office, by divine vocation, and finally by the sacrament conferred on him, reaches the dignity of the priesthood, he merits the love of his peers and of all those who belong to the most sacred orders. Being raised to a beauty that makes him in all things the image of God, he loves the souls who resemble him

---

[1] This does not tell us very much about the precise method of choice, and we shall find the same problem arising in the matter of the bishop's judgement in excommunicating (p. 195 below). The author seems to hold that the choice was decided not by a casting of lots in the ordinary sense; but however that may be, it is clearly his conviction that the choice was made by God, impelling, or at least guiding, the bishop to make the proper judgement. It is probable that he has in mind no visible extraordinary intervention but is thinking simply of what is called today the 'grace of state', the special assistance given by each sacrament—and even more generally for every state of life—operating through the 'gifts of the Holy Ghost' assisting, and in the Thomistic view even impelling and 'pre-moving' to a decision that is exactly in conformity with the will of God. Such impulse, speaking generally, may of course be resisted and, one is bound to add, frequently is resisted only too successfully.

and receives their holy love in return. This is the reason for the ritual kiss exchanged by the members of the priesthood, symbolising the community formed by souls which resemble one another, that joy in their common love which preserves fully in the whole hierarchy, in perfect radiance, its likeness to God' (513B).

(2) Rites Peculiar to Particular Orders

(a) *The Bishop.* The placing on his head of the book of the sacred scriptures signifies that it is through him that is transmitted to men 'all that God in his goodness has wished to transmit to the human hierarchy'. It should be noted particularly that it is not merely the words and their explanation, 'knowledge' in that sense that he transmits, but their content in the most literal sense of the word, that of which these words are the material symbols: the divine activity (θεουργία) of God manifested in human form (θεανδρία) presented here. I think this is implied by the phrase 'all the manifestations, all the words and all the acts' of God; it is certainly central to his thought,[1] and is perhaps intended to be expressed in the phrase of the final sentence: 'he is endowed with the most divine knowledge and the highest power of spiritual elevation'. What he transmits through the sacraments is a 'knowledge' which is life, an 'elevation' through increasingly perfect degrees of created being until the creature is one with God, a 'knowledge' that at every level, from the point at which it emerges as the material, animate and inanimate, things of everyday life up through rational apprehension and discussion to the Knowledge of the *Mystical Theology,* is never merely either material sign or, in the later terminology, 'abstract idea' of God, but degrees of reception of the Light which is God himself.

'Such, as I have said, are the rites common to all consecrations to the priesthood. The bishop, however, is the only one who has placed on his head the sacred scriptures. Since all the priestly power and knowledge of making perfect [i.e.

---

[1] Cf. with reference to the synaxis (p. 109) and the λόγια of sacred scripture, *passim,* and, e.g., *Letter* ix (1105D–1108C), where Scripture is said to have literally (in the context of the mysteries) the 'force of its words' and the sacred authors give us not a mere 'historical narrative' but a 'life-giving perfection'.

sacramental power, fulfilling, "confecting" in the technical phrase, the sacraments] have been given to bishops, by that divine Bounty who is the source of every sacrament, it is right that there should be placed on the heads of bishops the Scriptures that God himself has inspired, which reveal to us all that is known about God, all his work, all his manifestations, all his words and all his acts, in a word all that the Deity in his goodness has wished to transmit to the human hierarchy of what has been said and done by God. The bishop, in a word, who lives a life modelled on that of God and participates fully and completely in the power of the hierarchy, is not content with receiving, by divine illumination, authentic knowledge of all the ritual formulas and all the sacraments of the hierarchy. It is he also who transmits them to others, according to their rank in the hierarchy, and it is he who, because he is endowed with the highest [lit. most divine] knowledge and the highest power of spiritual elevation, performs the most sacred consecrations [i.e. sacramental acts] of the hierarchy' (516A).

(b) *Priests*. 'Regarding priests, what distinguishes the rite of their consecration is that they kneel on both knees, while the order of deacons kneel on only one knee to receive consecration by the bishop' (516A).

(c) *Deacons*. '—the order of deacons kneel on only one knee—'

(3) *Significance of the Kneeling in the Case of Each*

'The kneeling indicates that the aspirant approaches the sacrament with humility and places his undertaking beneath the protection of God. There exist, to repeat again, three classes charged with the task of initiation, with the function of submitting to the divine yoke by virtue of three sacraments three orders of initiates and of assuring their salvation through the sacred rites of the liturgy. It is natural, then, that the order of deacons, whose function is only purificatory, should be content to conduct the purified and place them before the altar, so that as souls freed from all stain they might be sanctified there in a supernatural manner [lit. 'in a hypercosmic manner'].

'The priests, for their part, kneel on two knees because their role is not limited to the purification of those whom they present for the reception of the sacraments. After raising souls spiritually through the sacred rites proper to them and freeing them from

MYSTERY OF THE PRIESTLY CONSECRATION

all stain they confer on them the sacrament by which they possess the permanent habitual power of contemplation.

'As for the bishop, having knelt on both knees he receives on his head the book of the Scriptures transmitted by God, for it is he who teaches those who, in accordance with their respective powers, the deacons have purified and the priests have enlightened, the understanding of the mysteries into which they have been initiated, in accordance with the laws of the hierarchy and the measure of their ability, and raises those brought before him to a perfection as full and complete as their capacity allows' (516C).

The exact significance of the kneeling may not be evident at first sight—on one knee, on two knees, on two knees with the book of scriptures on the head. The idea seems to be that the deacon kneels on only one knee in order to indicate that his duty will be simply to bring the catechumen to the altar and then retire; since he is not to remain there he kneels on only one knee. The priest, since he is to remain and co-operate with the bishop, kneels on two knees.[1] The bishop alone has the book of the Scriptures, because it is through him that the neophyte will receive the knowledge that will bring him to perfection, 'knowledge' in the double sense of the sacrament and such explanation of it as the author himself gives here, progressively, as he qualifies for it.

Perhaps this is all that can be gathered with certainty from these three paragraphs, and all the author intends to convey: the degrees of co-operation of subordinate clergy with the bishop in leading up the catechumen through purification and enlightenment to union with the Light, the continuation of the rhythm of the hierarchy of the Law, leading on to the hidden knowledge, 'worship in the spirit'. The author obviously has in mind a function at which the bishop officiates assisted by the other clergy, such as that described on pp. 67 ff., where as we saw, it is the bishop who appears to do everything, with the *assistance*, proximate or remote, of his clergy, and it is impossible to delineate exactly what each order does. But it is probable

[1] Stiglmayr suggests that the deacon kneels on one knee because he has only one activity in this (purificatory), the priest on two because he had a second activity (illumination). Perhaps the difference in interpretation is not so great; one cleric is more involved than the other.

that the distinction has little meaning for our author; what the clergy do the bishop does, since they receive everything through him, and whether the bishop baptises or anoints personally or through another, there is no essential difference. There is, however, here some at least verbal confusion over the matter of who 'purifies' the catechumen, and in this instance it is hardly sufficient to invoke the argument that all passing to a higher degree involves a measure of purification, a rising to a greater intensity of light compared with which all former light was darkness, so that even in the angels there is something analogous to it (p. 184). It is clearly the mind of the author, expressed repeatedly, that 'purification' of the catechumens is the office of the deacon, and in this passage he is said to 'place them before the altar as souls freed from all stain'. In spite of this we find in the following paragraph the priest 'freeing them from all stain', though admittedly he does more than this.

It may be, as already suggested (p. 152), that the deacon has trained the catechumen to reform his life and break with habits of sin and so brought him to the *point* of (sacramental) purification, for which he is consigned to the care of the priest. But this is not entirely satisfactory, since in the author's own example we find even the priest doing no more than co-operate with the bishop, calling out the candidate's name while the bishop performs the immersion and pronounces the formula (p. 65). It seems rather that the act of the deacon is conceived as folded up, telescoped, as it were, into that of the priest, and the priest's into that of the bishop, and the whole operation is one of bringing the catechumen, through these symbolic acts, into increasingly closer proximity to the Light until he is finally united with it in the synaxis, where what was signified by these acts in their varying degree is finally fulfilled. This does in fact seem to correspond with St. Thomas's teaching that baptism, for instance, does not produce its effect until the reception of holy communion.[1] The whole process of 'illumination' is considered, it would seem, as a single coming of light through the bishop as the being of the catechumen, an instantaneous 'passing from death to life' effected by a series of acts, of sacramental 'figures' and 'symbols' that of necessity spread it over an extent of space and time. The operation seems to be one of collaboration be-

[1] Cf. p. 84, n. 2.

tween the orders of clergy in the application of the appropriate signs in what is essentially a single act. There is obviously nothing to prevent deacon and priest officiating alone, on occasion, in the performance of their respective offices, applying the 'light' that flows through the bishop; but this example serves the author's purpose better as illustrating the 'hierarchy', the divine economy in the flow of Light.

One of a critical turn of mind might well wonder here what would happen to the neophyte or catechumen who should happen to die before the reception of holy communion, as might well happen in a later practice where the sacraments might be separated by a space of several years: would he find salvation? I think it would be the unanimous opinion of theologians today that he would do so, though they might explain the manner of it differently. There is in fact less difficulty in the author's scheme than in most modern expositions of theology. For this author the light is always there 'offering itself' (p. 71), even pursuing one who tries to escape from it; the aspirant has only to open his eyes to it; and this we see him doing in turning from west to east and raising his eyes to the true light.

In whatever way we interpret these words of the author, speculation on them does throw into prominence a question always in the background throughout this treatise, the precise relationship in the author's mind of the external material sign to the spiritual reality, more precisely of a spiritual reality, not so much *in*, but *as* a material sign; for though we may make a mental distinction, they are in fact for this author one thing. It is failure to appreciate the significance of this last fact, one of his fundamental principles, that has led critics to see in the author's teaching, but still more in that of the later writers who derive from him, a complete and final rejection of the sensible order. All he is saying—and no one, surely, will deny it—is that most men are content to stay on the surface of reality, enjoying the external aspect, without ever penetrating very far beneath it.[1]

But, to return to this question of the relationship between the spiritual reality and the material, sensible sign; it is, for instance, a defined dogma of the Church that the virtue, the spiritual power or faculty of faith, by which man is able to make an act of faith, is first infused at baptism, yet an adult coming to

[1] Cf. p. 92.

baptism is required to make an act of faith before what is considered to be the essential rite, the pouring of water with the appropriate form. How can he make an act of faith before he has the faculty, any more than a man can see without the faculty of sight? Or if he in fact has the faculty and is able to make an act of faith, why the sacrament? I have posed this question to doctors of divinity without receiving any clear, satisfying answer. It may be dealt with fully in some of the standard authors, but I have not been able to find it in those to which I have had access. On the other hand, at least one eastern rite[1] prays *after* the actual baptism that the catechumen who is already a neophyte may receive regeneration (in which is included the infusion of the virtue of faith) in the waters of baptism. St. Thomas, as we have seen, seems to hold that there is no effect until the reception of holy communion.

Again, in this sacrament and sacrifice of the Holy Eucharist, the Mass, the sacred elements are blessed repeatedly by the priest *after* the consecration, the act of transubstantiation into the body and the blood of Christ. In fact, they are signed with the cross, accompanied by words that leave no doubt the intention is to 'hallow and bless' them, more times after than before the 'consecration'. This is to assume the common belief that the consecration does take place at the pronouncing of the words of institution, though this has been questioned.[2] It has even been asked whether the host is already consecrated before the consecration of the chalice and, if the answer is in the affirmative, whether it would be consecrated if there were no intention of proceeding to the consecration of the chalice. The question whether the consecration is effected before the Greek *epiklesis*, or what in the present Latin rite is assumed to take the place of a possible former *epiklesis*, extends the conceivable limits still further in this direction. In the other direction it has been noted that in the Byzantine rite, at the procession with the uncon-

[1] Addis and Arnold, *A Catholic Dictionary*, have a reference to this.

[2] A discussion of the point is outside the scope of this work. The question is usually made to depend upon the position of the *epiklesis* (the prayer to the Holy Ghost for the transubstantiation of the elements). In one eastern rite this prayer occurs *after* the words of institution. When applied to the Latin rite the dispute centres round the question whether there is, or ever was, a true *epiklesis* in the Roman rite and, if so, whether its function is filled by one of the prayers *before* or *after* the words of institution.

secrated elements, the 'great entry', these tend to be adored by the faithful as though they were already consecrated, though I believe this is beyond the intention or wish of the clergy.

One might dismiss such discussion and say that at least Mass was begun and completed over a certain period; yet even this would require a certain qualification. This particular celebration is simply the temporal and local presentation of the one sacrifice effected in God 'before the foundation of the world (Eph. i, 4 ff.)', manifested in the act of Christ, and apprehended by us in the substance of this world of 'time before and time after'; as continued until the end of time in one direction, and even as present in some mysterious fashion in time before, so that even those under the hierarchy of the Law enjoyed a certain participation in it.

No explanation of this is offered by our author, nor, I think, would he feel the need of any explanation; or rather he would probably regard it as part of the ultimate mystery of our created existence. The spiritual assumes this particular material shape and form; this particular shape and form, from our point of viewing it, encircle and enclose it.[1] It is temporal and spatial extension of what transcends space and time, though all space and time are present in it; and the whole purpose of these

[1] It must be understood clearly that the mystery or sacrament is an 'effective sign' that actually produces what it signifies; the fulfilment of the rite is not merely the *occasion* of the production of the effect. A little reflection, however, will show the genius of this 'enclosing', 'encircling' of the Presence by sacramental signs, as we see it in the Eucharist, as the most perfect expression of the instantaneous presence of a spiritual reality in a material form, of the interpenetration of time and eternity; for it is a Presence that is active both before and after, reaching 'from end to end'. Looking out on this from the point at which our own being takes its origin, from our source in Christ (always the viewpoint of this author), the aptness is still more striking. We see the invisible activity of Christ taking this shape and form, spreading out in all directions, and because of our 'oneness', 'synaxis', with Christ, our sharing in his priesthood—all of us in our measure—we share in this activity, diffusing it further still over the hour, the day, the week and the seasons into the whole fabric of our lives. That is looking out into the visible world. Looking inward, into our invisible Source, we see our own being enfolded in the same pattern as it takes its origin from God—'*Gratia tua nos semper et praeveniat et sequatur* . . .' (collect of 16th Sunday after Pentecost): 'May thy grace [Light, in this author's vocabulary] both come before and follow us [be, that is, both the beginning and continuation of our being and activity, surrounding it and enclosing it].'

'symbols' is to lead man on to union with the single, simple Reality of which they are the extension. Our neophyte, for instance, will receive the final, definitive effect of his baptism only when he passes finally beyond this world to the synaxis of which the synaxis of this world was the effective sign and the pledge.[1]

To extend the question, it is less difficult in a scheme such as this to see the significance of the mysterious utterances of Christ about the Second Coming and the end of the world, the statement that 'this generation shall not pass, till all these things be done' (Matt. xxiv, 34). With the death, resurrection and ascension of Christ the spiritual reality and its extension into space and time have become one: all '*is* done'. Christ has returned to heaven taking the world of men with him; from our position in this world there is a lapse of time, in the other world there is no time. Meanwhile every moment of our time here is a mirror of that timeless world, and through it we are already beyond time.

This involves the further question of the interval of time that is to elapse between the 'particular' judgement of each and the 'general judgement', and—perhaps of even greater personal interest—of the time of waiting after death until reunion with the body. Philosophers have always experienced some difficulty in describing the mode of existence of a 'disembodied' soul, for a soul is not, like an angel, a pure spirit, living *in* a body or united to it accidentally; it is of the essence of a human soul to be one 'thing' with a body, in the Aristotelian terminology to be the 'form' of the body. But when we say that the souls of the departed must wait until the last day for reunion with their bodies what precisely does this mean? For us here in this world there is probably a further period of time still to come; it may be that vast ages must pass until the end of the world and the Second Coming. But surely for those who have passed beyond time and in God are united to all that is, to the whole of being and all space and time, this interval can have no significance? In a word, where there is no time there can be no temporal interval between the particular judgement of each and the general judgement, between the passage from this world and reunion with the glorified resurrection body. It would seem that there

[1] Having reached the point at which all the converging lines meet, he is then able to travel, so to speak, down any one of them without leaving their source, the source that is the reality and being of all these particular things.

could be even no interval of waiting, not only for reunion with all those who have gone before but also for union with all those who are still to appear on the temporal plane and achieve salvation.[1]

Our author does not consider these matters, but it is within a comprehensive scheme of this kind, enclosing the whole of man's being and experience, that such questions are inevitably suggested and are most likely to find their solution—if solution there is on our lower plane. For my part I shall be content to leave such matters as queries, hoping that others, less incompetent, may provide the answers.

Once again, in spite of obscurity in the details, and in the wider vistas that are opened up, the main lines of the author's scheme are presented clearly enough: the hierarchy and its operation; the dispensation of a Light which is life and being through the degrees of the clergy, with the bishop at its head, through the priest at one remove and through the deacon at the second in the line of transmission.

[1] For this traditional, biblical, conception of the relationship between time (and history) and eternity, with the conclusion that, 'the death of Christ is not only the "beginning of the end", but actually the end of time' (through contact with the mysteries), quoting I Cor. x, 11 and citing K. Rahner in support, cf. Dom Victor Warnach, op. cit. above, p. 80. Christopher Dawson is interpreting the same tradition when he writes (*Religion and the Rise of Western Culture*, p. 41), 'It is almost impossible to convey to the modern mind the realism and objectivity with which the Christian of those days viewed the liturgical participation in the mysteries of salvation . . . a sacramental and mystical re-presentation . . . [in which] the eternal world invaded and transfused the world of time.'

It is obvious that the question of the connection between the Particular Judgement and the General Judgement is involved in this. It is a matter on which there has been considerable fluctuation of opinion among theologians through the ages. Sacred scripture seems to know of only one judgement including both of these, and modern theologians, starting from Scripture in the tradition of our present author, are concerned to explain how this can be. Hans Urs v. Balthasar, e.g., writes (*Fragen der Theologie Heute*, 1957, p. 403): 'We . . . cannot deny that biblically there are not two Judgements and Days of Judgement but only one, and that we must therefore see the particular judgement after death in a dynamic connection with the final judgement, however difficult it may be to imagine this, or rather to envisage it in the concrete.' There is an excellent survey of recent speculation on the subject (from which the above quotation is translated) in an article by Dom Burkhardt Neunheuser in *Tod und Leben*, 1959, pp. 85 ff. (*Laacher Heft*, xxv).

6. Mystery of the Monastic Consecration

THIS chapter deals with the third main division of the ecclesiastical hierarchy, the laity, and if it should seem a short chapter to cover so vast a subject we must recall that the other two divisions have, in effect, covered the same ground; they have described the economy by which the 'people' become the 'people of God'. The three degrees of the laity were in fact enumerated at some length in the chapter on the Holy Eucharist, in speaking of the classes that are excluded from the mystery once they have profited from the more directly didactic parts of the service.[1] Here the author treats explicitly of the division of the laity into three orders, classes or degrees: (1) those still undergoing purification in preparation for admission to the mysteries (including the penitents, those who, having been admitted, have fallen into sin and are again in process of purification); (2) those who already communicate in the mysteries, the 'holy people of God' (532C), who are also the 'order of contemplatives' (536D); (3) the highest class, the 'order of monks', those who 'have been raised to the highest perfection' (532D) and have been given this special title as indicating the essential 'unity' of their lives. These receive a special consecration, spoken of in language resembling that of the sacraments, and indeed this class and its 'consecration' is the principal topic of this chapter.

So many topics of immense practical importance are raised, or at least suggested, by this chapter, destined to be developed and interpreted in varying and sometimes contradictory senses by later writers, that it may be useful to enumerate them briefly

[1] Cf. p. 99 above.

here, where they appear at their source and, which is more, in a context that is a single, coherent whole.

(1) *The 'Three Ways'*

It will be obvious that, speaking generally, these three divisions of the laity correspond to the classical division into the purgative, illuminative and unitive ways. Useful as it may be, however, in arranging one's ideas, to make these distinctions, it is clear that, as the author himself repeatedly says, purification is going on at every stage, as it is also a fact that every stage is a degree of union; the whole is one continuous progress from darkness to light, from non-being to being. It may be possible to assign people to one or other division according to the preponderance of their way of life, when compared with other people, to the extent that this is visible to the outward viewer; God alone knows to which class they really belong. We shall see later in what sense the monk may be said to be in a state of the highest 'unity' and 'perfection', and in what sense the bishop is in the 'state of perfection', though this author does not in fact make explicit use of the phrase.

(2) *'Contemplation' and 'Mysticism'; Public and Private Prayer*

That contemplation and the highest mystical union is simply the logical development of the normal Christian life has always been the traditional teaching of the Church, though obscured by the fashion prevailing at some periods. Here it is stated clearly: 'The order of contemplatives is identical with the holy people' (536D); they enjoy, in fact, 'the permanent possession of the power of contemplation' (532C). This in spite of some modern Trappist authors who would restrict 'contemplative' not only to 'religious', and among religious not only to 'monks' in the strict sense, but among monks to only the Trappists, Carthusians and Camaldolese.

What is still more significant is the fact that here 'contemplation' of the mysteries, admission to Mass and the sacraments and intelligent participation in them, is considered to be identical with 'contemplation' in its many later derived senses; the author makes no distinction, any variation is one only of degree. Even more, it is for the author the origin and source of all contemplation and mysticism. The neophyte is permitted to 'contemplate', to 'see' the mysteries in an active participation which transforms him into that which he contemplates; for this 'sight', 'contemplation', 'knowledge' is, we recall, not simply knowledge or sight in the ordinary sense, but a reception of Light which is a degree of being. Contemplation and mysticism are for this author simply the logical development of active participation in the Church's liturgical worship. 'He that seeth me seeth the Father,' our Lord said (John xiv, 9). He might well have added that in seeing the sacraments (with their full clothing of symbols, words, actions, readings and chant) we see him; see him, moreover, in a context in which we can actually receive him and be transformed into him. In every sense we see him better this way than we could have done at any one moment of his earthly life, in a manner better calculated to help our contemplation to pass beyond the symbols to a plane where material signs and the language based on them are less adequate even than formerly, and we arrive finally at the luminous darkness that is a 'cloud of unknowing' for all that can be said of it in human concepts. It is this penetration beyond the symbols that the author is describing in his *Mystical Theology*. We must not, however, exaggerate this matter of 'contemplation for all'. It is clear from the author's remarks in the chapter on the Holy Eucharist (p. 92) that he does not expect the mass of men to travel far below the surface of what they contemplate; still they are essentially, radically, 'contemplatives', and this is contemplation, no matter how superficial—and in fact the most superficial is very deep indeed—differing only in degree from the highest and deepest mysticism.

We find here, then, no sense of any conflict between public and private prayer. The one leads on logically to the other; private prayer, more particularly what modern authors call 'contemplative prayer', is the fruit of liturgical contemplation, reception of the Light as the life of the soul. Modern psychological determination of the precise moment at which prayer becomes 'contemplative', 'mystical' or 'infused' would, I feel, have had little interest for this author. All prayer is for him infused, in fact all, the whole being of man, without qualification. As for 'awareness', 'experimental perception' of God, for him every sight and every experience is a sight and experience of God in its degree.

That this again is the tradition of the Church is confirmed by the fact that the monastic rule (of St. Benedict), compiled in the same age, possibly even in the same century, as the Dionysian writings, makes no explicit mention of 'contemplative prayer',[1] still less of anything resembling modern 'methods' of prayer; nor is any time specifically allotted to this in the Rule.[2] It seems to be assumed that through active, almost hourly, participation in the liturgy of the hierarchy monks will all be 'taught of God' (John vi, 45); their prayer will gradually become contemplative in the more restricted modern sense of the term and will persist beyond the set times of public prayer. They will be performing more perfectly, in a more favourable environment, the work common to all the 'holy people of God'.

(3) *'Contemplative' and 'Active'*

There is no doubt that this author would have been surprised to hear that there were Christians who were not 'contemplative' in proportion as they were Christian. I think he would have been equally surprised at the idea that contemplative Christians were not also 'active', and that there might even be opposition between contemplation and action. There is in fact nothing in these writings to suggest that their author is aware of any conflict between action as such and the contemplation which is an ability to transcend sensible, material realities, or rather to penetrate beyond their external aspects. It is in fact for him a postulate of man's nature that he must always *start* from the sensible and material; there can be no question of avoiding it, of withdrawing from it in that sense if he is to contemplate at all.

It is obvious that excessive activity is liable to impede the reflection necessary to carry a man beyond the surface of things, but it is probable that the sense of an actual conflict has arisen largely from a misunderstanding of the passage of St. Thomas usually referred to in this context. Referring to the current tendency to divide men into 'contemplative' and 'active', he

---

[1] The *'oratio pura'* of the Rule appears, however, to be Cassian's 'truly contemplative and mystical prayer'. Cf. Abbot Butler's critical edition of Rule (Freiburg, 1912), p. 150.

[2] It is, however, certain that there was time allotted to prayer apart from that of the divine office. This may be gathered from passages of the Rule and of the *Dialogues* of Gregory the Great, such as the enchanting story of the 'little black boy' (normally invisible to the rest) who drew the monk away from his prayers.

explains how 'contemplative' is to be understood in this comparison. 'It is not,' he says, 'those who contemplate who are called contemplatives, but those who devote their whole lives to contemplation'.[1] This is sometimes understood to mean that not all 'contemplatives' do in fact contemplate, but they receive the name of 'contemplative' if they devote their whole lives to the pursuit of contemplation; and, it is implied, there are no other contemplatives. That this is not St. Thomas's meaning should be obvious from his consistent teaching throughout his work. What he is saying is that, though others may contemplate, the name of 'contemplative' is narrowed down in contemporary usage to those who devote their whole lives to it; it is this, and not the fact of contemplation, that confers the title. That this is his meaning is confirmed by the comparison he uses. All those who worship God are religious, but only those who devote their whole life to the worship of God are called 'religious' (i.e. in the restricted sense of members of religious orders). For our author all degrees of the Christian life are degrees of contemplation, though, as we know, the word means more for him than it had come to mean in common use by the time of St. Thomas; it is no less than the reception of a whole being that is translated into the actions of ordinary life. For him, therefore, all Christians are, or at least should be, advancing in contemplation, and logically he would have been compelled to give the name of 'contemplative' equally to 'active' religious—had he known any. Radically, in fact, St. Thomas's line of advance is the same as that of the Areopagite, though he begins with the concepts and terminology of his age; through action and contemplation to the 'mixed' life, in which action is an overflow without any diminution of the degree of contemplation.[2]

These three states of life do correspond roughly, it is clear, to the 'three ways', and in the estimation of St. Thomas they are ascending degrees of perfection, the highest resembling most nearly that of God himself, unceasing, motionless contemplation that is also a going out to the creation of the world. Ideally, theoretically, each man ends in this perfect harmony of intense activity and unceasing contemplation, and whether he begins as 'active' or 'contemplative' will depend on his disposition and

[1] S. Th. II–II, Q. 81, 1 ad 5.
[2] S. Th. II–II, Q. 182, 1 ad 3, and 188, 6 c; III, Q. 40, 1 ad 2.

accidental circumstances. There can be little doubt that many, perhaps most, men are most 'contemplative' when they are active; on the other hand, Thomas Merton, in his earliest and most uninhibited book,[1] came to the conclusion that few of his 'contemplative' fellow-religious were contemplative in the sense that they contemplated. As in the 'three ways' so here; the lowest is also a degree of the highest. Even the most superficial and distracted 'activity' proceeding from this state of life is, in our author's conception, an 'overflow' from a degree of contemplation. On the other hand, the 'contemplative' religious may be more active, within his enclosure, and more distracted, than his 'active' fellow-religious; what is more, his activity may proceed from a lower degree of contemplation.

It is useful, as we saw, to make such distinctions, and they do correspond to something in the nature of things; but it is necessary to move very cautiously in their application. Meanwhile there is no trace here of that dichotomy which has become a persistent tradition in Christian ascetical and devotional literature. The author's mind will emerge more clearly from the description of the highest of his degrees of the laity, the monk.

(4) *The Monastic Order*

The essential note of the highest order of the laity is for our author not the amount of their activity or contemplation, their abstention from activity, or even the devotion of their whole lives to contemplation in the restricted sense in which that is commonly understood today, but the *unity* of their lives, the degree to which a whole life is united in one single *service* of God. The *Times Educational Supplement* echoed this (probably unconsciously) in a leader some years ago,[2] when it summed up a series of articles by saying: 'Christians must regard the schools not as a piece of mechanism for the dissemination of useful information, or even as a society of individuals brought together with the object of improving their several characters, but as *a body dedicated ultimately and in all its activities to worship* [italics, the present writer's].' This, it is clear, is precisely what our author has in mind, a life that is a service, a worship, a liturgy; and it is significant that the monastic rule that was destined to become

[1] *Elected Silence.* [2] November 4th, 1949.

the one rule of the West, describes the monastery in these identical terms: A School of the Lord's Service.[1]

Members of this highest order of the laity are sometimes called *therapeutes*, he says, sometimes *monks* (533A), and these are names given officially by 'our divine masters'. Therapeutes means, roughly, *servitors* or *worshippers*, a name given because of the purity and completeness of their *service* and *worship* of God. There is hardly any adequate translation of the word in English. *Liturgists*, in the original, etymological sense of one performing a public service, might do were it not for the unfortunate associations this word has for many people, and were it not for the danger of its being taken to imply that monks are *propter chorum fundati*,[2] with no other work or obligations. That this is not his meaning is clear from the type of monasticism he must have known and from his alternative title, which in fact supplements the other.

It is very significant that he rejects the more obvious etymology of the word monk, *monachos*, as so called because he lives *alone* (*monachos*—alone), whether as a hermit or as a member of a community that lives *alone*, apart from the larger world, for an explanation that is all his own—so far, that is, as the etymology of the word is concerned. For him the monk is so called because of the *oneness* or *unification* of his life (*monos*—one, single) into one single service, worship or liturgy of God. The one title, it is clear, supplements the other.

Without knowing the exact date of composition of these writings we cannot tell if their author knew the *Rule of St. Benedict* or Benedictine monasticism. He knew it in the sense that he certainly knew the variations of monasticism of which this Rule was the distilled essence, formulating in a single code the essentials of monasticism in a form in which they were capable of being transmitted to any age, climate or race. In consequence, the life described in the Rule forms a perfect illustration of the Areopagite's principle, that of a whole, small, self-

[1] *Rule of St. Benedict*, Prologue.

[2] 'Founded for the choir', a phrase that became current in the Middle Ages, when, in consequence of the decline in the cultivation of serious manual work, offices in choir were multiplied in order, Abbot Butler bluntly says, 'to fill in the time' (*Benedictine Monachism*—I am obliged to quote from memory). Cluny was, perhaps, the most striking example of this; but how foreign it was to the intentions of the founder may be seen from a glance at the divisions of the monastic day as given in the Rule.

contained world, a microcosm; a perfect unity in which everything has as its direct aim the service or worship of God. The surrounding wall that protects its unity, with a gate kept by a 'wise old man', encloses, ideally, all that is necessary for human life 'such as water, a mill and a garden and the various crafts', so that the monks 'have no need to wander abroad, for this is by no means expedient for their souls'.[1] The most careful precautions are in fact taken to ensure the monk's both physical and mental stability and 'unification' within his enclosure, focusing all his attention on the central act of this small world, the worship of God in the stricter sense of the solemn celebration of the 'mysteries', the 'traffic of Jacob's Ladder', through which the monk ascends through the hierarchies to the eternal liturgy of heaven and returns to make the external circumference of his life a less inadequate expression of it. It is a world in which, ideally at least, the dichotomy between activity and contemplation, prayer and work, has been transcended, and work has become prayer and worship. From one aspect such an economy provides an environment for the most perfect celebration of the Church's liturgical worship, and one in which this can produce its greatest effect on the participant; an economy in which the whole of life is presented as co-ordinated in its service, as leading inevitably up to it and taken up by it into the worship of heaven. From another aspect all this more external clothing is an overflow from it, receiving from it a progressive perfection of being, a world of men modelled on the Heavenly Jerusalem.

It is easily seen how delicate is the balance in such a microcosm, in such a small self-contained world, embracing on such a small scale all the major basic human activities,[2] the arts and

[1] Rule of St. Benedict, Ch. LXVI.

[2] When I used this phrase before (*Dublin Review*, No. 466, 1954) the editor was kind enough to point out that monks do not in fact produce children, and that this is a 'basic activity'. This cannot be denied; nevertheless, there is a regular prayer that the community may be 'increased in merit and number', and children produced by others are traditionally found in Benedictine monasteries in greater or smaller numbers. The precise manner of their arrival is of less importance. The deeper explanation, of course, which cannot be developed here, is that virginity is, in the Christian tradition, not only higher but also spiritually more fruitful than the married state: bodily begetting and birth is the reflection on a lower plane of a higher spiritual activity and contained in this.

crafts, and the men of such varied natural disposition and character who exercise them. It is very easy for one aspect of the life, most especially one particular work or activity, to acquire an undue preponderance and threaten the 'unity' of the life, perhaps in the end even giving it a completely new orientation, causing it to face outwards and thereby eliminating the essential note of the monastic life. In the larger world, where the world is the enclosure (though even that enclosure is now on the point of being broken), it is not so easy for any one activity, no matter how intensively pursued by the individual, to dominate the scene; but it is a prevailing danger in monastic communities. A survey of the ebb and flow of monastic history would show that periodic movements of reform have commonly been inspired by an instinctive attempt to restore a balance and 'unity' that has been lost, or at least seriously impaired, often, in the attempt, going rather too far in the opposite direction, but in general bearing a witness to the norm.

This, then, is for our author the 'highest perfection' of the Christian life, yet differing only in degree from that of all the 'holy people of God'. Newman has described in his own inimitable style how lower degrees of the Christian life, showing a greater diffusion with a less intensity of being, but in their degree bearing the same essential of a life conceived as a single unity with the worship of God as its ultimate aim, have demonstrably in many cases appeared as a direct overflow from such a central core: '. . . by degrees the woody swamp became a hermitage, a religious house, a farm, an abbey, a village, a seminary, a school of learning, and a city'.

Mention of 'hermitage' and 'abbey' as stages in one continuous progress (though it is clear from the context that Newman means a small isolated community rather than a hermitage in the strict sense of the dwelling of one man) reminds one that many authors find it necessary, surprisingly, to explain, or even to apologise for, the fact that Benedict left his former eremitical life and became a cenobite, a monk dwelling in a community. This follows, surely, the classical lines of development of all monasticism, Christian and non-Christian: one man living in solitude approached by others with a request to teach them his way of life, so that the office of *guru* or spiritual teacher is forced upon him rather than deliberately chosen, and what was a hermitage becomes a *collegium*, a community. In terms of the hierarchy it is a transmission of light drawing them up to his own level. In terms of his own development it is a passage from the 'active' through the 'contemplative' to the 'mixed' life in an 'overflow' that, beginning as a small stream, became a mighty torrent rejoicing the city of God, reaching to the corners of the earth and spanning a period of some fourteen hundred years in time. In terms of the 'three ways' it is a progress from purgation, through illumination to union, beginning with the most complete and utter rejection of material things, and ending with their salvation, with their preservation and restoration to their place in the hierarchy, to the formation of a mode of life in which all things are united in one worship of God. But perhaps this can best be summed up in saying that Benedict is in this the living exemplar of the paradox inherent in Christian monasticism, that it has always done most for the world by leaving it alone; that in proportion as the monk has tried to retire from the world he has exercised an attraction and influence over it. He has in fact exhibited in this degree the pattern of all Christian life, in which nothing, not even the service of man, is to be preferred to the service of God.

(5) *The 'State of Perfection'*

There have been many interpretations of this phrase, none that I know quite satisfactory. Our author does not in fact use the phrase, though there is no doubt that it derives from him indirectly. He does say that the monk, through his 'consecration', is 'raised to the highest perfection' (532D); and monks are for him the 'highest' degree of the laity. He does not say this explicitly of bishops, but by analogy the bishop, too, is clearly in his view established in the 'highest perfection', the highest perfection, that is, of his own (clerical) order which is, as an order, superior to that of the laity. I think that the confusion and variety of interpretation of the phrase 'state of perfection' arises from a failure to appreciate what this author means by 'perfection', and since an understanding of this is essential for an understanding of the author's whole scheme of things, it is worth while examining it briefly.

It would be simple to say that he means by 'perfection' perfection of state or function, and this is commonly said. It is said that the bishop has received the 'perfection' or 'fulness' of the priestly consecration, with the power to administer all sacraments and consecrations; he stands at the fountain-head, controlling them in all their fulness. In this sense he is in the state of perfection. It is not a question of personal sanctity and perfection, but of function. Such is the argument. He is, the commentators say, in the state of 'perfection already acquired', and in making this qualification they are in fact preparing the ground for a logical fallacy, for they then go on to say that the monk is only in a state of 'perfection still to be acquired', which he has pledged himself to strive after, they use 'perfection' here in the quite different sense of personal perfection. There is in fact no such distinction in this author; both are 'perfect' in the same sense, within their own order, and each receives it by a consecration (the bishop) or a quasi-consecration (the monk).

It is, however, a demonstrable fact that neither all bishops nor all monks are perfect in the sense of visible personal holiness; and it must in fairness be said that neither body is commonly given to vaunting its claims to such personal holiness. Cardinal Manning held (apparently dissenting from St. Thomas) that not only bishops but all priests are in the 'state of perfection', though admittedly he seems to be using it as an argument for acquiring a perfection not yet possessed.[1] If one were allowed to search Jerusalem with lamps, it is doubtful if in fact the clergy would be found as a body notably of greater personal sanctity, or even

---

[1] *The Eternal Priesthood*. Speaking, however, from memory I think the Cardinal is less concerned with denying the superiority of the bishop than with emphasising the state of perfection of the priest, that in both cases it entails, or should entail, personal holiness. For our present author, it is clear, all the initiate are in a 'state of perfection'—it is a matter of degree— and that of the priest is the very highest, at one remove only from that of the bishop. It is higher, for instance, than that of the monk (of the monk as such; he may also be a priest). Understood in this sense (the priestly power or function as involving a personal sanctity), the Cardinal is undoubtedly expressing the constant tradition of the Church. Cf., e.g., the conclusion drawn by Dom Botte ('L'Ordre D'après Les Prières d'Ordination'. *Études Sur Le Sacrament De L'Ordre*, Éd. du Cerf, 1957, p. 35) from a study of the liturgical texts, that this 'represents the thought not of an age or a country, but the tradition of the universal Church. *Quod ubique, quod semper.*' He also concludes that it was the mind of the Church from the beginning, as shown in the liturgical texts, that 'la pleine efficacité des fonctions sacrées est conditionée par la sainteté de ceux qui les exercent'.

more diligent and efficient in the performance of their duties, than the better type of the 'holy people of God', though admittedly ministering something that is beyond assessment in terms of material values.

Nevertheless, it is certain that this author knows nothing of any distinction between perfection of state or function and personal perfection, neither for the bishop nor for the monk. Both 'perfections', personal and that of function or state are given simultaneously by the one act of consecration or quasi-consecration, and he uses the one word which means equally to make perfect or to confer a sacrament. If we ask why the higher degree of personal holiness is not always evident the answer can only be that the subject is failing to 'correspond', in the modern phrase, with what is given him; in the phrase of our present author, is 'closing his eyes'[1] to it in some degree. It may take him a lifetime to assimilate it all, and after that a period of purgatory. In the tradition of this author, extending into the Middle Ages, order (and in its degree also the monastic consecration) is seen as in essence a charism, a grace that is personal yet destined for the 'edifying [building up] of the body of Christ' (Eph. iv, 12). This, however, as we know, is simply the highest expression of a principle valid throughout the ecclesiastical hierarchy, that all receive what they receive both for themselves and others; each member of the hierarchy *is* this degree of Light, that is both a reception and a transmission to those subordinate. It is not easy for the modern mind to adapt itself to this manner of thinking, which is, nevertheless, that of the universal Church: Grace, Light, the interior sanctification of man, as an objective reality which may assume a visible material form and be transmitted to others in that form.

The 'consecration' of the monk is not a 'sacrament' in the full, restricted sense of the word as we use it today, though at the time these writings were composed there was no such sharp distinction. It is a 'consecration' analogous to that of the bishop yet performed not by a bishop but a priest, because it bestows

---

[1] Comparing this with the conclusion of Dom Botte above (p. 176, n. 1), one would have to say that the priest always (assuming the correct form and intention) transmits the minimum Light sufficient for the validity (*ex opere operato*) of the sacrament he administers, yet not all he might transmit. This also is surely a matter of common experience.

perfection of a lower order. It is, however, considered to bestow a 'grace that makes perfect',[1] a phrase that might equally well be translated 'sacramental grace', for the same word is used. In other words, the monk's 'perfection' is also, in the author's view, not only 'to be acquired', but 'already acquired'.

Again it is an instance of the common Catholic teaching that every man receives grace (Light) exactly proportionate to the obligations of his state. It is not then remarkable that in the case of the highest degree of the laity, the pattern and exemplar of all those beneath, this should be transmitted by a rite analogous to that of the episcopal consecration. The Light has sought out the monk and, analogous to its operation in the case of the bishop, established him permanently[2] in this 'highest perfection' —with all that the term implies. If all the 'Light' to be transmitted by the bishop requires a period of space and time for its diffusion—this is of the essence of his task, we remember, to present the spiritual in material, visible form—the same is true, normally at least, of the translation of his personal perfection into human acts. Both aspects, however, are for this author simply the Light, God, 'operative throughout the hierarchy'.[3] The same is true of the monk, in his own degree.

PLAN OF THE CHAPTER

The author, then, first distinguishes the three degrees of the laity; he next describes the 'consecration of a monk'; then goes on to the 'contemplation' of this rite. He concludes by a résumé of the divisions of the human hierarchy, then, almost as a postscript (he has compared the divisions of the ecclesiastical hierarchy with those of the celestial) and as answering a supposed objection, adds that even in the celestial hierarchy there is something that corresponds in a way to 'purification', since

[1] Cf. p. 181, n. 2 below.
[2] In the sense that he is established for ever in this state of life and, even should he not reach heaven, a certain character, analogous to that of the priest, distinguishing him as of this particular order or class remains. Cf. the *Magnificat* antiphon for first vespers of the Feast of All Saints in the Roman Rite, where the principal orders of the hierarchies, from the seraphim down to the 'holy people', are enumerated *in extenso*.
[3] *Eccl. Hier.*, 372A, 372C.

MYSTERY OF THE MONASTIC CONSECRATION

the angels rise through the mediation of the higher orders to a 'purer', more perfect, knowledge of God.

We shall now see the author's own words. Little is in fact added here to what we have already learned in the case of the two lower degrees of the laity, and it is clear that his principal concern is with the monk and the monastic consecration. Since the rites described in the chapter on Illumination form strictly the Christian initiation, it may seem a little odd that those still undergoing purification should be included among the 'initiate'. Still this class does, of course, include the penitents, those who have fallen and are making a fresh beginning; and for all of them this is at least the beginning of initiation. The various groups within this body are not more clearly indicated here than when they are mentioned in the Holy Eucharist, but it is sufficiently clear that they include catechumens and public penitents in various stages of preparation and probation.

(1) *Those Undergoing Purification (the Lowest Degree)* (529D)

'These, then, are the priestly orders, their functions, powers, activities and consecration. We must now describe the three orders formed by the initiate who are subordinate to them.

We would say that the order of those undergoing purification is constituted by all those, mentioned already, who are excluded from the sacraments. To begin with are they whose instruction and formation, whereby the teaching of sacred scripture may bring them to spiritual birth, has not yet been effected by the deacons. Next are they who had fallen away and are receiving that instruction in the Scriptures which is to bring them back to the life of holiness; then the lax, who are still affected by the deceits of the adversary and whom the power of holy scripture is in process of strengthening. These are followed by those who are again on the road which will conduct them from sin to the works of holiness, and, finally, by those who, although turned to God, are not yet perfectly established in stable godly habits.

Such then are the ranks of those undergoing purification, being brought to birth and purified by the power of the deacons. These, by their sacred powers, purify them so that, when they are perfectly purified, they may approach to contemplation of and communion in the sacraments most apt to enlighten them' (532B).

(2) *Second (and Middle) Degree; The 'Holy People', the 'Order of Contemplatives'*

'The middle order is composed of those who contemplate certain mysteries and, being perfectly purified, enter into communion with these mysteries according to their capacity. This order has been entrusted to the priests for illumination. Being purified, that is, from all that is profane, established on holy, immovable foundations, the members of this order rise through the agency of the priests to the stable possession of the power of contemplation and participate so far as they are able in the divine symbols. This contemplation and communion fill them with a holy joy, and they are raised, in the measure of their ability, through their powers of spiritual ascent, to those holy mysteries of which they now possess the knowledge.

'This degree I call the holy people,[1] for they have been subjected to a complete purification and are now worthy of initiation and communion in the most luminous sacraments, in so far as this is permitted to them' (532C).

(3) *The Third and Highest Degree, the Order of Monks*

'But the highest of all the orders of the initiate is the holy army of monks. They have been perfectly purified from every stain, their energy reduced to a unity giving holiness to all their activities,[2] and admitted, so far as possible to spiritual contemplation of and communion in all the sacred mysteries. After being subjected to the perfecting[3] power of the divine bishops, through whom they receive from the hierarchy according to their capacity illumination and initiation into the sacraments, they are raised through this sacred knowledge, and in proportion to their own merits, to the highest perfection. This is why

---

[1] Cf. epistle of Mass of Saturday in Easter Week (I Pet. ii, 9) '... a chosen generation, a kingly priesthood, a holy nation, a purchased people ...'.

[2] The obscurity of this author's writing is well illustrated here by his statement that this order of monks has been 'perfectly purified'. Since the middle order (and even the uninitiate catechumenate) is also, we are told, 'perfectly purified', it is difficult to see what in this respect these have that the others have not got. On the other hand, we shall learn soon that, even the angels are still undergoing 'purification'. The answer has already been suggested, that it is a matter of degree, of 'hierarchy'; all are complete, 'perfect', even in possession of all that is—within the limitations of their own order.   [3] I.e. or 'sacramental'. Cf. p. 137.

MYSTERY OF THE MONASTIC CONSECRATION

our masters, judging these men worthy of a sacred title, have called them sometimes 'servitors'[1] and sometimes 'monks', because of the purity of the performance of their duty of worship, or 'service' of God; and because their life, far from being divided remains perfectly one, and they unify themselves by a recollection which excludes all distraction. So they tend to a unity like that of God and to the perfection of the love of God. Moreover, our sacred institutions have bestowed on them a grace which perfects them[2] and have found them worthy of a special rite of consecration. This consecration is the duty not of the bishop (who officiates only to confer ordination to the priestly rank) but of priests, who are charged with this secondary rite of the liturgy of the hierarchy' (533A).

DESCRIPTION OF THE RITE

(1) 'The priest stands before the altar, pronouncing the prayer for the consecration of a monk. The initiate, standing behind the priest, does not kneel either on one knee or two, nor is there placed on his head the Scriptures containing the deposit of divine revelation. He is content to remain standing before the priest, while the latter pronounces over him the words of the monastic consecration. After this consecration the priest approaches the initiate. (2) He first asks if he renounces not only any action, but even the thought of anything, that could bring division into his life. He then reminds him of the rules of a fully perfect life, affirming publicly that it is his duty to surpass all the virtues of a merely mediocre life. (3) When the initiate has formally subscribed to these undertakings the priest makes the sign of the cross on him, then cuts his hair while invoking the three persons of the divine Beatitude. (4) Then, having completely unclothed him, he places on him a new habit. Finally, followed by all the others present at the ceremony, he gives him the kiss of peace and (5) admits him to communion in the mysteries of the Godhead'[3] (533C).

---

[1] *Therapeutes*, perhaps 'liturgists', but see p. 172. The word is unusual in patristic literature. Stiglmayr knows only Clement of Alexandria to use it.

[2] Or 'sacramental grace' ($\tau\epsilon\lambda\epsilon\sigma\tau\iota\kappa\dot{\eta}\nu$ $\chi\acute{\alpha}\rho\iota\nu$).

[3] I.e. that fuller measure of 'union', 'contemplation', deeper penetration of the symbols into the life of God in which this higher degree consists. This is explained partly by the 'contemplation' that follows. More directly the

MYSTERY OF THE MONASTIC CONSECRATION

CONTEMPLATION

(1) (Obviously contrasting the rite with that of the priestly ordination.) Significance of the fact that the monk stands instead of kneeling and does not receive on his head the sacred scriptures: his office not to lead others but to remain stable in the unity of his life.

'These rites signify that it is not the mission of the monastic order to direct others but, while remaining stable in its holy unity, it takes it place after the priestly orders, following them in willing obedience as a faithful companion of the journey along the route that leads them to divine knowledge of those mysteries at which they are permitted to be present' (533C).

(2) Act of renunciation, excluding all division and leading to union of 'one with the One'.

'The rite by which the initiate is made to renounce all actions, even all thoughts, that could bring division into his life signifies that perfect philosophy which confers on monks the knowledge of the precepts by which their life achieves unity. As I have said, theirs is not a middle rank among the initiate, but the most sublime of all. That is why what is perfectly licit to men of the second order is often completely forbidden to monks; for it is their duty to restore their lives to unity and to form only one with the One, to unite themselves with the holy Unity and to imitate, so far as they lawfully may, the priestly life, since they are in many ways related to it, are much closer to it than the initiate of the other orders' (536A).

(3) Significance of the sign of the cross and tonsure: mortifying of carnal desires and turning from visible beauty to the invisible.

'The sign of the cross signifies, as we have said, the death of all carnal desires. The tonsure symbolises a life pure and severed from all separable covering that might conceal inner deformity by artificial, extraneous ornaments, rising rather by "single-minded and unifying"[1] virtues to the highest possible conformity to the divine' (536A).

---

[1] The inverted commas are mine. There is a play on the word '*monachos*' (here in the adjectival form, ἐνιαίοις καὶ μοναχικοῖς κάλλεσιν). In the author's etymology (p. 181 above) it may mean both 'monastic' and 'unifying'. Here he uses two words practically synonymous, one serving to explain the other.

---

reference is to the celebration of the Eucharist which we shall find following, or, better, accompanying the rite.

(4) The stripping and clothing indicate the passage to a greater perfection; the kiss, a sign of unity and congratulation.

(The divesting of the ordinary dress and the taking of the monastic habit symbolises the passage from the ordinary 'moderate' holiness of the 'middle order' to a 'greater perfection', just as at baptism the new dress signified the passage from purification to contemplation and enlightenment.)

'The laying aside of the former dress and the taking of the habit represent the passage from a moderate holiness to a greater perfection. We have seen already that the ceremony by which God is born in souls also entails a change of dress which signifies the spiritual ascent from purification to the higher stages, those of contemplation and illumination. As for the kiss given to the initiate by the consecrating priest and all the others present, this should be seen as a sign of the union in which all who have become like God are united in the joyous bonds of a mutual, charitable congratulation' (536B).

(5) Reception of holy communion signifies that the monk's union with God is now of a higher order, even 'in a manner different' from that of the 'holy people'.

'At the conclusion of all these ceremonies the priest summons him whom he has just consecrated to take part in the holy communion. This shews in a sacred manner that if the candidate truly comes to this monastic and unifying discipline,[1] he will contemplate the holy mysteries presented to his sight and communicate in the sacred symbols not merely like the members of the middle order; rather, through his divine knowledge of the mysteries in which he will participate, he will be admitted to communion with God in a manner different from that of the holy people.[2] It is for the same reason that, after the ceremony

---

[1] ἀναγωγήν: raising up, elevation, rearing, discipline. There is again this play (obviously deliberate) on the word 'monastic' as meaning also 'unifying' or 'bringing to unity'; while ἀναγωγή may equally well be rendered 'elevation', or even 'rearing', remembering the Benedictine phrase of 'school of the Lord's service'.

[2] ἑτέρῳ τρόπῳ. It is a 'different manner' of union or 'synaxis'. It seems clear that in the author's view a special character is given. We are not told in what the difference consists, except that we know it is a different degree of what the others have. The difference must not be exaggerated, yet neither should it be under-rated: each degree opens up a new dimension, a new world not accessible to those below.

of their consecration and to conclude the sacrament of their ordination, the priestly orders receive the communion of the most holy Eucharist at the hands of the bishop who has just ordained them. It is not merely because the reception of the divine mysteries crowns all participation in the hierarchy, but because all the sacred orders, according as the spiritual elevation and consecration have deified them in a greater or less degree, receive each in his own measure, the divine gift of this same communion' (536C).

CONCLUSION

I. *A Brief Résumé of the Whole Chapter*

'To resume, then, the sacraments effect purification, illumination and perfection. The deacons constitute the order that purifies, priests the order that enlightens and bishops, living in the likeness of God, the order that makes perfect. The order of those undergoing purification, in so far as its members are still in the stage of purification, is not yet admitted to initiation and to participation in the sacred mysteries. The order of contemplatives is identical with that of the holy people.[1] The order of the perfect consists of the monks, because they have unified their lives.[2] In its holy, harmonious division into orders our own hierarchy thus presents the same structure as the celestial hierarchies, as given by divine revelation, preserving carefully, proportioned to its human character, the characteristics in which it resembles God and imitates him' (537A).

II. *Afterthought, Foreseeing a Possible Objection*

The degrees of the ecclesiastical hierarchy mirror those of the celestial hierarchy; but how can angels be said to undergo purification?

'But, you may object, in the celestial hierarchies no trace is found of an order of purified, since it would be sacrilegious and false to assert that there exists in heaven an order of sinners. For me to deny, however, that the angels are completely immaculate and possess the perfection of supernatural purity would mean that I had lost all understanding of the most sacred

---
[1] θεωρητικὴ δὲ τάξις ὁ ἱερὸς λαός.
[2] ἡ τῶν ἑνιαίων μοναχῶν.

mysteries. If one of the angels were to give way to evil he would be immediately excluded from the heavenly, harmonious company of divine spirits. He would fall into darkness where dwell the host of the renegades. Nevertheless it is correct to say that in the celestial hierarchy there is something corresponding to the purification of lower beings. It is illumination which gives them access to mysteries they had not known before; which leads them to a more perfect understanding of divine knowledge; which, finally, leads them by means of higher and more divine spirits to higher and brighter illuminations from the contemplation of God.

'In this sense it is possible to distinguish on the one hand orders that are enlightened[1] and made perfect and, on the other hand, orders that purify, enlighten and make perfect. The higher spirits, the most divine, have indeed the threefold task, in accordance with the corresponding degrees of the celestial hierarchy, of purifying from all ignorance the heavenly orders subordinate to them, of imparting to them the fulness of divine illuminations, and finally of perfecting them in the luminous knowledge that comes from the contemplation of God. As we have already said, the heavenly orders are not equal in their knowledge of the illuminations which come from contemplation of the divine mysteries. It is God who enlightens immediately the first orders, and by means of them that he enlightens the lower orders, in proportion to their capacity, with the radiance of his divine light' (537C).

[1] There is no mention of a degree that is 'being purified', and one can only conclude that the author's courage has failed him; he cannot bring himself to say in so many words that there is an order of angels undergoing purification. It is, however, evident that it comes within the logic of his scheme, as he himself has explained.

7. Mystery Over Those Who Have Fallen Asleep in Holiness

THIS final chapter is almost in the nature of an appendix, since the tale of the degrees of the hierarchy has already been completed. It has, however, a certain artistic relevance. We began with the initiation of the neophyte and followed him through the stages by which he was raised to perfect union in the monastic order, studying on the way the orders of the clergy through which the light was transmitted to him. It is not unfitting that the treatise should close with a glimpse of journey's end, his final passing from the visible world to definitive, indissoluble union with the One, body and soul in heaven. Characteristically the author takes the opportunity of tying up a few loose ends.

The subject is the Christian funeral rites, and it is difficult to see how an author who devotes nearly a fifth part of his treatise to a not strictly relevant account of the disposal of the human body after death can be justly accused of a lack of interest in the body and the world of the senses. No one can deny his insistence on the need of passing beyond the senses, but this is only part of the paradox of all created being, that we find things in our present state only by walking away from them; and here the resurrection and eternal existence of the body is stated explicitly and with emphasis.

The chapter is arranged on the plan of the others, with introduction, description of the rite and contemplation. A number of important questions are raised in the course of the chapter, but it will perhaps be best to consider these as they arise. One MS.

ends with the dedication: Denys the Areopagite, Bishop of Athens, to Timothy, Bishop of Ephesus.

INTRODUCTORY

(1) The joy and confidence with which the 'saints' (the 'holy people', the laity) look forward to death and the subsequent resurrection of soul and body (553A).

'Having made these points we must now, I think, speak of our funeral rites. These differ according as it is a question of the holy or the profane; as their lives were different, so also are their deaths.

'They who have led a holy life will remember those promises of God whose truth they have in a way seen in the contemplation of his resurrection, and will reach the moment ordained for their death filled with holy joy and inspired with a firm and sincere hope, seeing it as the end of their warfare, for they know with certainty that through the complete resurrection which is to come for them their entire being will be saved and live fully for ever. For not only holy souls, which during their earthly life have not given way to evil,[1] will acquire in their regeneration the highest immutable likeness to God, but also their purified bodies that bore the same yoke as the souls, fulfilled the same pilgrimage, were enrolled with them and fought the same warfare. They also will receive in return for their labour in the service of God, and at the same time as their souls, the reward of that resurrection which will make them share with souls that unfailing security assured by life in God. United to the souls whose companions they were here below, become in a way members of Christ himself, they will enjoy everlasting peace and immortal happiness in a life like that of God. One can understand, then why the saints meet death with joy, in unquenchable hope, when the end of their warfare arrives.'

(2) This certain knowledge compared with the false theories of those outside the Church (533B).

'Among those outside the Church some have the absurd idea that the dead return to nothing.[2] Others imagine that the bond

---
[1] This is the reading of M and minor MSS. and seems to be the sense required here, though the MS. is very corrupt. Cordier's text in Migne has the opposite sense, omitting the negative: 'souls who *have* given way to evil'.
[2] Epicureans.

uniting body and soul is broken for ever,[1] for they say it would not be fitting for souls to retain this bond amid beatific peace and in full likeness to God. These, however, through insufficient instruction in divine knowledge, forget that in Christ we have already begun such a life in the closest possible likeness to that of God. Others again attribute new incarnations to souls,[2] and in this they seem to me very unjust towards their bodies, which have shared the labour of the soul; for they deprive them unfittingly of the reward due to them at the end of a course in union with God. Others, finally, who have fallen into quite materialist ideas,[3] have claimed that the repose in perfect happiness promised to the saints is like the happiness in this world. To those who have become like angels they have sacrilegiously attributed the need of nourishment proper to a perishable life.

'However, none of the true saints will fall into such errors; they know that their being in its entirety will receive the repose that will make them like Christ. When the end assigned to their earthly life approaches, then, as they draw closer to it, they see very clearly the way that leads to immortality. They praise then the gifts of the deity and, filled with divine happiness, they no longer fear falling into evil but realise clearly that they will possess for ever the reward they have earned.

'As for those stained and defiled by sin, though they have received some initiation into the sacred mysteries—an initiation they have rejected in order to abandon themselves to their wicked desires—when the end of their life on earth comes the divine law of the Scriptures no longer appears to them so contemptible. They regard then with other eyes the pleasures that have wrought their destruction, to which their passions attached them, as also that holy life they have foolishly abandoned and which they are now compelled to praise. Because of their sinful life they leave this world reluctantly and with lamentations, encouraged by no ray of hope.'

(3) The happy passing of the 'holy people' (556B).

'Nothing like this happens at the death of the saints. The just man is full of holy gladness when he comes to the end of his warfare, and it is with great joy that he advances towards his

---
[1] Manicheans.   [2] Pythagoreans.   [3] Chiliasts.

THOSE WHO HAVE FALLEN ASLEEP IN HOLINESS

new life.[1] His acquaintance, his neighbours in God, whose lives resemble his own, congratulate him on having attained the victory and the goal of his desires. They sing hymns of thanksgiving in honour of him who is the author of this victory, asking him to grant them also the grace of such a repose. Then they take the body of the dead and carry it to the bishop as if for the award of the crown of victory. The latter receives it with joy and, in accordance with the rules, performs the sacred rites instituted for those who have died a holy death.'

DESCRIPTION OF THE RITE

'Having assembled the congregation, the bishop proceeds in this way: (1) If the dead belongs to one of the orders of the priesthood he is placed at the foot of the altar. (2) Then the bishop begins by invoking God and giving thanks. (If the dead has the rank of monk or of the faithful people the bishop places him outside the sanctuary, at the entrance to the holy place reserved for the priests. He then recites the prayer of thanksgiving.) (3) The deacons then read the text of the faithful promises contained in the divine scripture on the subject of our resurrection and sing the psalms relating to the same theme. (4) The principal deacon after this sends away the catechumens, and then (5) reads the names of those who have already died a holy death, estimating him who has just finished his earthly life as worthy to be commemorated with them and like them. Finally, he exhorts all those present to pray for ultimate happiness in Christ. (6) The divine bishop then recites a prayer over the body. (7) When this is finished he kisses the dead, followed in this immediately by all those present. (8) When all have given the kiss of peace the bishop anoints the body with holy oil and prays for all the dead. (9) He then places the body in holy ground by the side of other saints of equal dignity.'

CONTEMPLATION

(1) The placing of the dead in his appropriate place in the church signifies that the reward he will receive in the resurrec-

[1] In the mind of the author all that has happened so far has been, in a sense, his 'initiation', the activity in space and time in which his 'birth from God' his regeneration, his new life, has been effected (cf. p. 81 above). This is his final, definitive entry into that life.

tion will correspond to his life in this world. The profane have no understanding of these rites: we have been enlightened by God to see their spiritual significance (557A).

'If those outside the Church were to assist at these rites or be told of them they would, I think, smile and express pity for our delusion. We should not be surprised at that. As Scripture says 'One must believe in order to understand'.[1] We, whom the light of Jesus has initiated into the spiritual sense of these sacred rites, can affirm that it is not without reasonable cause that the bishop brings in the body of the dead and places it in the part of the church reserved for those of his order. It signifies that at the general resurrection each will have his lot corresponding to his life here below. He who has led in this world, in the measure permitted to a man to imitate God, a life like that of God, perfectly holy, will possess for ever in the ages to come peace and divine happiness. If, while leading a holy life, he has yet remained at a stage below the fullest likeness to God, he will receive rewards proportioned to his merit.'

(2) Prayer of thanksgiving (557B).

'It is to praise this divine justice that the bishop makes the act of thanksgiving and praises the Deity, who delivers us all from unjust tyranny in order to submit us to the perfect equity of his own judgement.'

(3) Recalling of the divine promises signifies the happiness of the dead and encourages the living (557B).

'The singing and the reading of the divine promises signify first what happiness and peace are enjoyed for ever by those who reach divine perfection. Giving for an example to the living him who as died a holy death, they teach that the living also should tend to the same perfection.'

(4) Though at the celebration of the sacraments all those undergoing purification are sent away, here only the catechumens are dismissed so that the others may have a salutary reminder of death (557C).

'Notice this, however. In this ceremony, instead of sending out, as usually happens, all those who belong to the order of those undergoing purification, only the catechumens are

[1] Is. vii, 9.

THOSE WHO HAVE FALLEN ASLEEP IN HOLINESS

excluded from the congregation. These latter, being not yet initiated into any of the sacraments, could not assist without irreverence, however little, at any of the ceremonies of the sacred liturgy; for God is not yet born in them, he who is the source and distributor of light, and so they have not yet received in any degree the power of contemplating the mysteries. On the other hand the rest of those undergoing purification have already been initiated and received the sacred gifts. It is true that they have in their folly returned to evil instead of rising, as was their duty, to a higher perfection. That is why it is not wrong to exclude them from that contemplation of and communion with God made visible under the sacramental symbols.[1] If they were to participate unworthily in these sacred ceremonies they would suffer for their audacity and would only increase their contempt of divine realities and due consideration for themselves. None the less, it is lawful to admit them to the funeral rites, for this spectacle teaches them clearly the uncertainty of the hour of death, the rewards promised to the good by the infallible Scriptures, and the punishment without end with which they threaten the wicked.'

(5) Solemn reading of the names of those who have died a holy death (551D).

'It will, then, be a lesson not without value for these latter to assist at this solemn proclamation by which the deacons affirm that he who has died piously is truly admitted for ever into the community of the saints. They will then, perhaps, experience a desire for a similar fate and may realise, in listening to the deacons, how true it is that all are happy who die in the peace of Christ.'

(6) Prayer for the dead (560A).

(a) 'Then the divine bishop comes forward and recites a prayer over the dead. After the prayer he kisses him, followed by all those present. The prayer, addressed to the divine Goodness, asks him to pardon the dead all the faults due to human weakness and to establish him in the light and the land of the living,

---

[1] As we have seen, assistance at the Holy Eucharist at this period was expected to entail reception of holy communion: the 'contemplation' was also a 'union' transforming the communicant into the object of his contemplation.

in the bosom of Abraham, Isaac and Jacob, where sorrow, sadness and weeping are known no more.[1]

'Such, then, is the happiness clearly promised as a reward to the saints. What could be compared to immortality freed from all suffering and filled with light? Yet, though it is good that this should be translated into images adapted as far as possible to our weakness, still those promises remain beyond all understanding, and the terms in which they are expressed are inadequate to the truth they contain. For we must believe that it is not without reason that Scripture says: "Eye hath not seen, nor ear heard, neither hath it entered into the heart of man, what things God hath prepared for them that love him" (I Cor. ii, 9).

The bosom of the patriarchs and of other holy men means, I think, the divine repose and perfect happiness encompassing all those who live in conformity with God in perfect happiness without end.'

(*b*) Difficulty foreseen in the question of prayer for the dead. The author's explanation (560C).

This prayer for the dead suggests a problem to the mind of the author; or more probably he is replying to current criticism by heretics. It is not a question of assisting souls in purgatory, a matter which is not mentioned,[2] but the more general question of how the prayer of the Church can affect the reward or punishment which must inevitably follow as a consequence of divine justice; if the soul is already in heaven or hell nothing can alter the fact, nor can the place, the degree of happiness in heaven, be affected.

The author's argument is not easy to follow, but the basis of it is clear, that the bishop is acting here consistently with his fundamental role of manifesting in material terms spiritual realities. His prayer, that is, is less a prayer at this stage than a manifestation, a revelation in material signs of the fate of the deceased. The prayer in the strict sense, one might almost say, has been made already during the whole course of initiation and progress to perfection of the one now dead, producing infallibly its effect—with the regular qualification of the author,

---

[1] Apoc. xxi, 4.

[2] There appears to be no explicit mention of purgatory before Augustine, but it is considered to be contained implicitly in the universal practice of prayer for the dead.

THOSE WHO HAVE FALLEN ASLEEP IN HOLINESS

'according to the capacity' and the disposition of the recipient. Having now passed beyond the visible world, he is no longer, of course, subject to the jurisdiction of the bishop, whose office is precisely to stand between the invisible and visible planes, transmitting the light from one to the other translated into visible, material form. This final prayer is thus, one might say, the conclusion of the whole process of prayer that was the conferring of the sacraments; as these manifested in visible, material form the effect that was invisible, spiritual, beyond bodily sight, so this, its conclusion, manifests the final result of the whole operation, with the same qualification—according to the capacity, the merit, the disposition of the deceased. As the degree of divine life given by the conferring of the sacrament varied in each case according to the dispositions of each[1]—if it was received unworthily nothing was received, rather sin was incurred—so it is also here. Only when the life and end of the deceased has manifestly been such as to offer no hope that he has reached such a happy state is the rite and the prayers omitted.

'You might reply that we are without doubt right in all this, but that one point remains obscure. Why does the bishop pray to the divine Goodness to pardon the faults of the dead and to grant him the rank and illumination of those who have lived in conformity with God? If each one receives from divine justice the reward that corresponds to the merit or demerit of his earthly life, once the dead has ceased from activity here below by what prayer could the bishop obtain for him a repose other than that which is his by right, corresponding to the life he has led in this world? I, for my part, am not ignorant of the fact that each one is bound to enjoy the lot he has merited, for I believe in the teaching of Scripture, which tells us: 'The Lord has judged and every one shall receive in accordance with his bodily actions, good or evil'.[2] Moreover that the prayers of the just here below, and still more prayers for the dead, are of value only to those

---

[1] The sacraments produce their effect, in the technical phrase, *ex opere operato*; they do not depend for their effect on the sanctity or merit of the minister or the recipient; nevertheless, the *degree* of grace (Light) received may vary according to the dispositions of the subject.

[2] The general sense is that of II Cor. v, 10. The author appears to be quoting from memory.

who merit them is indeed the true doctrine delivered to us by the Scriptures. Was Samuel able to obtain anything in favour of Saul?[1] In what did the people of the Jews profit from the prayers of the prophets? In the same way, in fact, that a man who has lost his eyes would be foolish to claim a share in the light of the sun, which sheds its gifts only on eyes that are intact, so it would be impossible and a vain hope to claim the intercession of the saints at the very moment when one is frustrating the natural action of their sanctity by abuse of the gifts of God and rejection of the clear commands of divine Goodness.

'I declare, all the same, in conformity with Scripture, that the prayers of the saints [i.e. the "holy people"] are perfectly useful in this world in the case of a man who desires the gifts of God, who disposes himself to receive them with consciousness of his own unworthiness and goes to some good man to beg him to help and add the assistance of his prayers. Such assistance cannot fail to be eminently useful. It will procure him the divine gifts he desires. The divine Goodness will communicate himself to him because of his good dispositions, because of the veneration he shews for the saints, by reason of the laudable zeal with which he implores the divine gifts to which he aspires, and finally because of his manner of life, in harmony with his desire and conformed to that of God.

'It is indeed a law established by the judgement of God that the divine gifts, as perfectly befits their divine character, are granted to those who are worthy to receive them through the medium of those who are worthy to distribute them. Should it happen, then, that anyone abuse this sacred rule, and led by a fatal presumption, should believe himself capable of entering by himself into contact with the deity, disdaining the mediation of the saints; if also it should happen that one unworthy and wicked should pray to God for them without giving proof to the best of his power of a solid desire of the divine gifts, he would receive no fruit from his unworthy prayer.

'Regarding, then, the prayer mentioned, made by the bishop on behalf of the dead, this must be explained in accordance with the traditions our divine masters have handed down to us.

'The divine bishop is, as the Scriptures say, the revealer of the divine judgements. He is, in fact, the messenger [angel] of

[1] I Kings xvi, 1.

almighty God.¹ Consequently he knows, since God has taught him by means of the Scriptures, that to those who have lived good lives it is granted, according to their merit, and weighed by the justice of God, to live a life of light in God, because the Deity, in his love for men, closes his eyes to the faults they have committed, since no man, as Scripture says, is free from stain.² The bishop knows well the promises contained in the infallible Scriptures. He prays, therefore, that they may be realised and that those who have lived honourably may receive their reward. In this he models himself on the divine Goodness whom he imitates, asking as though they were graces for himself gifts intended for others.

Knowing, then, that the divine promises will be infallibly realised, in this way he teaches to all those present that the gifts he asks in virtue of a holy institution will be fully granted to those who live a perfect life in God. For the bishop, in interpreting divine justice, will be very careful to avoid suggesting anything that is not fully in agreement with God and that does not correspond to the divine promises. Moreover, when it is a question of those who have died in a state of sin he does not recite this prayer at all, not only because in so doing he would be going beyond his role of interpreter, because he would presume to perform the functions of the hierarchy on his own initiative and not under the inspiration of him who is the source of every sacrament, but also because his impious prayer would be rejected and God would reply in the words of Scripture: 'You ask and receive not; because you ask amiss'.³

The bishop, then, man of God, asks only for what corresponds to the divine promises, what is agreeable to God, what God will grant fully. He thus manifests before God, the lover of the good, his own love of the right and good and reveals to those assisting what gifts will be received by the saints.'

(c) The question of excommunication (564B).

The preceding passage leads to a consideration of the power of excommunication, linked in the text with the power of for-

---

¹ Zach. ii, 8.
² Job xiv, 2. The idea seems to be that God will overlook the small 'venial' faults such as no one can entirely avoid without a special grace.
³ James iv, 3.

giving sins, of binding and loosing. The author's explanation is fundamentally the same. Excommunication is for him the visible manifestation or interpretation, effecting on the visible plane of this world something already effected in the invisible sphere. By a certain mode of action a man has already severed his connection with God; this is now made manifest in the visible body of the Church by the bishop—he is cut off from it. The bishop does not act arbitrarily, from mere caprice. In the exercise of his office, under the guidance of the Holy Spirit, he gives solemn, formal effect on the visible plane to what he sees to be already reality on the invisible. It seems that what the author wishes to emphasise is simply that here, as in the administration of the sacraments, the bishop is transmitting to his subordinates, in a manner adapted to their capacity, what he has received from God. In this he must, it is obvious, use human judgement, but the grace of his office gives him a more than human judgement, a more than merely human power of discernment, an 'inspiration' and 'movement' by God similar to the inspiration by which Peter declared Christ to be 'the son of the living God'.

This power of excommunication, as all the powers of the hierarchy, is to be used only in the measure that the bishop is 'moved by the Deity himself'. Since we are not told how the bishop is to recognise the impulse of the Spirit, it seems evident that this means no more than that the bishop may rely on divine guidance when, after careful examination of his motives, he acts in the light of ordinary human prudence, that he will then, in fact, be exercising more than merely human prudence. If a bishop were quite perfect, 'transparent', and sensitive to the divine action, he would, in the author's way of thinking, be perfectly subject to divine guidance and impulse in such matters.

One might ask what would happen should the bishop, instead of being 'moved by the deity', act from unworthy motives, on his own inspiration. One might quote the case of Joan of Arc excommunicated by her bishop, yet later canonised. As in the hypothesis of prayer for an unrepentant public sinner after his death, it is obvious that such an action would have no effect; it would not be a manifestation and interpretation of the spiritual reality; the bishop would not be acting in accordance with his office. His action would, it is true, deprive the excommunicate of the sacraments, cutting him off from the visible body of the Church; yet grace may be obtained apart from the sacraments and even outside the visible body of the Church, though it still remains the grace of Christ, the 'source of every hierarchy', with the hierarchy as its normal, infallible, divinely instituted channel.

'In the same way, in virtue of his office as revealer of divine judgements, the bishop has the power of excommunicating, not indeed that the all-wise Deity bows obediently, if one may venture to say so, to his whims, but because the bishop obeys the Spirit who is the source of every sacrament and expresses himself through his mouth, because it is by reason of their sin that he excommunicates those whom God has already judged. It is written indeed: "Receive ye the Holy Ghost. Whose sins you shall forgive, they are forgiven them; and whose sins you shall retain, they are retained."[1] And to him who received the divine revelation from the Father it was said, according to Scripture: "Whatsoever thou shalt bind upon earth, it shall be bound also in heaven."[2] By this is indicated that St. Peter himself and all the bishops similarly have the duty in virtue of their office of revealers and interpreters, in accordance with the revelations they receive of the judgements of the Father, to admit the friends of God and exclude his enemies. When Peter made his inspired declaration[3] it was not, as Scripture witnesses, on his own initiative nor by revelation of flesh and blood, but under the impulse of God who himself initiated him spiritually into the divine mysteries. In the same way the bishops, these men of God, are obliged to use their powers of excommunication, as all other powers of the hierarchy, only in the measure that they are moved by the Deity himself, the principle of every sacrament. Other men are obliged to obey the bishops, when these act in virtue of their office of bishop, as being moved by God himself, for it is said: "He that despiseth you despiseth me." '[4]

---

[1] John xxii, 22. [2] Matt. xvi, 19. [3] Matt. xvi, 16.

[4] Luke x, 16. Some have thought to find in the above passage (beginning, p. 195. 'In this he models . . .'; Migne, para. 7, 564) an indication that the author did not believe that the sacraments are effective *ex opere operato* (cf. p. 193, n. 1). The present writer can say only that he is unable to find this; but writing in a remote spot, far removed from adequate libraries, it is

(7) The kiss of peace (565A).[1]

'Let us now return to the rites that follow the prayer of which we have just spoken. Having finished it the bishop gives to the dead the kiss of peace, followed immediately by all those present; for he who has led a godlike life is in perfect harmony with all those who live in conformity with God.'

(8) The anointing of the dead; signifying that the deceased has fought to victory (565A).

To the average modern reader it will no doubt be surprising to find that the last anointing here is not our sacrament of extreme unction but an anointing given to the dead body immediately before burial. This was, however, the general practice in the Greek Church; and in the Latin Church we find Archbishop Theodore of Canterbury (c. 680) speaking of it being given to the bodies of monks and so, we may suppose, also to the clergy. Our 'last anointing' (extreme unction) did not in fact acquire this name until the late Middle Ages; before that it seems to have been most commonly known as the 'anointing of the sick', a title which better describes its purpose, the full and final restoration of the body to its original power, certainly for the next life and probably for a further period in this present world.

This sacrament is presumably covered in this treatise by the

[1] This practice was forbidden later by conciliar decrees.

---

not possible for him to know the exact passages to which objection is taken. It is sufficiently clear that there is here no question of administration of the sacraments. In the one case the person is already dead and beyond the scope of the sacraments; in the other it is question not of administering sacraments but of witholding them—the power of 'binding' and 'retaining'. The author does indeed draw an analogy between his action here and in administering the sacraments; in both cases he is presenting an invisible reality in a visible, material form. But there is an essential difference. In the case of the sacraments the sign is an effective sign, producing what it signifies; in these present cases the bishop is seen as simply revealing, giving material expression to something that has already happened in the invisible sphere. His prayer for the dead is less a prayer than an official pronouncement of this, of the reward of the good; his sentence of excommunication gives visible effect to something that has already happened on the invisible plane, the severance of the sinner's connection with God, the breaking of the line of transmission of the Light.

general statement concerning holy oil (p. 122), that it is used 'in almost all the ceremonies of the hierarchy'. Still it is rather odd that the author, given his habit of ranging back and forth, does not mention it explicitly; it could, one feels, reinforce his remarks on the future destiny of the body.

'After the kiss of peace the bishop anoints the body of the dead with holy oil. You will remember that in the ceremony of birth from God it is, before baptism, by anointing with holy oil that the initiate is permitted for the first time to participate in the sacred symbols, immediately after he has been stripped of his former dress. Now, on the contrary, it is at the end of all that holy oil is poured out over the dead. Then the sacred anointing summoned the initiate to a holy warfare; now the pouring of the oil signifies that in this combat he has fought to victory.'[1]

(9) Placing of the body of the dead in a place corresponding with his dignity: teaches that the body is to share with the soul the joys of the resurrection (565B).

'Having completed these rites the bishop places the body in a suitable place with the bodies of other saints of equal dignity. If the dead has lived, body and soul, a life pleasing to God, his body will merit to share in the honours of the soul whose labour and warfare it has shared. That is why divine justice associates the body with the soul when it gives to this last the final reward it has earned, for it too has shared in the course of the same pilgrimage the holiness or wickedness of one identical life. Accordingly our sacred institutions grant communion with God both to the one and to the other: to the soul by pure contemplation and inner understanding of the sacred rites; to the body through the figure of the holy oil and the sacred symbols of holy

---

[1] It is by no means clear how this is signified, and the author offers no explanation. It is probably seen as the final healing and salving of the wounds incurred in battle, in preparation for the entry of the body into eternal life. This, however, is properly the effect of the sacrament of what we now call the 'last anointing', the removal of the 'vestiges' of sin from body as well as soul, restoring it to its original perfection for the life of heaven. It is conceivable that this anointing is seen simply as the completion of the sacramental anointing, with special emphasis on the *bodily* resurrection, ultimately as the completion of the anointing begun in baptism (cf. p. 76 f. above).

communion with God.[1] Thus they sanctify the whole man, accomplishing the holy work of his complete, integral salvation, and demonstrating by the comprehensive nature of these liturgical rites the fulness of the resurrection which is to come.'

There follow now what are in the nature of afterthoughts or appendices to the whole work, and finally a conclusion:

(i) Why, here and throughout, the formulas of the sacraments are not committed to writing: the initiate learns them when he receives the sacrament; at the same time he receives the illumination necessary to penetrate their inner reality (565C).

'As for the formulas used in the administration of the sacraments, it would be unlawful[2] to explain these in writing and to unveil to the general public their mystical significance and the power of God working in them. As tradition teaches, if you learn them through initiation, where they are exposed to no danger of public derision, then as you rise spiritually through the practice of a holy life and become perfect in the love of God and of good works, you will be enlightened by him who is the source of all the sacraments, and attain to the highest knowledge of the mysteries.'

(ii) The question of infant baptism; how to explain it to pagans (565D).

[1] This passage forms an excellent résumé of the author's fundamental conception of the sacraments, the mysteries and of the relationship between body and soul. Man is one, spiritual with a material bodily expression; the sacraments, through which he receives ultimately his being, are similarly spiritual realities with an external material, visible form or expression. The conclusion is especially noteworthy. It is the sacramental *symbols* that allow the body to share in the contemplation of the soul; and it is the twofold nature of the sacraments which, for this author, demonstrates the resurrection of the body. This follows simply as the logical conclusion from his premises: all that is in the lower degrees flows from the higher; here the very eternal being of the body is received through the sacraments, the body of man through the body of Christ.

[2] This, alluded to before (p. 47), was in fact a general rule, as is evident from St. Basil's statement that it is not permitted to commit to writing what only the initiate are allowed to see. In consequence, the 'matter' of the sacraments is not referred to directly and, for instance, the overturning of the chalice in a pagan riot is, in a letter to the Pope, the 'spilling of the blood of Christ on the ground', but, in a general communication, 'the overturning of the symbols'.

THOSE WHO HAVE FALLEN ASLEEP IN HOLINESS

Here it is not apparently the actual conferring of the sacrament on an infant, as the spectacle of the bishop teaching the divine mysteries to one unable to understand them, and a third person making promises on the child's behalf which the bishop sees as constituting a problem for pagans. His explanation is less an explanation than a suggestion of how best to present the problem to those who enquire about it. He admits there is a problem; but they must be told that no one is capable of understanding completely the divine mysteries. Many are beyond the understanding of even the highest angels: it is a matter of degree. It is not, however, unreasonable that a child should be admitted to the sacraments on condition that a sponsor should undertake to rear him in accordance with the obligations of the Christian life so that, bred in good habits—and aided in this by these same sacraments—he may himself, when he comes of age, keep the promises made on his behalf.

'But, you may say to me, what does seem to call for the derision of the wicked is the fact that infants, though incapable of understanding the divine mysteries, should nevertheless be admitted to the sacrament by which they are born of God, as also to the sacred symbols of holy communion; the fact that one may see bishops teaching the divine mysteries to one not capable of understanding, delivering our holy traditions in vain to one who does not understand them. What lends itself still more to scoffing is the fact that others, in place of the children, pronounce the ritual abjurations and make the promises.

'Now it is your duty who, as bishop, understand fully these rites, not to be irritated by those who are at fault in this, but prudently to enlighten them, refuting their objections charitably and replying, in accordance with our holy law, that our own knowledge is far from extending to a complete understanding of the divine mysteries. There is more than one that remains beyond our understanding; nevertheless, though the full understanding of their nature eludes us and is known only to the orders superior to our human one, they have their origin in God. Many mysteries are beyond the knowledge of even the highest spirits and are known fully only to the Deity, all wise and source of all knowledge. We may, however, say on this point what our teachers, themselves initiated into the earliest traditions, have handed down to us.

'These state, what is indeed true, that children bred according to our rules will develop good habits and will escape all error and temptations to a life of wickedness. Realising this our masters have thought it good to admit infants to the sacraments on condition that the natural parents of the infant concerned entrust him to some good teacher, himself initiated into the sacred mysteries, who should be able to effect his religious instruction as his spiritual father and the guarantor of spiritual well-being. One who thus undertakes to lead the child in the way of a holy life is asked by the bishop to agree to the ritual abjurations and to make the promises. It is untrue, however, as the scoffers claim, that the sponsor is initiated into the divine mysteries in place of the infant, for he does not say that he abjures or makes a promise in place of the child, rather it is the child himself who abjures and promises. This amounts to saying: I undertake, when this child is able to understand sacred truths, so to form and train him by my instruction in the divine that he may withstand all the temptations of the adversary, may undertake the promises and fulfil them in deed.

'There is, then, to my mind, nothing absurd in admitting the child to the sacraments that are to raise him spiritually, on condition that a master and guarantor form him in good habits and arm him against the temptations of the devil. If the bishop admits him to participation in the sacred symbols it is so that he may be nourished by them and, through this nourishment, his whole life may be passed in unremitting contemplation of the divine mysteries, that entering into communion with them by progress in holiness and thus acquiring lasting habits of holiness, he may be led to holiness under the direction of a loyal sponsor who himself lives in conformity with God.'

Conclusion of the whole (568D):

'Such, my child, are the hidden realities accessible to contemplation[1] and capable of unifying our souls that I have seen in our hierarchy. Other souls, no doubt, with greater power of spiritual sight, will not be limited to these contemplations; they will have enjoyed a sight of realities more resplendent and with a closer likeness to God. On your eyes too, I think, will shine

---

[1] Lit. θεάματα, 'spectacles', but in the sense implied here of spectacles containing a hidden content accessible to the contemplative (cf. p. 67 f.).

splendours brighter and more divine, if you follow the course I have indicated to rise to a fuller illumination. Do you then, when the time comes, dear friend, share with me such more perfect enlightenment and reveal to my eyes all you have been able to apprehend of beauties more harmonious and in closer union with the One. I am confident of waking by my words sparks of divine fire that lie hidden in you.'

'Denys the Areopagite, Bishop of Athens, to Timothy, Bishop of Ephesus.'

Index

Aaron, 155
'Active Life', 169f., 175
Activity, excess of, 66, 101; with contemplation, 16, 108; motionless of God, 78; motionless of God reflected in Bishop, 96n[1]
'Adaptation', in missionary work, 26
Aelred, St., of Rievaulx, 51n[1]
Agape, 36
Alleluia, 140
All Saints, Feast of, 178n[2]
Altar, symbolic of Christ, 136, 154n[2]
Ambrose, St., 8n[1]
Angels, order of in *Celestial Hierarchy*, 11; teaching of Aquinas on, 12n[1]; mode of communication of, 10; compared with men, 22n[2]; guardians of nations, 143; 'purification' of 184; *see also* Hierarchies and *passim*
Animals, in relation to hierarchies, 13
Anointing, in Illumination, 76, 82; *see also* Unction
Anthropology, 4
Apathy, 4
'Appropriation', in operations of Holy Trinity, 61
Aquinas, St. Thomas, 9n[1], 12n[1], 14n[2], 15n[2], 16n[2], 17, 26, 32, 35, 68n[1], 84, 87, 170n[1,2]; place in Catholic theology, 30n[2]
Aristotle, 6, 14n[2], 37f.
Ascension of Christ, significance for cosmos, 164f.
Asceticism, evaluation of, 36
Assimilation, to God, 60f., and *passim*
Assumption of the Blessed Virgin, 80n[1]
Athens, Bishop of, 9n[2]
Athletes, in Illumination, 76f.
Atomic explosion, 5, 8

Augustine, St., 11n[3], 16n[1], 23, 68f., 73, 74, 192n[2]

Balthasar, H. U. von 165n[1]
Bang, 'The Big', 5
Baptism, 28; *see also* Illumination and *passim*
Barden, W., O.P., 21n[1]
Basil, St., 47, 200n[2]
Beautiful, The, name of God, 51
'Becoming', state of, 19f., and *passim*
Belloc, 12n[3]
Benedict, St., 17, 169; *Rule* of, 172f.
'Birth from God', 60, and *passim*
Bishop, 28; visible head of hierarchy, 49; approached through the deacon, 63n[1]; must never lose sight of invisible realities, 66; functions of, 149; source of all activity of clergy, 63, 159; 'revealer of divine judgements', 194; 'messenger' (angel) of God, 194; and *passim*
Body, the human, eternal existence of, 8, 186; relation to soul, 14n[2], 161f., 187, 200n[1]; resurrection of, 22n[2], 164; the 'spiritual', 80; care for, 186
Bombs, atom, 6
Botte, Dom, 176n[1], 177n[1]
Bouyer, Père, 138n[1]
Bread, 'The True', 24
British Army, 5
Butler, Abbot Cuthbert, 172n[2]
Byzantine rite, 162; communion of saints in, 107n[1]

Campbell, Rev. T., 48n[1], 53n[1]
Canon, of the Mass, 104
Capacity, as deciding place in hierarchy, 58 and *passim*; *see also* Merit
Cassian, 169n[1]

205

INDEX

Cat, The Cheshire, 6
Catechumens, 179, 28, 99f., 189, 190; 'Mass of', 47
'Cave', Plato's, 39
Celestial Hierarchy, The, 11; *see also* Angels, Hierarchies and *passim*
Cenobites, 174
Charism, 177
Charity, 60
Cherubim, confused with Seraphim, 133
Children, in monasteries, 173n[2]; as lectors, 90n[1]
Chiliasts, 188
Choir, monastic, 172
Christ, incorporation into through the hierarchy, 19; 'imitation of', 42; as 'First of the Athletes', 77; and *passim*
Church, and science, 6
Cinema, 8
Clement of Alexandria, 172n[1]
Clergy, 27; assistant, 89; correspond to Seraphim in celestial hierarchy, 132; personal sanctity of, 175f.; and *passim*
Clothing, in monastic habit, 183
Cloud of Unknowing, The, 4
Cluny, 172n[2]
'Commemoration', Jewish concept of, 23n[2]; in the Eucharist, 112f.
Commandments, The, observance of, 61
Communion, Holy, 85f.; reception of, regular part of assistance at Mass, 27, 88
'Completion', as effect of 'sacraments', 139
Confessions, The (of St. Augustine), 69
Confirmation, Sacrament of, 29, 66, 82, 119; effect of, 121; *see also* Unction
Consciousness, and matter, dualism of, 7
Contemplation, 15; meaning in present context, 67f.; and possession, 68; in St. Thomas, 68n[2]; in tradition, 167f.
'Contemplative', 28; identified with 'initiate', 166, 180, 184; c. life, 169f., 175
'Co-operation', with the Light, 58
Cornelius, St., 90
Cosmic explosion, 5
Cosmology, 4

Cosmos, development of, 9; nature and constitution of, 68; and the Eucharist, 112f.
Creation, 'continuous', 5n[2]; and the hierarchies, 13f., 21
Creed, origin of and date of treatise, 90
Cyril of Alexandria, St., 8n[1]

Dawson, C., 165n[1]
Deacon, 28, 89; functions of, 151; and *passim*
Dead, prayer for, 192f.; anointing of, 198
Death, 22; symbolic in baptism, 78f.; joy at approach of, 187; false theories of, 187f.; entering into life, completion of initiation, 80, 84, 188f.
De Civitate Dei (Augustine), 70
De Cura Pastorali (Gregory the Great), 66
Deification, 58, and *passim*
Denys, pseudo-, the Areopagite, identity of, 9n[2]
Desire, of sacraments, 59, 161
Determinism, 12n[3]
Didache, 86n[1]
Dies irae, 5
Dissolution, final, 5
Divine Names, On the (pseudo-Denys), 10, 35, and *passim*
Doctrine, in pagan mysteries, 138n[2]
Downside, 3
Drama, origin in England, 69
Dualism, of consciousness and matter, 7
Dupont, Rev. J., O.S.B., 23n[2]

Earth, 'the New', 6, 21, 22n[2]
Eastern theology, 87; liturgies, 96n[1], 162; religious thought, 9, 25
Easter Vigil, 82
Ecclesiastical Hierarchy, divisions of, mode of operation, 27f., 47f., and *passim*; relation to Celestial Hierarchy, 11, 26f., 130, and *passim*
Ecstasy, 35
Eddington, Sir Arthur, 7n[1]
Educational Supplement, Times, 171
Effort, necessity of, 57
Elected Silence (Merton), 171
Enclosure, monastic, 173
End of world, 5, 164
Energy, 6
'Enlightenment' (Illumination), 28, 60, and *passim*

206

INDEX

'Enlightened' (initiate), 51
Enthusiasm (Knox), 37
Epicureans, 187n^1
Epiklesis, 162n^2
Epiphanius, 8n^1
Eremitical life, 174
Eros, motive force of hierarchies, 35
'Eternal dwelling', 6
Eternity, source of cosmos, 18n^2; and time, 77, 113f., 161f., and *passim*
Eucharist, uses of word, 85, 66, 104; as Mass, Synaxis, 22, 29, 162, and *passim*; centre of sacramental rites, 88; 'Eucharistic Prayer', 104
Eusebius, St., 90
Evagrius, 18n^1
Evil, nature of, 3, 14n^1
Excommunication, 195f.
'Expanding universe', 5
Exsultet, 32n^2
Extension, as quality of matter, 6; spatial and temporal, 18f., and *passim*; of mysteries (sacraments) in space and time, 77, 109f., 161f., and *passim*
Extreme Unction, 198

Faith, and 'sight', 67f.; in baptism, 161f.
Faithful, 'Mass of', 47
Fall, The, 7, 18f.; effects, 75n^1; *'felix culpa'* of, 32
Fathers of the Church, 8n^1; and Plato, 25, 37
Fire, of charity, 61
Font, baptismal, 78f.
Fragrance, of unction, 120
Free-will, 12n^3
Funeral rites, 186f.; description, 189; 'contemplation', 189f.

Gandillac, M. de, 12n^3, 48n^1, 53n^1, 57n^1
German, 'resistance', 5
Gifts, of Holy Ghost, 156n^1
Gilson, E., 10, 113n^2
Gloria in excelsis, 90
God, The Unknown (Noyes), 7
God, 'The Unknown', 9n^2; yet revealed in all things, 10; 'essentially unknowable'?, 34; as 'Thought', simple 'Act', 50; immediate contact with through the hierarchies, 57, 126n^2; and *passim*; *see also* Light
Good, Idea of The, 38f.

Gospel, 'good tidings', duty of bishop to preach, 63; the Fourth, 97. *See also* Scriptures
Grace, 19n^2, 31; and nature, 19n^2; 'habitual', 'actual', 75n^1; 'of state', 156n^1
Greek, Church, 198; Fathers, 10, 18n^1; theology, 58; fire in, 61
Gregory, St., The Great, 17, 66, 169n^2
Gregory, St., of Nyssa, 13n^1, 18n^1
Guru, 174

Heaven, 50; liturgy of reflected in liturgy of earth, 96n^1
Hell, 20, 192
Hierarchy, defined, 3, 48f.; in visible creation, 10; *The Celestial* (pseudo-Denys), *The Ecclesiastical* (pseudo-Denys), described, 11f.; 'thick-headedness' in, 12n^2; relationship between Celestial and Ecclesiastical, 30f., 52f.; ultimate position in, 126n^2; function and personal sanctity, 126n^2; Ecclesiastical contains all that is in Celestial, 130; whole reflected in each part, 141; whole and each division threefold, 141; synopsis of mode of operation, 141f.
'Hierarch' (Bishop), visible head of hierarchy, 50n^1
History, and the hierarchies, 18n^2, and *passim*
Holy oils, number of, 119n^1; *see also* Unction
Hoyle, Prof. Fred., 5n^2, 33n^1
Humanism, Christian, 4
Humanity, of Christ communicated to men, 113n^2
Hybris, 58

Ideas (Forms), of Plato, 38
'Ignorance', in *Mystical Theology*, 138n^1
Illumination, introductory notions, 27f.; approach to, 61f.; Mystery of (baptism, initiation, 'birth from God'): Introduction, 60f.; enrolment, 62f., 73; stripping, abjuration of Prince of Darkness, turning to Light, 64, 75; anointing, 65, 76; baptism, 65, 78; baptismal robe, 65, 82; confirmation, 66, 82; and *passim*
'Illumination', of mind and will, 12n^3
Illuminati, 51

INDEX

'Imitation', in the hierarchies, 11 and *passim*; of Christ, through his Mysteries, 49; of Christ on visible plane criterion of spiritual progress, 42, 144n^2
Immanence, of God, 10f.
Incarnation, place in the hierarchies, 17, 18n^2, 57n^1; unique of Christ, 57n^1; significance in the Eucharist, 111f., 113f.
Infant baptism defended, 200f.
Initiate, 27
Initiation, significance of term, 27, 138, 84, 199n^1
'Initiators' (clergy), 27
'Intelligence', name of God, 52
Introversion, in approach to Light, 74
'Invisible' God, movement towards in Sacrament of Unction, 125f.
'Invisibility', passage to through baptism, 79

Jacob's Ladder, 83, 173
Jeans, Sir James, 6
Jerome, St., 8n^1
Jerusalem, 'The New', 32; 'The Heavenly', 173
Jesus, Incarnate Word, invisible head of hierarchies, 49; adored as God by Seraphim, 131, 134
Jews, 22n^1; alone in O.T. accepted Light, 143
John, St. (Ev.), 10, 14n^2, 97
John, Pope, xxiii, 67
Journey's end, 186
Judgement, 'particular' and 'general', 164f.
Julian, of Norwich, 17
Jungmann, Rev. J. A., S. J., 90n^2

Kabir, 9n^1
Knowledge, identified with the Light, 10 and *passim*; all is knowledge of God, 11; and Being, 14, 144n^1, 157; of God, also union and possession, 34, 51, and *passim*; man's before Fall, 15n^2; by infused species, 18n^2; rational in hierarchy, 19n^2; mystical compared with rational, discursive, 27, 55, 92
Knox, Mgr. R., 24, 37
Koinonia (Communion, Mass), 60f.; *see also* Eucharist, Synaxis

Krasinski, Cyril von K., Rev. O.S.B., 9n^1

Laity (initiate), 27, 166f., and *passim*; place in hierarchy, 62; maturity, 92; holiness, 126n^2; 'contemplative', 183
Lapsed, 28
'Last Day', 5, 164f.
Latin Fathers, 10
Law, Hierarchy of, and purpose in Old Testament, 22n^1, 141f.
Lector, office of, 89f.
λειτουργοί (assistant clergy, deacons), 89
Life, 'This is Your', 8
Light, God described as, 10f. and *passim*; transmitted through hierarchies, includes whole being and activity of creature, 11f.; always present to man in all things, 19n^2; whole present at each stage, 57n^1; shines on all and 'pursues them', 71; before Illumination (baptism), 62n^1; already present in O.T., 95n^1, 22n^1; gradual approach to in Illumination, 67; itself seen in contemplation, 69; received in 'pattern' of Christ, 78f.; offered to all, 21f., 143; *see also* Knowledge
Liturgical Year, 5; extension of unity of Eucharist, 95; l. worship, didactic value of, 15n^1, 24, 92, 97n^2; dramatic character, 69; in monastic order, 171f.
λόγια, sacred scripture as, 54f.
Love (*eros*), as motive force of hierarchies, 35f.; universal unitive force within Trinity and in created being, 60f.

Maharshi, Ramana, 35n^2
Man, head of visible creation, 10; being of lower creation transmitted through, 13f.
Manicheans, 188
Manning, Cardinal, 176
Manual work, 172n^2
Marmion, Abbot, 95n^1
Mass, alternative names, 85; author's view of central rite, 109f.; 'of Catechumens', 'of Faithful', 47; and liturgical worship, 15n^1; for Dead, 5, 6n^1; *see also* Eucharist, Synaxis, and *passim*

INDEX

Mathematics, 6
Matrimony, 119, 173n^2
Matter, constitution of, 6, 7; dualism of consciousness and, 7n^1; 'spiritualisation' of, 13n^1; not evil, 14n^1; relationship to spirit, 51; and *passim*
Material, world, reality of, 7; nature of m. cosmos, 18n^1
Matthias, election of, 156
Maximus Confessor, 12n^3, 13n^1
Maya, 35n^2
Medicine, Tibetan, 9n^1
Memory, in Augustinian psychology, 23n^2; and the Eucharist, 23n^2, 112f., 113n^2; Semitic concept of, 113n^2
Men, higher than angels?, 30
Merit, decides place in hierarchy, 57 and *passim*; significance of term here, 58
Merton, Thomas, 171
Microcosm, 9; monastic community as, 173f.
Microfilm, 8
Migne, 10n^1, and *passim*
Military Government, 5
'Mind' of God, 19n^3
Missarum Sollemnia (Jungmann), 90n^2
'Mixed Life', 170, 175
Monastic Order, 29, 171f.; etymology, 172, 182; Consecration, 29, 166f.; rite of, description, 181; 'contemplation', 182f.
Monk, place in hierarchy, 43, 180; of 'order of perfect', 175f., 183
Moses, 37, 153, 146, 155
Music, 23f.
Mystery, meaning here, 138, 69; 'The' of St. Paul, 138n^1; ms. of life of Christ, 21n^1; ms. (sacraments) of ecclesiastical hierarchy, 26, 55 and *passim*; unveiled only to initiate, 47f.; of life of Christ, physical, efficient cause of salvation, 113n^2; in ideal environment, 173; some beyond understanding of highest angels, 201; pagan, 94n^1, 120, 138n^1
Mystic, etymology, 138
Mystical knowledge, compared with rational, 54f., and *passim*
Mystical Theology, The (pseudo-Denys), 4, 35, 48n^1, 58, 157
Mystici Corporis Christi, 73
'Mysticism', 167

Nature, and grace, orders of, 19n^2
Nature, and the light, 19n^2; redemption of, 34
Neo-Platonism, 37
Neunheuser, D. Burkhardt, 165n^1
Newman, Cardinal, 7, 22n^1, 23, 174
Noyes, Alfred, 7, 23

Oil, Holy, 29; mixed with baptismal water, 65; consecration of, 119f. *See also* Unction
Okkulte Phänomene (Wiesinger), 12n^3
Old Testament, Hierarchy of, 141f.; rites of, 163
Oratio pura, 169n^1
Order, Holy, 28, 141, and *passim*
Orders, minor, 28, 89
Origen, 18n^1
'Otherworldliness', 4, 22n^2, 161f., 186; *see also* Imitation
'Overflow', of contemplation into activity, 44, 170f., 174, 175; *see also* Imitation of Christ

Pagan mysteries, metaphors from, 94n^1; imagery from, 120
Pantheism, 58
Paradise, Earthly, 18n^1
Paris, Bishop of, 9n^2
'Particulars', of Plato, 37f.
Paschal Vigil, 32n^2
Patristic tradition, 4
Patrologia Graeca (ed. Migne), 10n^1, and *passim*
'Pattern', in hierarchies repeated throughout, 11f. and *passim*; *see also* Light
Paul, St., 9n^2, 47, 79
Penitents, public, 28, 179, 195; class of, 102 (dismissed at Synaxis); present throughout funeral rites, 190
Pentecost, liturgy of, 61
Perfection, meaning in present context, 84, 137f., 198; degrees of in hierarchies, 83; relative, 92, and *passim*; personal and of state, 176n^1, 177n^1; 'state of', of bishop, 175f., of monk, 175f.
Perfume, of holy oil, 82, 120, 129
Peter, St., 196, 197
Philosophy, Aristotelian, 6
Philosophy of Physical Science (Eddington), 7n^1

209

INDEX

Philosophy, *History of Christian Ph. in Middle Ages* (Gilson), 11n[1]
Physical Science, 6
Pinckaers, Rev. S., O.P., 69
Pius xii, Pope, 73
Plato, 10, 16n[3], 18n[2], 21n[1], 25, 37f.
Plato's Theory of Ideas (Ross), 38n[1]
Platonism, 37
Possessed (*energumens*), 100f.
Position, in hierarchy, 126n[2]
Prayer, public and private, 167f; for the dead, 193f.; 'of the saints', 194
Preface (of Mass), 6n[1], 104
Priest, 28 and *passim*; functions of, 150
Priesthood, Rite of Consecration to: 141f.; kneeling, 153, 154, 158; imposition of hands, 153, 154; sign of cross, 153, 155; proclamation, 153, 155; kiss of peace, 153, 156; book of sacred scripture, 153, 157
Priesthood, The Eternal (Manning), 176n[1]
Profane, defined, 102; 'sacrilege to be allowed access to sacred symbols', 56 and *passim*; excluded from contemplation of mysteries, 27, 62, 71; salvation for?, 72
'Prophetic words', 'effective' power of, 14n[2]
Prospero, 7
Pseudo-Denys. *See* Denys
Punishment, eternal, 191, 193
Purgation, 67, and *passim*; entails a measure of union, 28; and 'Three Ways', 167
Purgatory, 192n[2]
Pythagoreans, 188n[2]

Quietism, 12n[3]

Rahner, K., 165n[1]
Rational knowledge, place in hierarchy, 19n[2]
Reality, spiritual the higher, 50f.
'Recapitulation', in Christ, 20, 69f.
Reconciliation, essential for assistance at Eucharist, 105
Redemption, The, 18n[2], 20n[1], and *passim*
Reformation, Counter-, 24
Regeneration, 60n[3]
'Remembrance', Plato's doctrine of, 18n[2]

Renunciation, 4; significance in present scheme, 36; monastic, 182 and *passim*
'Re-presentation', in Eucharist, 113
Republic, The (Plato), 40
Res sacramenti, 138n[1]
Resurrection, of body, 8, 164
Reunion, of East and West, role of present scheme, 26
Revelation, of God, in visible creation, 10; in sacred scripture, 54; in synaxis (Eucharist), 109f.
Reward, eternal, 192, 195
Rome, 90
Roques, M. René, 14n[1]
Ross, Sir David, 38
Rulers, of the State (Plato's), 42
Russia, mentality, 25

Sacrament, interpretation of word, 36, 137f.; restricted sense of, 177; seven, 119; formulas of not committed to writing, 200; not equal in dignity, 87, 121; others 'incomplete' without Eucharist, 84; mode of operation of, 21n[1]; effective signs, 163n[1]; extension in space and time, 83, 200n[1], and *passim*; producing effect *ex opere operato*, 177n[1], 197n[4]; and sanctity of minister, 12n[2], 176n[1], 177n[1], 126n[2]; desire of, 84; *see also* Mystery
Sacramental system, 3
Sacrifice, 'of Cross', 114
Saints, mediation of, 194
Salvation, outside the Church?, 72
Samkaracharya, 18n[1]
Samuel, 194
Sanctity, personal of clergy, 175f.; *see also* Sacraments
Saul, 194
School, 'of the Lord's service', 172
Science, physical, 6, 23; and religion, 6
Scientific knowledge, place in hierarchy, 19n[2]
Scotus Erigena, 13n[1], 20n[3]
Scripture, sacred, series of manifestations of the Light, 54f.; 'substance' of ecclesiastical hierarchy, 53f.; and tradition, 10; relation to Eucharist, 53f., 114f.; content revealed only to initiate, 55; use in Illumination, 55, 100; in consecration of bishop, 29, 157; *see also* Testament

INDEX

'Seal' (with sign of cross), in Illumination, 64n[1]
Second Coming, The, 164
'Secrecy', of Christian mysteries, 47. *See also* Profane
Seeing, all a 'sight' of God, 68, and *passim*
Senses, knowledge through, validity of, 6; world of, 186; and the invisible Word, 21f.; means of approach to spiritual, 74f.
Seraphim, symbolism in Unction, 120f., 130f.
Service, end of education, 171; of God, 171; of man, 175
Shakespeare, 7
Sheed, Dr. F., 50
Sight, bodily of spiritual realities, 15f.
Sin, 18n[2], 32n[2]; 'against the Light'? 71n[3]; venial, 195n[2]; forgiveness of, 197f.
Sinai, Mt. and the Law, 143, 146
Solidity, 6
Soul, 'disembodied', 164
Space, place in present scheme, 19n[2], and *passim*
'Spark', of the soul, 23n[2]
Speculari, significance in this tradition, 69f.
Spirit, The Holy, action symbolised by qualities of holy oil, 83; and Mystery of Unction, 139; visible manifestation, 121
Spiritual order, as containing the material, 50f., 161f., and *passim*
Stiglmayr, Rev. J., 11n[3], 48n[1], 53n[1], 57n[1]
Subdeacon, 89
Subordination, principle of in hierarchies, 52f., 148, and *passim*; of clergy, seen in Illumination, 67
Sun, and Plato's Cave, 41
Symbols, sacramental, nature and function, 67f., and *passim*; of essence of ecclesiastical hierarchy, 53f., and *passim*; relation to spiritual reality, 161f.; genius of in liturgical worship, 95f., 97n[2]; content accessible according to capacity of initiate, 92
Synaxis, significance of term, 85f., and *passim*; Mystery of: 85f.; incensation, 89, 94f.; chant, 89, 97; epistle and gospel, 89, 98; dismissal of catechumens, etc., 90, 99f.; creed(?), 90, 103; offertory, 91, 104; kiss of peace, 91, 104; reading of diptychs, 91, 105; *lavabo*, 91, 107; consecration, 91, 109f.; communion, 91, 116; *see also* Eucharist, Mass
Synoptics, 97
Syriac Didascalia, 63n[1], 89; and unity, 105n[1]

Tabernacle, of Old Testament, 146
Tauler, 146n[2]
Teaching, and transmission of Light, 63, 71n[2], and *passim*
'Telescoping', of functions and degrees of being, 160f.; of all being (recapitulation) in Eucharist, 113f.
τελετή, as translated by 'sacrament', 137f.
Tempest, The, 7
Testament, Old assumed into New, 54f.; Christ already present in Old, 22n[1]; *see also* Law, Hierarchy of, *and* Scripture
Thanksgiving, at funeral rites, 189
θεῖος (divine), sense in which used, 50n[3]
Theodore of Canterbury, 198
Theology, 4; schools, 6; text-books, 26
Theology and Sanity (Sheed), 50
Therapeutes, 172, 181; *see also* Service
θεωρία (contemplation), significance in this author, 67f.
Thomas, St., Aquinas. *See* Aquinas
Tibetan Medicine, 9
Time, 5, 20n[3], 22n[1], 77; significance in this context, 18n[2]; end of, 20, 161f.; 'moving likeness of eternity', 21n[1]
Timaeus (Plato), 21n[1]
Timothy, Bishop of Ephesus, 47
Tonsure, monastic, 182
Tradition, oral, 10; in Hierarchy, 53; of Christian philosophy, 7
Transcendence, of God, 10
Transubstantiation, moment of, 162f.
Trinity, The Holy, 20; source of the hierarchies, 49; external activity of, 61n[1]; participation in life of, 50

INDEX

Ullathorne, Archbishop, 3

Unction, 28 and *passim*; effect of, 136; extreme, 119; Mystery of, rite, 119f.: incensation, 122, 128; chant, reading, dismissal of catechumens etc., 122, 128; preparation of oil—perfume, 122, 129; covering of oil, 122, 134; by twelve-winged veil, 122, 130f.; uses of oil, 135f.; *see also* Confirmation, Holy Oil

Uninitiate, salvation for?, 72

Union, 27f., 35f., 167 and *passim*

Unity, 'Sacrament of' (Eucharist), 87n[1]; return of cosmos to through Eucharist, 95f.; essential note of monastic order, 171, 182n[1], 183

Universe, 'the expanding', 5

Universe, The Nature of The (Hoyle), 5n[2]

'Universals', of Plato, 37f.

Unknowing, Cloud of, 4

'Unknowing', knowledge by, 35, 168

Unseen world, reality of, 7

Veil, in Unction, 120f.

Virginity, 52n[3], 173n[2]

Visible, relationship to invisible, 7f.; first stage of approach to invisible, 19n[2], 74; 'making visible the works of God', 112f.; and *passim*

Vladimir, 96n[1]

Vocation, 153n[1], 155f.

Warnach, D. Victor, 80n[1], 165n[1]

Ways, 'The Three', 167, 175

West, common religious heritage of East and, 9

White robe, in Illumination, 82

Wiesinger, Abbot, 12n[3]

Word, The, 'echoed' down the hierarchies, 13n[2]; uncreated source and pattern of cosmos, 19

World, destructibility of, 8; objective reality of external, 13n[1]; w. of senses material expression of Light, 14f., and *passim*; end of, 5, 20n[3], 164

Yogi, In Search of a, 18n[1]

For Product Safety Concerns and Information please contact our EU representative GPSR@taylorandfrancis.com
Taylor & Francis Verlag GmbH, Kaufingerstraße 24, 80331 München, Germany

www.ingramcontent.com/pod-product-compliance
Lightning Source LLC
Chambersburg PA
CBHW061443300426
44114CB00014B/1811